AF527144

The New Age of Terrorism

The New Age of Terrorism

Dr. S.K. Awasthi

MD Publications Pvt Ltd
New Delhi
www.mdppl.com

Copyright © 2009 by MD Publications Pvt Ltd.

All rights reserved. No part of this book may be reproduced or utilized in any form or by any means, electronically or mechanically, including photocopying, recording, or by any information storage and retrieval system, without the prior permission in writing from the publisher.

Published by :

MD Publications Pvt Ltd
"MD House", 11, Darya Ganj,
New Delhi - 110 002
Phone : +91-11-41563325 (Customer Service)
+91-11-41562846 (Editorial)
E-mail (orders): order@mdppl.com
Website: www.mdppl.com

ISBN: 978-81-7533-209-6

Published and Printed by Mr. Pranav Gupta on behalf of **MD Publications Pvt Ltd** at Times Press, New Delhi.

PREFACE

The world is gradually waking up to the threat of an unprecedented terrorist attack, which leaves behind tremendous political and scientific implications. Reports that terrorist groups had planned to gas European Parliament building in Strasbourg, aimed at killing all the 625 European Members of Parliament in February this year is indicative of the shape of terror to come.

Terrorism has become bloodier, is less dependent on state sponsors, has evolved new models of organization, has become adept at exploiting new communications technologies, involves global campaigns, and has had a strategic impact. None of these trends will allow prediction or extrapolation. Also, terrorists have yet to achieve their stated long-range goals, and use of weapons of mass destruction has not been materialized.

The catastrophic events of September 11, 2001 have renewed focus on the war risk exclusions in insurance contracts. Before the dust settled and fires were extinguished in New York City and Washington D.C., President Bush and Members of Congress were calling the attacks "acts of war" and declaring the United States at war against world terrorism.

The applicability of the exclusions to claims arising out of the September 11 attacks are not quite as simplistic as the news media suggests. There are valid concerns that retaliation, triggered by our country's war against terrorism and military efforts in Afghanistan, is likely and insurers will again face September 11 events. Further, some question whether insurers' determination not to apply their policies' war risk exclusion with respect to September 11 claims could preclude the assertion of the exclusion in the future on grounds they have waived the right to do so. These issues and others have insurers and policyholders scurrying for a solution to a risk that was once theoretically discussed and is now real and foreseeable, not only abroad, but in the United States.

I am very grateful to Mr. Pranav Gupta, Director of MD Publications Pvt Ltd, New Delhi, for his cooperation and support for this book.

Dr. S.K. Awasthi

Contents

1

Introduction

The catastrophic events of September 11, 2001 have renewed focus on the war risk exclusions in insurance contracts. Before the dust settled and fires were extinguished in New York City and Washington D.C., President Bush and Members of Congress were calling the attacks "acts of war" and declaring the United States at war against world terrorism. At the same time, government officials were urging insurers not to exercise the acts-of-war exclusion to deny coverage relating to the attacks.

A number of major insurers, including Northwestern Mutual, Chubb Corp., Swiss Re, Hartford Financial Services Group, Ace Ltd., Met Life Inc., Prudential Financial, and CIGNA have acquiesced, agreeing the acts on September 11 were terrorism and therefore did not trigger the war exemptions. However, not all insurers, in particular reinsurers, have committed on whether they will invoke the act-of-war exclusion and thus, the debate continues. The applicability of these exclusions to claims arising out of the September 11 attacks are not quite as simplistic as the news media suggests.

There are valid concerns that retaliation, triggered by our country's war against terrorism and military efforts in Afghanistan, is likely and insurers will again face applicability of the war risk exclusion under a different set of circumstances while still experiencing the financial fallout of the September 11 events. Further, some question whether insurers' determination not to apply their policies' war risk exclusion with respect to September 11 claims could preclude the assertion of the exclusion in the future on grounds they have waived the right to do so.' These issues and others have insurers and policyholders scurrying for a solution to a risk that was once theoretically discussed and is now real and foreseeable, not only abroad, but in the United States. This article will briefly address the legal history of the war risk exclusion, its potential applicability to claims resulting from the attacks of September 11 and actions insurers are taking to reduce their exposure for similar risks in the future.

The War Risk Exclusion

The attacks on the World Trade Center and Pentagon triggered claims under a variety of policies each having its own variation of the war risk exclusion and some none at all. Many of the claims will be governed by the following exclusion published by the Insurance Services Office, Inc. in contemporary policies which utilizes several broad terms besides "war" to describe the exclusions' scope.

War and Military Action

Warlike action by a military force, including action and hindering or defending against an actual or expected attack, by any government, sovereign or other authority using military personnel or other agents or insurrection, rebellion, revolution, usurped power, or action taken by governmental authority in hindering or defending any of these.

No court decisions have addressed the exact language of the war exclusion clause in the current commercial property forms. Although the language in the exclusion provisions appears sufficiently broad to cover an attack of the magnitude on September 11, 2001, decisions addressing past war exclusions reveal courts have traditionally adopted narrow meanings of the terms "war" and "military action" in construing these exclusions. American courts, following British precedent have adhered to a strict doctrine of what constitutes war, applying the exclusion only in situations where the damages arise from a genuine warlike act between sovereign entities.

The law established in Pan Am will be pivotal in any coverage issue arising from the recent attacks on the World Trade Center and Pentagon. The applicability of the war risk exclusion was addressed in this case under the following circumstances. Two men acting for the Popular Front for the Liberation of Palestine (PFLP) hijacked a 747 El Al plane from Amsterdam and forced the crew to fly to Beirut where a demolitions expert and explosives were put on board. The aircraft was then flown to Egypt under PFLP control. In Cairo, after passengers were evacuated on short notice, the aircraft was blown up and totally destroyed. There was no loss of life. The 747 was insured by all-risk private insurers, war risks insurers from London, as well as the United States Government. The all-risk insurance and war risk coverage provided by London Underwriters included war exclusions.

The courts were asked to decide the issue of whether any of the war risk exclusions applied. If so, then the insurers would not be liable and the United States would have to pay the $9.8 million excess. If inapplicable, then the insurers would share the loss and the United States would pay nothing. Both the trial court and the court of appeals concluded the exclusions were inapplicable requiring the all-risk insurers to share the loss.

The Court of Appeals for the Second Circuit in affirming the decision of the trial court issued a thirty-three page opinion that examined in detail the meaning of specific policy terms in light of the facts and prior case law. It took into consideration decisions from early British and American cases on war involving the American Civil War, World Wars I and II, and the Korean Conflict. Based on this legal history, the court held:

> The cases establish that war is a course of hostility engaged in by entities that have at least significant attributes of sovereignty. Under international law, war is waged by states or state-like entities ... and includes only hostilities carried on by entities that constitute governments at least de facto in character.

Because the PFLP never claimed to be a state, the Second Circuit reasoned this activist group could not be acting on behalf of any of the states in which it existed when the plane was hijacked, especially since those states uniformly and publicly opposed hijacking. The hijackers were agents of a radical political group and not a sovereign government. The court concluded a gorilla group or radical political group must have at least some incidence of sovereignty before its activities can properly be defined as war.

Subsequent to the decision in Pan American, there has been little case law published which specifically addresses war exclusions, particularly in the context of first-party property or business income insurance.

Cases since Pan Am have expressly followed its precedent or dealt with other issues consistent with its holding. In Holiday Inns, Inc. v. Aetna Insurance Co.,8 the court, extensively quoting from Pan American, declined to apply the war risk exclusion to a claim for damages to a hotel that was shelled during battles in Beirut, Lebanon. The court focused on the faction occupying the Holiday Inn at the time of the fighting and concluded that it was not a sovereign entity. It noted that even if the group could be argued to possess the necessary sovereignty, it was not fighting with another sovereign government at the time of damage.

In TRT/FTC Communications, Inc. v. Insurance Company of the State of Pennsylvania, the applicability of war risk exclusions was addressed under a manuscript policy in the context of the 1989 United States invasion of Panama. The Panamanian National Assembly passed a declaration proclaiming a state of war existed between the United States and the Republic of Panama on December 15, 1989. Five days later on December 20, the United States military forces invaded Panama City resulting in civil disorder. TRT/FTC Communications occupied space on the ground floor of a building in the business district of Panama City. Several persons dressed as civilians but carrying AK-47 military assault rifles broke into TRT's ground floor facility on December 21 and stole merchandise and equipment.

In the coverage litigation that followed, the court concluded the war risk exclusion applied to preclude coverage. It determined the men who robbed TRT were part of an arm of the Panamanian Government's forces involved in the war effort. The court noted that regardless of whether the men were part of the Panamanian forces or a band of looters, there was ample evidence to support the conclusion that their actions against TRT were enabled by the military hostilities occurring between Panama and the United States.

Another consideration to be taken into account in the application of war exclusions is precedent that provides the loss must arise from a hazard existing only in wartime and not in peacetime. For example, in Queen Insurance Co. v. Globe & Rutger's Insurance Co., I" the Supreme Court ruled damage from a collision of two merchant ships sailing with separate convoys during World War I, with no hostile warships apparently present, was not a war risk. The damage caused by the collision was such that it could have occurred at any time, not just during war. In Aircraft International, Inc. v. United States, an insured was denied coverage based on the war exclusion for aircraft lost in

Vietnam during the war when it collided with a military aircraft. The court held the loss was due to an aviation risk even though the two aircraft were flying over Vietnam only because of the war.

The Florida Supreme Court in American Fire & Casualty Co. v. Sunny South Aircraft Services, Inc., concluded the war exclusion should not apply against a claim for loss to an aircraft hijacked to Cuba and then damaged by a Cuban military plane. It reasoned theft rather than warlike activity caused the loss. The theft was determined not to be a hazard separate and distinct from that of peacetime even though the plane was damaged by a warplane.

Unless additional facts are revealed that prove the terrorist attacks on September 11 were directed by some government or sovereignty at least de facto in character, then it will be very difficult for insurers to succeed in any coverage dispute involving war risk exclusions. Although recent events have changed our common understanding of the word "war," it is unlikely courts will reverse their traditional narrow view of the standard war exclusions.

Terrorism Exclusions

In response to the new realities of the insurance market, the questionable applicability of war risk exclusions to losses related to acts of terrorism, and faced with reinsurers refusing to reinsure terrorism related losses after January 1, 2002, property and casualty insurers have turned to newly drafted terrorism endorsements. This was done to minimize their exposures and ensure their continued ability to negotiate acceptable reinsurance treaties. Insurance companies, insurance service organizations, attorneys, underwriters and others involved in drafting insurance policies began writing terrorism endorsements with the intent of excluding from coverage any loss, cost, expense, exposure or other damage, of any kind, that might emanate from terrorism or threats of terrorism.

Meant to clarify that the policies to which they are attached do not provide the insured with coverage for damages that fall within the scope of the exclusion, or only provide limited coverage, these endorsements are as varied as the companies and underwriters drafting them. However, without exception, these forms clearly have at their core the intent to limit coverage that might otherwise be available for losses that result from terrorism or terroristic activities. Manuscript terrorism exclusions are perhaps the most broadly worded. By way of example is the following form, drafted to be used on property policies:

- Acts of Terrorism or Terroristic Threats

We will not pay for loss, damage, cost or expense of whatsoever nature caused directly or indirectly by, resulting from or in connection with "acts of terrorism" or "terroristic threats." Such loss or damage is excluded regardless of any other cause or event that contributes concurrently or in any sequence to the loss. We will not pay for loss, damage, cost or expense of whatsoever nature caused directly or indirectly by, resulting from or in connection with any action taken in defending, controlling, preventing, suppressing or in any way related to "acts of terrorism" or "terroristic threats."

If such acts or threats also come within the terms of the War and Military Action Exclusion, that exclusion supersedes this Terrorism exclusion. If an act of terrorism involves nuclear reaction, nuclear radiation, or radioactive contamination, this Terrorism exclusion will apply to losses that result from such nuclear reaction or radiation or radioactive contamination in place of the Nuclear Hazard exclusion.

Added Definitions: "Acts of terrorism" means any act or activity that is dangerous to human life or property, is disruptive of public, private, governmental or business services or operations, or is in any way threatening to the health, welfare, or economic well-being of the general public, whether such act or activity is committed in the United States or anywhere else in the world, and which act or activity has the apparent intent of, or otherwise results in:

- Terrorization, harm, intimidation or coercion of a civilian population; or
- Exertion of influence on the policy or conduct of a government by intimidation or coercion, assassination or kidnapping; or
- Direct or indirect interruption or disruption in public, private, governmental or business services or operations; or
- Direct or indirect interruption or disruption in the manufacture, supply, distribution or sale of goods, products, or services; or
- Direct or indirect interruption or disruption in the use of technology or the Internet; or
- Harm to persons or property.

"Terroristic threat" means a threat to commit any "acts of terrorism" or other act, activity or crime of violence with the purpose to terrorize another or to cause evacuation of a building, place of assembly, or facility of public transportation, or otherwise to cause serious public inconvenience, or in reckless disregard of the risk of causing such terror or inconvenience. "Acts of terrorism" and "terroristic threats" include, but are not limited to, acts or activity that are of a criminal nature as provided for by the laws of the United States or any State of the United States, regardless of where in the world such acts or activity may occur.

"Acts of terrorism" or "terroristic threats" further include any such act or threat encompassed within the meaning or intent of any antiterrorist statute or law of the United States or State of the United States.

Other manuscript terrorism endorsements utilize differing definitions of "terrorism," some using language that is more focused on the activity and the apparent intent of the terrorist, while others utilize language focusing on the result. One of the challenges of these endorsements is to distinguish between acts of violence that typically could lead to covered losses and acts of violence that are in the nature of terrorism. The new terrorism laws provide some guidance in this regard, but those definitions may be too limiting. Note the importance in not limiting the exclusion to acts of terrorism directed to a government.

As we saw after September 11th, and which we continue to see, the breadth and depth of damages that can emanate from an act of terrorism affects businesses in ways that would previously have not even been considered. Hence, disruption to business, technology (which might not involve a violent event), and other day-to-day public and private operations is a key exposure to be eliminated or minimized by these endorsements. A variation on complete elimination of coverage would be having a sub-limit for terrorism losses. However, that has its own potential problems if there is ever an issue as to whether the sub-limits or the entire limits might be available in the event of a covered loss.

In addition to manuscript terrorism endorsements, the Insurance Services Office, Inc. (ISO) and the American Association of Insurance Services (AAIS) have filed terrorism exclusion forms excluding coverage for terrorism related damages under various types of property and casualty policies. Both ISO and AAIS began filing their forms in November 2001 on behalf of their member companies, in anticipation of January 1, 2002 reinsurance renewals.

On December 21, 2001 the National Association of Insurance Commissioners (NAIC) announced that, "[w]ith the inaction by Congress [in enacting insurance terrorism legislation], state regulators have been placed in the unfortunate position of having to approve some exclusions in order to protect the solvency of companies in the commercial lines market. By doing so, they will ensure the continued availability of coverage other than terrorism," said NAIC President and Iowa Insurance Commissioner Terri Vaughan. "We urge Congress to act on this issue immediately upon their return. Only Congressional action can bring stability back to the market in the short run... Given Congress' failure to act, regulators will begin allowing insurers to exclude terrorism losses if a terrorist act causes total insured losses exceeding $25 million."

In making its comments, the NAIC noted that its members had been working with ISO to create limited exclusionary language acceptable to both regulators and the insurance industry. It commended ISO for its work in this area as well as its decision to offer the forms to non-ISO property and casualty companies without charge. Insurers that are current licensees of ISO for policy forms can use the new language pursuant to their current ISO agreements and state approval of the forms. Non-ISO companies can contact ISO for copies of the terrorism exclusion forms, and permission to use them, by contacting the ISO customer service department."

As noted, AAIS has also filed forms of terrorism exclusions on behalf of its members, in those states that are accepting terrorism endorsements for commercial lines of insurance. In particular, as of February 26, 2002, AAIS announced that it is not pursuing the approval of its terrorism endorsements in California, Florida or New York, based on the positions established by the insurance commissioners in those states. The AAIS commercial lines endorsements are referred to as War, Military Action and Terrorism Exclusions.

AAIS also has terrorism forms for personal lines policies but is not filing these endorsements with state regulators, that required obligation being left to the individual insurance companies wishing to use the forms." Basically, the homeowner forms are either a "complete" terrorism endorsement, or include a more limited exclusion for nuclear, biological and chemical events." Unlike the war exclusions in the commercial lines endorsements, these forms specify that the discharge of a nuclear weapon is deemed an act of war, even if accidental. A state-by-state list of contact persons for questions regarding Terrorism Exclusions is maintained by the NAIC.

As we enter this new age of terrorism, both war and the war risk exclusions as we have known them are evermore changed. The war risk exclusions of "old" are being modified and updated to include terrorism exposures through any combination of means, whether reduced coverage limits, caps on coverage amounts, outright exclusions or any one of a multitude of other variations. Simply stated, with terrorism as a fact of post-September 11th life in the United States and Western Europe, the insurance market and the risks that it will insure have been forever altered. How businesses, governments and the insurance industry respond to this new risk will have a major impact on the economic growth and vitality of the free world. Managing this exposure has become the challenge for our times.

The Technique of Terrorism

We are living in a radically new age of global terrorism, and we must seek substantially new ways of comprehending its nature, means, and manifestations. When we speak of terrorism today, we are no longer dealing with the historically and relatively discrete, small-scale, sporadic, and marginalized individuals or groups that employed weapons of limited scope and consequence. The latter is what Walter Laqueur has referred to as "nuisance terrorism" in his discussion of The New Terrorism. Today, neither historical precedent nor political prescription can guide us through our global struggle with terrorism. Today, we must ponder the implications of weapons of mass destruction (WMD)—chemical, biological, radiological, and nuclear—as well as cyber terrorism, narcoterrorism, and transnational groups and networks using increasingly powerful and sophisticated means and methods of mass communication, information, and propaganda. Today, we must weigh the causes and consequences of frequent, horrific, and unpredictable terrorist events, such as hijackings, kidnappings, suicide bombings, 9/11, the recent bombing attacks in Madrid and London, and the continuous violence and mayhem in Iraq and elsewhere in the world.

Today, we must confront the increasing lethality, destructiveness, lawlessness, and fanaticism displayed by contemporary terrorist organizations, whose means and methods collectively surpass anything we have witnessed historically. Likewise, we must carefully consider the possibility that many acts of terrorism emerge from the "clash of civilizations" that Samuel Huntington so eloquently outlined in the mid-1990s. Indeed, we need to understand the nature and scope of this "clash"—especially in the present conflicts between the West and Islamist fundamentalism—because these conflicts have produced the most serious and substantial confrontations and threats to world peace at this time. In sum, any definition of terrorism that does not take all of these matters into consideration is destined to mislead and misinform its audience, among other serious consequences. We live in a unique historical context, and our comprehension of this fact must constitute the first major step we take towards understanding the prevalence and originality of contemporary terrorism.

There is, however, an additional concern related to our understanding and analysis of contemporary terrorism. And this concern has to do with the entire process by which we conceptualize and define it. Defining what we mean by "terrorism" in a clear, comprehensive, and generally acceptable manner has proved to be a persistently problematic task. In fact, there are literally hundreds of definitions of terrorism from a wide variety of sources—e.g., academics, politicians, government agencies, security experts, journalists, and militants—yet none has been able to capture the essence of the phenomenon to the general satisfaction of most. I agree fundamentally with Jessica Stern's observation that defining terrorism is much more than an academic exercise: "The definition inevitably determines the kind of data we collect and analyze, which in turn influences our understanding of trends and our prediction about the future ... How we define it profoundly influences how we respond to it."

One thing is certain: We can no longer indulge the conventional illusion that "one person's terrorist is another's freedom fighter." This kind of moral relativism clouds our thinking and presents an imposing obstacle to understanding and defining the realities and threats of modern terrorism. If an individual or group resorts to terrorist means, then he or it cannot legitimately avoid either the terrorist label or its consequences. A terrorist is one who employs terrorist means, for whatever stated or unstated purpose. Perhaps a single, unified definition is neither desirable nor achievable, but that is not the essential issue in this context. The real obstacle lies in the fact that many analysts focus almost entirely on the ends or goals of terrorism and attempt to grapple with the political, legal, moral, and normative implications of terrorist beliefs and behavior, while others get bogged down in attempting to sort out the multitude of subjective aims and ideologies that typify particular terrorist groups or movements.

The end result of these approaches is that they are too often politically biased and value-laden, leading to the wide variety of sometimes confusing and inconsistent individual definitions. This leads in turn to the practical impossibility of reaching general agreement about the nature, extent, or characteristics of terrorism as a whole. What we have now, therefore, is a multitude of definitions that reveal as much about the analysts as they do about the terrorist phenomenon itself. Symptomatically, Alex Schmid and associates initially surveyed a number of leading academic experts almost two decades ago in order to identify and isolate the most salient elements of terrorism in the experts' definitions.

Schmid's findings revealed a wide selection of elements that were based on their statistical recurrence in the survey data: i.e., violence, force (83.5%); political factors (65%); fear, emphasis on terror (51%); threat (47%); psychological effects and anticipated reactions (41.5%); discrepancy between targets and victims (37.5%); intentional, planned, systematic, organized action (32%); methods of combat, strategy, tactics (30.5%); publicity aspects (21.5%); and criminal intent (6%). Although the weight given to some of those elements may have changed somewhat since the events of 9/11, Schmid's findings are still representative of a rather vague "consensus" among some of the experts about which factors they consider to be most relevant to the study and definition of terrorism today.

Bruce Hoffman, a well-known expert on terrorist matters, reviewed many of the same definitional issues ten years later in his work, Inside Terrorism. Hoffman attributed many of the deficiencies in definition to the tendency towards "equivocation" by many authors, which he believed had led to the fact that "there is no one widely accepted or agreed definition for terrorism." I concur generally with Hoffman's overall assessment but find that he offers a rather weak alternative to the issue of equivocation when he proposes to define terrorism as "the deliberate creation and exploitation of fear through violence or the threat of violence in the pursuit of political change." Hoffman's emphasis on the elements of fear and violence is perfectly legitimate and consistent with other experts, but his analysis is incomplete, and his mention of the "pursuit of political change" leaves much to the imagination, as do virtually all definitions that focus on the purely political or ideological goals of terrorism.

In order to address further the definitional issues I have raised so far, I propose something more than the addition of another idiosyncratic definition to those that have already been amassed. As stated above, I believe that contemporary terrorism must be understood in a broader social context than has previously been the case. It must be understood as a significant sociological reality that reflects most of the basic features of the technological societies and civilization in which we live. In fact, one could convincingly argue that the cumulative effects of technology are among the major causes of terrorism today. Because the world of technique and technology is characterized by the predominance of technical means over subjective, hypothetical, theoretical, or moralistic ends, we must recognize that terrorism itself is a matter of means: i.e., a vast but interconnected system of ideas, methods, weapons, tactics, and strategies that must be understood as an inseparable whole.

Indeed, it is my contention that terrorism is a technique in the sense that it is an effective means to a stated or implied objective, just like any other vehicle for achieving any goal whatsoever. Although my contention is somewhat unorthodox, I believe that it captures the sociological essence of terrorism in a manner that is more complete and comprehensive than other, more traditional approaches. It also allows us to focus upon what I would argue is the determining factor in contemporary terrorist operations: i.e., the search for the most efficient and effective technical means to accomplish their proposed objectives. To clarify my conception of the technique of terrorism I will concentrate on the following three interrelated propositions that I will use sequentially to define and delineate the terrorist phenomenon.

Proposition 1: The technique of terrorism is defined by the totality of means employed or advocated by an individual, group, or organization in furtherance of express or implied political, ideological, social, cultural, economic, or religious objectives.

Contrary to what some specialists assert, modern terrorism is a direct by-product of the technological civilization and technical processes that characterize our world. Just as technological development has become an increasingly powerful and determining aspect of modern advancements in virtually every field of human endeavor, so it has triggered a virtually simultaneous rise in the violence, destructiveness, weaponry, and organization of terrorism throughout the world. Technology and terrorism are inextricably linked together in a complex system of means, methods, ideas, strategies, weapons, and organizations—the whole of which is substantially greater than the sum of its parts. It is precisely in this sense that I use the term technique of terrorism to characterize modern terrorism.

As stated earlier, terrorism is a means to an end—i.e., a technique that is used by terrorists to achieve a calculated objective by applying a variety of deliberately violent means and methods to that specific goal. Nevertheless, as is often the case in our technological civilization, the technical means employed tend to overpower and transform the ends pursued, which is invariably what occurs when terrorists use violence to achieve their objectives. In his impressive analysis of the Techniques du terrorisme, Jean-Luc Marret demonstrates extensively, for example, the interconnections between the technological developments in modern weaponry, such as bomb making, and the ever expansive technologies of terrorism. Marret argues convincingly that terrorist methods expand by a process of "contagion," during which innovations are introduced, successful actions copied, and refinements made—all of which influence a variety of terrorist groups and movements almost simultaneously. Thus, the innovations in terrorism follow the same exponential pattern of technological development and diffusion that we witness generally.

In other words, to the extent that terrorism forms an inseparable whole, it is characterized by the same technological imperatives that propel and animate the larger technological civilization. This is not, however, an entirely "mechanical" process in which the ends pursued are always realized to technical perfection. Terrorism is not a "science" that produces altogether predictable results; imprecise execution, amateurism, and clumsiness, for example, can definitely alter outcomes, as has been the case in many terrorist plans and aspirations (Note, for example, the brief terrorist career of shoe bomber Richard Reid). Nonetheless, it is important to understand that terrorists are engaged in a continuous process of searching for the best and most efficient way to accomplish their aims, and that this process of searching is actually what animates and defines the technique of terrorism. The important thing to remember with terrorism is the fact that it is the totality of means terrorists employ or advocate that defines them, not their express or implied intentions, ideology, or ultimate motives or mistakes. This point is amply illustrated in the following three characteristics we find in terrorism today.

First of all, terrorists may be classified as individuals acting on their own—such as the Unabomber Ted Kaczynski or Carlos "The Jackal"—or acting in concert, such as Timothy McVeigh and Terry Nichols. They can form relatively small groups, such as the Abu Sayyaf in the Philippines, or complex organizations or networks, such as Hamas, Hezbollah, or al-Qaeda. Regardless of size, each terrorist configuration has its own "signature" or modus operandi, which in fact further underlines the centrality and commonality of technique in its operations. The weapons or tactics it utilizes generally become its defining characteristic, such as hijackings (Popular Front for the Liberation of Palestine, al-Qaeda), kidnappings for ransom (Abu Sayyaf, al-Qaeda), "kneecapping" (IRA, Italy's Red Brigades), and suicide bombings (Tamil Tigers, Hamas, Hezbollah, Iraqi insurgents, al-Qaeda).

Furthermore, the arsenal of weapons available to contemporary terrorists is limited only by financial resources, technological feasibility, and technical imagination. The steadily increasing lethality of terrorist weaponry is a function of both the exponential proliferation of weapons technology among terrorist groups worldwide, and the development of a sophisticated class of terrorist technicians, such as the al-Qaeda tactician Kalid Sheik Muhammed, or the infamous bomber Ramsey Youssef. Indeed, the "technicians of terror" deserve far more scrutiny and study than they have received to date.

Second, the "new terrorism" is different from previous types of terrorism because it is characterized by often vaguely formulated political objectives, indiscriminant violent attacks, attempts to achieve maximum psychological and social disorder, and the potential to use weapons of mass destruction. The Aum Shinrikyo millenarian cult in Japan is a curious example of this new trend. In 1995, members of the cult placed packages containing Sarin nerve gas in the Tokyo subway system, killing more than a dozen victims and injuring about five thousand. Under Shoko Asahara, the cult's leader, the goal was to seize control of Japan, and then the world, as part of the projected coming of Armageddon. Although the cult accumulated an impressive arsenal of weapons of potential mass destruction, it ultimately failed because of poor technical execution of its terrorist plans. Even though the 1995 attack ended in failure, it was a first attempt to use and justify WMD as part of an overall terrorist strategy.

Moreover, Asahara attracted literally thousands of adherents in several different countries to his secular-religious movement—a perfect illustration of how beliefs can become instruments of terror. Third, many features of the "new terrorism" have become an integral part of the signature operations of al-Qaeda in particular.

The fact that al-Qaeda has developed the techniques of terrorism to such an advanced stage qualifies it as the quintessential contemporary terrorist organization. Peter Bergen, for example, carefully demonstrates how Usama bin Laden has effectively operated as a "terrorist CEO" and "venture capitalist," while adroitly merging modern organizational and managerial techniques with the ideology of the "clash of civilizations," Islamist piety, and the concept of jihad, or "holy war." In many regards, bin Laden and al-Qaeda are prime reflections of the contradictions of our times—promoting jihad against the "Crusaders," the "Great Satan," "modernity," "globalization," and "the West," while simultaneously utilizing every material and self-serving component of the technological civilization that they otherwise claim to despise and reject absolutely. It remains to be seen how long this flagrant contradiction can be effectively maintained as a technique of al-Qaeda's terrorist strategy.

On the other hand, it is perhaps the surest sign we have that bin Laden's cynical manipulation of Islam will ultimately fail in the face of technological modernization and globalization, which will determine, inexorably, the ultimate path of modern history. Since bin Laden's brand of terrorism has no finality—with the sole exception of self annihilation—the remaining question may only be the price we will have to pay until it inevitably consumes itself.

Proposition 2: The technique of terrorism incorporates the planned, calculated, and systematic acts or threats of violence that generally typify the modes of operation and selection of victims of terrorist groups.

The history of terrorism correlates strongly with those parts of the human historical experience where violence has been perceived as a morally justifiable means to a projected end. Thus, the violent tactics and tools of terrorism have tended to mirror the general historical development of weaponry and warfare—from the ancient swords and daggers, through the invention of firearms, the guillotine, and dynamite, down to the contemporary age of deadly explosive devices and weapons of mass destruction. The twentieth century has generated more violence, death, and destruction than any previous era of human history, and modern terrorism has tended to emulate those traits uniquely. Because of its sheer lethality, destructiveness, and high public visibility, terrorism has become, with few exceptions, the exclusive method of choice in most modern attempts to bring about political and social change.

Both left-wing ideologues and right-wing extremists have resorted to terrorism in impressive numbers, and currently, we see groups and individuals of every persuasion joining the ranks of various secular-religious movements that have become appreciably more dangerous and violent as time goes by. Terrorist violence has many dimensions, but what makes it particularly dangerous today revolves around three dominant characteristics. The first characteristic involves the fact that terrorism typically involves acts or threats of violence that indicate carefully planned, rationally calculated, and systematic behavior on the part of terrorist groups. For example, the hijackings and suicide attacks of 9/11 were without precedent in the annals of terrorism. The attacks were the end result of systematic, detailed, patient, and audacious planning, rarely seen in previous terrorist operations. Al-Qaeda's success demonstrated conclusively that there were no "rules" or "limits" governing terrorist actions, only utilitarian results.

The "symbolic" value of 9/11 in terms of utter destructiveness, loss of life, and fear of future attacks, was sufficient justification and validation for bin Laden and his followers in their struggle against the "Great Satan." By boldly and violently attacking the United States, bin Laden and his supporters achieved several specific aims: first, they managed to mobilize and reinforce the profound adhesion of a wide cross-section of the Muslim and Arabic world through persistently anti-American propaganda, both before and after the events of 9/11. What had once been latent hostility and animosity in the relationship between segments of Islam and the West now became overt expressions of violent and aggressive emotions, supported by pan-Arabic propaganda. Thus, the United States specifically became the ideal scapegoat for radical Muslim militants in particular. A second aim revolves around the fact that terrorists were able to normalize acts of violence in the relations between Islam and the West—a profound propaganda effect that has since been used to legitimize countless terrorist attacks against "Western" interests throughout the world, especially in Iraq.

Finally, the normalization of violence has led to a situation in which the mere suggestion or threat of violent terrorist actions is enough to cause fear and anxiety in a wider social audience. In the age of global mass communications, this effect occurs with unprecedented regularity, and the threat of violence alone is often an adequate substitute for its real-life application. Bin Laden seems to have understood and encouraged this effect in most of his threatening media communications since 9/11. A second major characteristic of today's terrorism denotes the inevitable dialectic or cycle of violence that in turn engenders the highly predictable syndrome of terrorism/ counterterrorism we have seen in recent years. For instance, in the aftermath of the attacks of 9/11, there was an extraordinary development of safety and security techniques and technologies, both within and outside the United States.

This development led to the accelerated creation of the Department of Homeland Security, the passage of the Patriot Act, and numerous security, surveillance, and intelligence initiatives and protocols that are now part of the United States' counterterrorism measures and techniques. Inasmuch as these measures were taken in response to the necessities of the moment, however, they have sometimes generated serious legal and civil liberties controversies, which is perfectly consistent with the political intent and technique of organizations like al-Qaeda. Furthermore, democratic ideals and institutions are meant to be among the many casualties of modern terrorism. In this connection, I am reminded of a February 10, 2006, Associated Press news photo of a Muslim woman carrying a banner alleging that "Freedom of Expression is Western Terrorism."

A third, and somewhat daunting, characteristic of contemporary terrorist violence is the formidable presence of the suicide bomber. The technique of suicide bombing has proliferated among contemporary terrorist groups through the same process of "contagion" identified earlier, to the point that suicide bombers have become one of the most recognizable and feared "weapons" in the terrorist arsenal. As David Brooks cogently points out, "Suicide bombing isn't just a tactic in a larger war; it overwhelms the political goals it is meant to serve.

It creates its own logic and transforms the culture of those who employ it." Suicide bombing is perhaps one of the ultimate expressions of the cycle and logic of violence that typifies Islamist terrorist groups in particular. Although not without historical precedent—e.g., the Japanese Kamikaze pilots in WWII—contemporary suicide bombing originated with groups such as Hezbollah and Hamas, and spread rapidly to other organizations, like al-Qaeda. Islamist bombers have not tended to be loners or entirely uneducated or alienated individuals.

As Brooks observes, most are products of the "culture of martyrdom," in which tightly run terrorist organizations widely recruit, indoctrinate, train, and reward bombers for their "martyrdom." For organizations like al-Qaeda, suicide bombers fulfill a well-defined need, as their role in terrorism is notoriously inexpensive and effective, and they are less complicated and compromising to employ than other possible terrorist techniques. As Bruce Hoffman notes, the suicide terrorist is "the ultimate smart bomb."

The technique of suicide bombing is fairly simple in that bombers often carry explosive devices strapped to their bodies, which they may detonate at will. Or they may use other means of delivery, such as cars, trucks, and other vehicles, as well as boats, bicycles, or aircraft. The impact of the bombings is immediate, and they produce considerable shock, intimidation and anxiety in a wider audience. We have seen this kind of effect in Israel's experience with terrorism, as well as in the insurgents' use of IEDs in Iraq. Most bombers are religiously inspired Muslims who have been trained and indoctrinated by Islamist ideologues and clerics to sacrifice their lives for the ultimate cause of Islam. In fact, martyrdom is given the highest priority by al-Qaeda in programming its followers for death.

As Walter Laqueur observes, "awaiting them in paradise are rivers of milk and honey, and beautiful young women. Those entering paradise are eventually reunited with their families and as martyrs stand in front of God as a new-born baby." Thus, the positive value placed on this ultimate act of self-sacrifice helps explain why legions of young Muslims are more than willing to become martyrs in a self-perpetuating cycle of suicidal violence. As a technique of terrorism, suicide bombing epitomizes the variously attributed Chinese military adage: "Kill one, terrorize a thousand."

Proposition 3: The technique of terrorism involves the unique application of psychological and sociological instruments of propaganda with the intent to generate fear, anxiety, intimidation, and demoralization in a wider social audience, as well as to indoctrinate and mobilize its followers.

In order to fully understand and define modern terrorism, we must include perhaps the most important dimension of its impact on the contemporary world: its relationship to modern forms of propaganda. There is a powerful symbiotic relationship between terrorism and propaganda that combines the material, spiritual, psychological, and sociological techniques necessary for the perpetuation of both. Terrorism must use propaganda in order to achieve any or all of its stated or implied objectives, and propaganda provides the necessary techniques for terrorism to be effective. In this context, I use the term propaganda broadly to imply the cluster of psychological and sociological techniques of persuasion and influence, combined with the techniques of organization discussed earlier, that are designed specifically to mobilize, integrate, and orient its followers toward terrorist actions.

Terrorist propaganda is not about telling lies in order to make its adherents believe certain ideas. Rather, it is designed to bypass or overwhelm cognitive and intellectual processes in order to obtain a desired behavior or action from its followers, as in the earlier example of the suicide bomber and martyr. That is the essence of what is referred to as "propaganda by deed," which is the new reality of propaganda in the modern age. To clarify my definition, we must examine three major aspects of this relationship: the instruments of propaganda themselves, the purposes they serve, and how they are used to mobilize followers.

First of all, modern terrorism is entirely dependent on our technological civilization, the mass means of communication, and global information systems to survive politically, publicize their purposes, and influence a wider social audience. As Ray Surette points out, terrorists have become increasingly media-wise as a consequence. Various terrorist groups have recognized the power of the media to crystallize public opinion and to set the social agenda through extensive coverage and commentary—especially involving terrorist violence. Surette is correct in underlining the fact that "terrorism has become a form of mass entertainment and public theater and thus highly valuable to media organizations."

"Terrorism is theatre," as Brian Jenkins suggested many years ago. And Martha Crenshaw made a similar observation when she stated, "The most basic reason for terrorism is to gain recognition or attention." Prime examples of the role of the media in the "new terrorism" emerged during the Middle-Eastern "skyjacking" incidents in the early 1970s. The Popular Front for the Liberation of Palestine (PFLP) was very successful in gaining worldwide recognition and limited support for their cause as a result of a series of air piracy attacks on commercial airlines. Thus, terrorist actions of this type became influential media events and powerful instruments of propaganda. Another emblematic, widely publicized, and emotionally charged incident occurred during the hostage taking of Israeli athletes by the Palestinian "Black September" group during the Munich Olympics in 1972.

Generally classified as propaganda-by-deed actions, these terrorist techniques soon became part of an identifiable process of imitation and contagion among terrorist groups, with many broad ramifications. For example, it is precisely in this context that we find the propagandistic struggle over control of the terminology of terrorism, especially in regard to the distinction between who will be labeled the "terrorist" and who will become the "freedom fighter." Control of media discourse on this matter is always crucial and remains contentious even today. As media outlets such as the Al-Jazeera network begin to play a more substantial political role in the conflicts between the West and the Islamic world, there will be, of necessity, an increasingly obvious propaganda war over issues such as the war in Iraq. More fundamentally, however, the "clash of civilizations" will be waged in "cyber-space," through the Internet and other multimedia technologies, with often unforeseeable consequences. In sum, the global means of communication and information have become major instruments of propaganda in our technological civilization—with decidedly ambivalent effects.

On the one hand, as massive purveyors of information, the media are by nature attracted to the violent, spectacular, visual, and destructive aspects of terrorism, and they give generous attention and coverage to terrorist events, such as the now unforgettable images of 9/11. On the other hand, they sometimes unwittingly engender further violence, destruction, and terrorism by the very nature of their coverage and excessive emphasis on the explicit and graphic means and methods of terrorist groups. Propaganda feeds on information, and the more immediate, dramatic, and audiovisual the information, the more effective it is for propaganda purposes.

Television is, of course, the present medium of choice for terrorists, because it prioritizes the dissemination of striking images on a global scale, encourages immediate visibility through satellite feeds and other technologies, and attracts huge audiences to its various formats. The Internet has also become an increasingly important and popular tool for terrorists for similar reasons. Moreover, one can actually become either a "virtual" or actual terrorist today simply by consulting terrorist websites regularly, joining web-based terrorist groups or sympathizers, consulting training manuals and other published terrorist materials, or learning how to make terrorist explosives—all through the convenience and collaboration of the world-wide web.

A second major characteristic that is often mentioned in definitions of terrorism is the idea that the ultimate purpose and conscious intent of terrorism is to generate fear, anxiety, intimidation, and demoralization in a wider social audience. Obviously, according to most definitions, the purpose of terrorism is to terrorize! Boaz Ganor summarizes this perspective when he concludes that "terrorism is the intentional use of, or threat to use violence against civilians or against civilian targets, in order to attain political aims." The strength of this definition lies in its emphasis on the intentional or threatened use of violence for political purposes. I have already discussed the indisputable use of violent means as a decisive aspect of all acts of terrorism; moreover, terrorist violence is often rationalized for political and ideological reasons. Nevertheless, I find Ganor's definition lacking in two areas.

First, it does not address other potential forms of violence—such as spiritual, psychological, or intellectual—besides the purely political. The study of propaganda reveals numerous forms of violence that are often more fundamental to the manipulation of human behavior than political agitation. Second, the idea that terrorism is somehow reserved for "civilians" or "innocents" exclusively leaves out important effects of terrorist violence on both combatants and society in general. Terrorists do not neatly distinguish between military and non-military targets, especially when their attacks are directed against "symbolic" targets, such as those included in the 9/11 attacks. Thus, on what basis did al-Qaeda actually discriminate between "civilian" targets in the WTC attacks, and "military" targets in the Pentagon attack, not to mention those "secondary" targets that were never attacked? Such a distinction was in fact immaterial to al-Qaeda's calculated plans to attack all major symbols of American power and presence in the world, and to kill as many Americans as possible in the process. Thus, the 9/11 attacks were undertaken primarily for their propaganda value and the additional social-psychological "collateral damage" the attacks were designed to provoke in American society.

Since the attacks, bin Laden's role has been to try to create a quasi-permanent sense of anxiety, fear, intimidation, and demoralization in the United States and elsewhere. One way bin Laden attempts to accomplish this is through incessant verbal, visual, and allegorical threat techniques, such as those regarding the safety and security of American interests, the issuance of periodic proclamations and fatwa's in videotapes and audiocassettes, and the deliberate cultivation of "mystery" about the nature of his leadership and geographic location. To a degree, bin Laden has been quite successful in his propaganda of intimidation throughout the Western world. Although he is no "mastermind" or "genius" of modern terrorism, bin Laden has learned how to cleverly combine previously developed techniques of propaganda into the structure, organization, and ideology of al-Qaeda. Indeed, of necessity, bin Laden has managed to forge a terrorist network that has transformed sectarian violence into an Islamist virtue.

Finally, al-Qaeda has become an effective model for the recruitment, training, indoctrination, and mobilization of contemporary terrorist organizations. Few experts have fully understood how effective al-Qaeda has been in indoctrinating and mobilizing followers for the purposes of "jihad." Bin Laden understood very well the political propaganda value of the defeat of the Soviets in Afghanistan in the 1980s. He also understood the sociological value of the "mujahideen" from Afghanistan in organizing the local leadership cadres for the cellular structure of the al-Qaeda network. Although he was not formally educated in the theology of Islam, bin Laden was able to grasp the secular-religious implications of the Islamic faith and transform it into a workable Islamist ideology. This secular-religious ideology became the necessary belief and behavior system around which al-Qaeda was organized and initially led by bin Laden and his closest associates. Upon this foundation, bin Laden was able to attract large numbers of disaffected, educated, alienated, and illiterate Muslims from all walks of life by constant references to "Allah," and the insinuation that bin Laden is always carrying out Allah's divine wishes in his terrorist actions.

In addition, al-Qaeda intensely recruits and indoctrinates all followers into a sociological and psychological mold of absolute conformity to the secular-religious beliefs and values of the group. The culture of self-sacrifice and martyrdom and the rewards to be reaped in the afterlife from waging jihad are integral parts of that same sociological and psychological mold. Most importantly, the ultimate purpose of this kind of propaganda is, again, not to change ideas or opinions, or to make adherents "believe" a certain set of preconceived ideas; most followers of Islam are already true believers in the precepts of their faith. Rather, the primary purpose is to obtain a behavior or an action at a desired moment—i.e., to create a kind of "orthopraxy" in which an individual is propelled through indoctrination to reflexive action for the sake of the cause. When fully understood, this form of propaganda can help us better understand the phenomenon of the suicide bomber who dispassionately carries out a suicidal mission, or the presence of followers of differing backgrounds and socioeconomic statuses in the ranks of suicide terrorists.

Al-Qaeda has certainly understood the techniques of propaganda necessary to generate public anxiety about these kinds of attacks, as well as the mobilization techniques needed to ensure the constant supply of Muslims willing to become martyrs in the future. Interestingly, the most recent orgy of violence over the unfortunate cartoon depictions of the Prophet Muhammed should also provide pause for reflection about the propaganda effects mentioned above. Once certain reflexes are created, mythical beliefs are exploited, scapegoats are identified, and media attention is mobilized, there must be a "release," or "focus," toward which the militants can direct their pent-up, emotional rage. In this case, the release was not provided by a specific terrorist group, but spilled over into locally orchestrated and irrational rampages of indiscriminate, anti-Western violence based on a deliberately calculated release of the cartoon information to the Arabic media.

This kind of effect was also seen recently in the month-long 2006 rioting in France and has become a frequent occurrence in many contemporary societies, including the United States, for diverse reasons. This is certainly one of the most troublesome sociological characteristics we must confront in correctly defining and comprehending contemporary terrorism, as the phenomenon itself becomes increasingly global and apparently limitless in nature. From the outset, I have attempted to establish the need for a means-based approach to understanding and defining modern forms of terrorism.

Because of the difficulties in defining terrorism along traditional lines, in which the emphasis upon the political, ideological, and other subjective motivations predominate, I proposed a more comprehensive, holistic conception based on my contention that terrorism is best understood as a technique, rooted in the very characteristics and means of the technological civilization that surrounds us.

In order to develop my idea further, I set forth three interconnected propositions that collectively illustrate and define what I wished to imply by the technique of terrorism. In the context of the new, global forms of terrorism, I developed abundant examples and illustrations for my basic ideas and contentions. As a result, I am convinced that the facts of modern terrorism generally support my three propositions for defining the technique of terrorism.

First, it is obvious to me that looking at terrorism as the totality of means used by terrorist groupings to further their objectives is a much better way to understand terrorism than emphasizing the often confusing and sometimes misleading aims and ideologies set forth by terrorists themselves.

To focus entirely on the justifications or motives of terrorists is to ignore the more fundamental and determining factor in all of their operations: the means they employ. Moreover, the most common and unavoidable instrument of terrorism is violence. Violence has common effects on anyone who uses it, and terrorists participate in a cycle of violence that has a certain logic and predictability in its effects and outcomes.

The amount of terrorist violence we see today seems to be a function of both the widespread availability of conventional and non-conventional (WMD) weapons, and the pervasiveness of the mass means of communication and information. Both of these characteristics are products of our technological civilization, and both are crucial components of the dialectic of terrorism and counterterrorism we see on a regular basis.

Finally, the most intractable aspect of modern terrorism involves the relationship between terrorism and propaganda. The manipulation of modern societies by the mass media has led to the accelerated application of modern propaganda techniques on a global scale.

As a consequence, terrorism has become a substantial and extremely dangerous presence in world affairs, and a constant source of fear and anxiety to those who are directly or indirectly victimized by its violence. In the specific case of al-Qaeda, we see a terrorist organization that provides a model to others, and that effectively uses modern propaganda techniques to recruit, indoctrinate, and animate masses of followers. Al-Qaeda's systematic and calculated use of psychological and sociological techniques of integration and indoctrination help explain the suicidal trends in Islamist terrorism, and the veritable "clash of civilizations" that has emerged in attempting to address and control aspects of contemporary terrorism. Only a focus on the techniques of terrorism will supply us with the necessary insight and information to both comprehend and combat terrorism in this day and age.

2

The New Age of Global Terrorism and Bin Laden

When hijacked planes were crashed into the World Trade Center and the Pentagon on September 11, 2001, people reacted in many different ways. However, most speculated that the acts were the work of religious fanatics. A number of commentators warned against making premature judgments about the identities of the hijackers, but the idea that the actions could have been undertaken by religious militants was clearly credible to almost everyone. By the beginning of the twenty-first century, the world has become accustomed to terrorists and militant revolutionaries with religious identities. As a result, no one was surprised to learn that those responsible for the destruction on September 11 appeared to be identifiable as Muslim activists, and that they are alleged to be associated with an Islamically identified terrorist organization.

What is surprising is that no one was surprised by the prominent role of religion in this very public act. The lack of surprise reflects the remarkable transformation of the role of religion in modern (and post-modern) society and how both scholars and the general public understand that role. The change is highlighted by a remarkable coincidence. Almost exactly a century before the destruction of the trade towers, a president of the United

States was murdered. On September 6, 1901, William McKinley was shot; he died of his wounds eight days later on September 14. His murderer, Leon Czolgosz, was identified as part of an international, ideologically inspired network striving to destroy the existing world order and replace it with a new visionary Utopia.

The inspiration for Czolgosz's act of violence and opposition was not, however, a "religious" vision; it was the vision of anarchism. Few observers at the time were surprised by the fact that Czolgosz was an anarchist, and there is no evidence that anyone's first thought was that the murderer might be a religious fanatic. Throughout much of the twentieth century, the first suspicions in any major act of political or public violence were not directed toward religious adherents. The first suspects in the minds of security forces as well as the general public were relatively secular revolutionaries, ranging from anarchists in the early years of the century to "Bolsheviks" and then, during most of the Cold War era, more generally "communist" revolutionaries of various types, directed from the Kremlin or by Castro or some other secular revolutionary.

In the Middle East by the early 1970s, plane hijacking and terrorism were often associated with radical Marxist Palestinian organizations like the Democratic Front for the Liberation of Palestine (DFLP). One reflection of the changing context is that when there was a report that responsibility for the acts of September 11 had been claimed by the DFLP, an organization with a historical record of "terrorist" acts, an informed observer could describe the report as "comically implausible."[1] Of course, the murder of an Israeli cabinet minister in October 2001 by members of the Popular Front for the Liberation of Palestine (PFLP), another old-style leftist radical group, was clear evidence that not all acts of public violence are now committed by religious zealots. However, the credible prominence of religious militants in the arena of public violence at the beginning of the twenty-first century is a sign of a major change in the dynamics of revolution and violent activism.

The rise of religious activism is seen by many as a significant development in contemporary world history. Many analysts have noted that "religious resurgence" on a global scale during the late twentieth century calls into question important aspects of the way the processes of modernization have been understood. Some have gone so far as to declare that the theory of secularization as a necessary part of modernization is, in the words of Peter Berger, one of the early formulators of that theory, "essentially mistaken. However, the rise to prominence of movements of religious resurgence may reflect an even broader phenomenon of the transformation of the nature of social movements of opposition and militancy and of advocacy of radical social change.

In interpreting the rise of new social movements in the 1960s and later, some of the scholars active in developing contemporary social movement theory describe a change in the basic nature of these social movements. In a classic discussion of this change, Jurgen Habermas noted in 1981 that the "new conflicts [in society] no longer arise in areas of material reproduction. Rather, the new conflicts arise in areas of cultural production, social integration and socialization. In short, the new conflicts are not sparked by problems of distribution, but concern the grammar of forms of life."' Using somewhat different terminology, Ronald Inglehart distinguishes between "materialist" and "postmaterialist" value priorities, noting that "postmaterialist values underlie many of the new social movements" and that "the emergence of new value priorities has ... been an important factor" in the rise of new social movements. The religious resurgence can usefully be viewed in this broader context of the emergence of movements based on postmaterialist values, where some of the movements have a traditional "religious" identity and others do not. In the new global context of these value-based movements, it is not surprising that some of the most militant (and violent) movements will be identified as "religious."

The militant Muslim movements that are most visible at the beginning of the twentyfirst century reflect these postmaterialist priorities. The Taliban in Afghanistan, for example, do not have the industrialization of their society as a high priority. The old ideology of the politics of material distribution that dominated the programs of the communist regimes in Afghanistan has been replaced by the politics of competitive cultural reproduction, in which the Taliban and others seek to determine the grammar of the forms of Afghan life.

The old materialist goals of the radical socialists in the Muslim world of the 1960s have been replaced by effectively postmaterialist (not anti-materialist) values. When the Front Islamique du Salut (Islamic Salvation Front or FIS) defeated the long-dominant Front de Liberation Nationale (FLN) in elections in Algeria in 1990-91, it was not on a platform that offered more rapid industrialization or increased productivity. Instead, the FIS offered a new set of value priorities. The challenge of Islamist movements to existing regimes throughout the Muslim world is articulated in terms of new values, not more effective implementation of materialist values. The appeal of Osama bin Laden's message is not that he promises material prosperity to Muslims, but rather that he calls Muslims to break out of what he sees as their submission to foreign domination to affirm values that are different from those of the current ruling elites.

The emerging picture of Bin Laden's organization, al-Qaeda, also reflects the changing nature of social movements in the contemporary world. The old-style revolutionary parties were often hierarchical and had some form of a relatively clear organizational structure. In the new world of global social movements, the network pattern of association is emerging as the more effective mode of operation. The "information revolution favors the rise of network forms of organization. The network appears to be the next major form of organization - long after tribes, hierarchies, and markets - to come into its own to redefine societies, and, in so doing, the nature of conflict and cooperation."

The picture of al-Qaeda as the core of a transnational, non-state network provides the basis for understanding the conflict emerging after September 11 as a "netwar," which is "an emerging mode of conflict in which the protagonists . . . use network forms of organization, doctrine, strategy and technology attuned to the information age." This style of conflict is very different from the Gulf War of the early 1990s, in which the immense military power of the United States could crush the armed forces of Saddam Hussein's Iraq in a clash between two hierarchically organized forces.

In the current netwar context, the worldview framework of the Muslim militants plays an important role that some discussions of social-movement theory can help to explain. Movements are framed by the interpretations, visions and symbols through which they define their identity and goals. Contemporary Muslim movements like Bin Laden's are framed in terms that are identifiably Islamic and familiar to all Muslims. Throughout the Muslim world there are people who are dissatisfied with their own condition and the position of the community of Muslim believers in the contemporary world. These people can form what some scholars have called "sentiment pools" or groups of individuals "who share common grievances... but who lack the organizational base for expressing their discontents and for acting in pursuit of their interests."' The frame of the basic shared concepts can provide the linkage that bridges the gap between existing social-movement organizations like al-Qaeda and the widely scattered sentiment pools throughout the world of Islamic communities.

Such "frame bridging" has been mostly studied within the context of advanced industrial or post-industrial societies, but, in the global information age, the bridging is possible in all types of societies and across all types of boundaries, whether national, civilizational or economic. Many different types of movements reflect these new dynamics. Insurgent indigenous peasants in rural Mexico would, under old global conditions, have had little visibility or chance of success. However, the Zapatista insurgency "can be thought of as a new type of transnational social-movement activity emerging in the global order to counter globally defined threats and the shrinking of national political-action spaces. The intercontinental encounters and the subsequent efforts to form networks of communication and resistance can be seen as constitutive parts of an incipient global civil society."

Al-Qaeda and the Zapatistas are very different types of organizations, but both draw strength from utilizing network modes of action in the emerging global civil society. The strength of al-Qaeda as an organization rests, then, not on the numbers of members directly and organizationally tied to Bin Laden. It rests instead on its ability as a flexible network of relationships to appeal to widely dispersed sentiment pools within which people can be recruited. In this structure, there is no hierarchical core whose destruction would bring an end to the system. Instead, the destruction of some part of the network in a highly visible way might simply add to the strength of the concept and symbol frame of the movement by creating a new symbolic narrative and highly appealing symbols of martyrdom.

The strength of Bin Laden's message rests at least partially as well on the nature of the role of religion within the emerging postmaterialist global civil society. His call is not to rouse the lower and working classes to a revolution defined by material values and class conflict. Instead, the appeal of the message of the militant religious movement rests on its call to fight for a religious vision of the future. Most mainstream Muslims condemn both Bin Laden's rigid religious vision and his terrorist methods, but Bin Laden frames his message in the mode of the new age of social movements advocating postmaterialist values. It is essential to recognize that Bin Laden and al-Qaeda are not simply mindless religious fanatics or anachronisms. Instead, they represent the extremes that can emerge in the new age of desecularized modernity and social movements of protest and revolution that are organized as networks and frame their message in ways that are congruent with the age of the "resurgence of religion."

Analyze Terrorist Strategies

The way to answer the questions at the end, according to Sun Tzu, is to analyze and counter the strategy of the enemy in this war. Strategies are nebulous things to analyze, so to do this objectively, this study needs a systematic method of analyzing and using terrorist groups' strategies. This chapter explores the most common method of comparing terrorist groups: the typology. It explains why this method is not deep enough for analyzing and comparing strategies. Instead, it develops what it calls an analytical framework, which consists of factors cited by scholars as those, most important to consider when analyzing terrorist groups. It explains how this framework can (and will) be used to develop an assessment of a terrorist group's strategy. One way of attacking the problem is by grouping the terrorist organizations within a terrorist typology, which is merely a classification system that attempts to delineate the different types of terrorism. For instance, some classify groups entirely by ideological motivation, which generally yields anarchism, communism, fascism, nationalism/

separatism, religion, and pro-state classes. Others include catchall categories for groups that do not quite fit, such as Latin American or new world. The classes or types within the typology are usually driven by its analytical purpose. To adequately represent the spectrum of terrorist groups, one would have to develop a multidimensional typology that differentiates with respect to all variables significant to the analysis.

The claim, for instance, that there is a new terrorism suggests a typology with the classes "new" and "old." But this is not entirely useful, because undoubtedly there would be differences among the old groups and among the new groups. A comparison strictly based on this two-class typology would stand little chance of finding a difference. To be effective, the typology would need subclasses, and the subclasses should be the same for "old" and "new." The weakness of this approach is that it implies the nature of terrorism is stable.

It is entirely possible, if there is a new terrorism, that none of the new groups would fit within the subclasses of old terrorism. To compare, however, an analyst would be tempted to fit the groups within these categories any- way, and this would blur reality. If the purpose of the classification is to determine the nature of the terrorist threat to states and to tell whether this threat has changed, this type of classification exercise is not nearly deep enough. The factors that produce these classes and subclasses are a good point of departure. If ideology is important enough to have inspired entire typologies, then it is a factor that should be considered in the analysis. Similarly, other factors that may be used to differentiate groups should be considered as well. This study develops an analytical framework consisting of the factors that are important in determining the nature of the terrorist threat.

The difference between this analytical framework and a typology is that the study makes no attempt to put names to the different factor variations. It will not call one group a left-wing group and another a right-wing group, as a typology would. Rather, it will perform a more difficult subjective assessment. Developing this analytical framework is difficult due to the diversity of terrorist groups. Like snowflakes, no two are identical; to ignore a nuance may be to incorrectly understand the threat a group imposes. Understandably, few experts have developed comprehensive analytical frame- works. O'Neill proposes the way to determine the nature of the insurgent group by identifying its goals, the means, or form of war, it uses. For a terrorist group, the means would be terrorism, as opposed to guerrilla or conventional war. The next step is to identify the strategy being used. These strategies would differ with respect to six factors: environment, popular support, organization, unity, external support, and government response.

A RAND Corporation study identified 10 categories of terrorist- group attributes that could be used to analyze terrorist groups and to answer broad analytical questions: organization; leadership; demography; ideology, doctrine, and goals; psychology, mind-set, and decision making; funding and logistics; operations and modus operandi; communications; external relations; and environment and government response. Some also include strategy in the list. At first glance, it may seem that these analytical frameworks have little in common. However, they can all be stripped to a common core of factors. For the moment, remove strategy from consideration. Strategy relates means to ends, so it will be addressed later as the overarching link among all other factors. The group's desired ends are often difficult to discern, given that the group may not have explicitly stated them and may have stated false ends just to cloud the issue.

As our exploration of the nature of terrorism revealed, often the ends are only one of many methods a group will use to motivate its members and target audience. Therefore, any stated ends can be considered in the same category as ideological motivation during the analysis. The rest of the factors in each of the above frame- works relate to a group's means. When placed side by side, the factors can be massaged into four categories that form a simple, four-factor an- analytical framework.

The operations factor refers to the type of acts the group carries out. The analyst must look at the types of tactics the group uses, the frequency of its attacks, and the number and type of targets it attacks. A group that at- tacks mostly materiel targets has a different strategy than one that attacks mostly people. A group that assassinates public officials with whom it disagrees has a different strategy than one that drives a planeload of people it does not know into a building of more people it does not know. O'Neill pro- poses that this has much to do with the type of environment in which the group is operating.

For instance, the Tupamaros showed that an urban campaign is possible within the proper societal context. The choice of the urban campaign revealed that the Tupamaros:

- Wanted close proximity to the more politically active city-dwellers,
- Wanted to be near the more lucrative political targets, and
- Knew that the city was a better environment from which to resist any military intervention.

These are bits of information that can aid in piecing together the group's strategy. The increasing lethality of modern terrorist acts and the fact that these acts are committed on seemingly innocent bystanders are probably the most oft-cited factors in the determination that today's terrorism is new. Motivation is another factor that is considered to have undergone a revolutionary change. In the context of this framework, motivation refers to the driving force that inspires the collective group (not the psychological motivation of the individuals). Whereas older groups usually had a political objective in mind (as well as a matching political ideology), many experts say today's groups are interested in causing total world chaos so as to usher in a new world order.

That this will have an impact on the terrorists' strategy is evident from Taheri's summary of the Islamic ideology used by many modern terrorist groups: "Considering itself as an expression of Islamic revival which must, by definition, lead to the conquest of the entire globe by the True Faith, . . . it is clearly conceived and con- ducted as a form of Holy War which can only end when total victory has been achieved." This motivation is an important factor in understanding the group's strategy, because it is the message that the group must transmit to its target audience to gain and maintain its legitimacy and, there- fore, sustain moral and materiel support, which is the third factor in the analytical framework. There are basically two types of support the groups need: materiel and moral. In the past, especially during the Cold War, external relations with states were common sources of funding and weapons.

That should have been a hint to these states that such ties were a potential starting point for counterterrorism: "It is a curious anomaly of covert warfare that governments understand the importance of financing groups they support, but fail to appreciate how vital cash is to the terrorist forces they oppose." Obtaining this materiel support forms a major portion of the terrorists' strategy. But just as important is obtaining the moral support of followers. "Terrorism is aimed at the people watching, not at the actual victims." The tough question here is, "Which people watching are the terrorists aiming to influence?" For example, when the airliners slammed into the WTC on 9/11, citizens of the United States were angry. That evening President Bush proclaimed in a speech that: The pictures of airplanes flying into buildings, fires burning, huge structures collapsing, have filled us with disbelief, terrible, sadness, and a quiet, unyielding anger. These acts of mass murder were intended to frighten our nation into chaos and retreat. But they have failed; our country is strong.

A great people have been moved to defend a great nation. Terrorist attacks can shake the foundations of our biggest buildings, but they cannot touch the foundation of America. These acts shattered steel, but they cannot dent the steel of American resolve. Whether the terrorists correctly predicted the American public's reaction to the attacks on the WTC is a matter for hypothesis. But more important is the fact that Americans were probably not the target audience for the attacks. It is quite possible the attacks were meant to show others in the world that the terrorists were carrying out their sacred duty to fight against the evil West, no matter what the cost. In that case the strong response can play into the terrorists' strategy. To correctly understand the terrorist group's strategy, the analysis must correctly identify the target audience. Usually, the audience is one that, if properly influenced, will in- crease the group's materiel and moral support. Once all the means are in place, the terrorists must organize to put them into action. In organizing, the group needs to satisfy several somewhat conflicting needs. There is a need to maintain covertness but also a need to maintain contact with the target audience to proselytize. There is a need for cooperation among members but also a need for anonymity in case one member gets arrested. Not only is there a need for functional specialization but also a need for duplication of some efforts. And there is a need for control from the top and a need for freedom at the operations level.

The Basque *Euskadi Ta Askatasuna (ETA)* solves these needs by organizing along three different lines: a basic cell structure, where a handful of individuals who do not know each others' names are responsible to a single individual; a division into legals, illegals, and supporters to maintain some covertness and some overtness; and a committee structure which assures the various functions such as finance, politics, and military operations are accomplished. As new terrorism evolves, organizations are increasingly becoming flatter, less hierarchical, and capable of forming a matrix with other organizations. This strategy indicates a difference in that this type of organization would be capable of operations on a much larger, global scale with the possibility of multiple operations immediately. Advanced technology communication would allow all the operations of a large network of terrorists to be effectively controlled by a single command section. Identification of these terrorist means and ends does not constitute assessment of the group's strategy. A strategy is a much more esoteric, subjective thing that one might describe as: "a product of the mind and will that adapts and distributes available means to attain desired ends in an atmosphere of uncertainty."

It is rarely written in one place while it is being executed. Even the top members may not be able to clearly communicate how the available means will translate to the desired ends. It is not an easy task to discern the group's strategy. But doing so is critical to determining the appropriate counterstrategy. The problem in Uruguay was that the government did not understand the Tupamaros's strategy and ended up playing right into it. Identifying the four factors in the analytical framework is the first part of identifying a terrorist group's strategy. The next part is identifying the mechanism that turns these factors into a strategy. In this context, a mechanism is an intellectual explanation for the translation of force, applied on a given target set, into political change. It is the theoretical reason for the success or failure of a given method to produce a desired outcome. Since this is the esoteric part of strategy, this is the part that must be surmised. Sometimes in retrospect, terrorists may hint at a mechanism in their writings. Carlos Marighella was a Brazilian legislator—turned terrorist in the late 1960s—who wrote a practical manual on how to conduct an urban terrorist campaign.

Many groups have adopted his methods. His basic mechanism was that spontaneous and random violence, combined with a propaganda campaign, would convince the government and its people that the government had lost control. Such action would cause the government to crack down with some type of martial law that would take away the people's freedoms and would show how repressive the government can be. At this point, the "urban guerrillas," as Marighella called them, would be the underdogs—victims of the same repression that the people were experiencing—but willing to fight in spite of it. The people would turn away from the government and join the guerrillas. Presumably, Marighella then aimed at increasing the terrorist forces through recruitment of the people until the government forces could be overthrown, although this is not clear from his manual. Another possibility would be that he expected the pressure of public opinion to force the government to give in to his demands.

A similar mechanism had worked for another group 20 years earlier— the Israeli group, Irgun, led by Menachim Begin. The Irgun had used violence, although mostly in the form of attacks on British government forces, to induce the British to impose military discipline on the Palestinian region. Simultaneously, the violence and counter-violence gained international recognition for the Irgun's cause. Finally, outcry from the British public and other countries, including the United States, forced the British to acquiesce to the formation of an Israeli state in Palestine. Lacking strategic foresight, the British played right into the Irgun's strategy. Since then, the Irgun strategy has been ineffective, even though many groups have followed Marighella's writings and used his method to spread terror in different parts of the world. These points out the need to identify a terrorist group's overall strategy, including its mechanism, when determining the counterstrategy.

Identifying a mechanism in a terrorist group's strategy is not as simple as putting oneself in another's shoes. The tendency when assessing a mechanism is to treat the enemy as a single, rational individual, when that is not the case at all. Not those terrorists are not rational, but no organization of human beings can be depended upon to act like a single, rational human being in all of its actions. The tendency is to think that an organization's actions are the results of choices made by its leaders. An organization is a black box that covers many smaller organizations that may be performing according to their own rules and procedures or that they may be serving goals that are only partially compatible with the organization's overall goals. This agrees with Crenshaw's observation that many terrorist organizations espouse ideological goals only as a way to appear legitimate. These organizations commit terrorist acts because that is what they do—violence attracts more recruits, who are trained to commit more violence, in a self-perpetuating cycle. Many of these organizations could be considered criminal in nature, and there may be no higher mechanism than tactical modus operandi.

This is why the analyst must identify the organization's operations, ideological motivation, support, and organizational structure and infer from them the nature of the group's strategy. Any incongruence among these factors could signal an incomplete or irrational strategy. The task of defining the nature of the terrorist threat to determine whether there is a new terrorism is a complex one. It involves much more than simply developing a typology that classifies terrorist groups by one or several characteristics of the group. This study follows the advice of Sun Tzu and assesses the strategy upon which the terrorist groups are staking their hopes of success. The first step in this two-step method is the development of a consistent analytical framework that completely describes the means at the disposal of a terrorist group. This study uses framework that is a hybrid of those used by several terrorist experts and consists of four primary factors: operations/lethality, motivation, support, and organization.

The second, and more difficult, step is determining the mechanism by which these four factors could translate into success for the terrorist group. The two steps, taken together, form an assessment of the terrorist group's strategy—a strategy that the group may or may not even be able to articulate among themselves. This strategic assessment forms the analytical foundation of the natural threat posed by terrorist groups and the appropriate strategy to defeat them. The remaining analyze a small sample of old and new terrorist groups and use this process to determine whether the nature of the new terrorist threat holds implications for our strategy in a war on terrorism. The delineation between old and new is that the new groups are those who have been influenced by both the Islamic fundamentalist revolution and the end of the Cold War—groups that have begun their terrorist activities in the 1990s and have ideologies that deal with worldwide struggle and conversion.

The revealed truth is the group's motivation in terms of ideology and goals. This allows the group to continue its operations—the armed struggle, in its ecosystem, which is the underground organization and its materiel and moral support. Communication of the motivation is the energy to maintain this support. This chapter analyzes three of the old terrorist groups: the Red Army Faction (RAF), the Palestine Liberation Organization (PLO), and the Irish Republican Army (IRA).

Red Army Faction

The RAF of West Germany was a good example of what most terrorist experts would label ideological or left-wing terrorism. They were born of the anti-everything movements that predominated in the West in the 1960s—when students with a social conscience were protesting the Vietnam War and there was a perceived repression of the Third World by the United States in the name of anticommunism.

As Hoffman puts it, "Perhaps the unprecedented economic prosperity of these years allowed the luxury of introspection and self-criticism that, in more radical political circles, generated a revulsion against the socioeconomic inequities endemic to the modern, industrialized capitalist state." The RAF evolved into one of the more dangerous European groups of the modern era and committed spectacular acts of terrorism against high-visibility targets, emerged from the ashes twice when their entire leadership was imprisoned, and attempted to organize a European-wide anti-imperialism front by combining with Action Directe of France in 1984 and the Red Brigades (PCC Faction) of Italy in 1988. But the fall of the Berlin Wall in 1989 started the process of politically marginalizing the group by taking away their ideological relevance, and the group declared a truce in 1992. As such, they make an excellent group to examine to learn the nature of the old terrorism.

The RAF evolved from a group formed by two German college students. On 3 April 1968 two Free University of Berlin students, Andreas Baader and his girlfriend, Gudrun Ensslin, set fire to two department stores with incendiary bombs. Their subsequent radical actions gradually drew the attention of the politically engaged, disaffected Berlin youth, including Ulrike Meinhof, a journalist-turned-political activist who became one of the group's core members. Andreas and Ulrike became the founders of the Baader-Meinhof Group (BMG). In 1970, Baader, Ensslin, Meinhof, and six others fled Germany to a terrorist training camp in Jordan to be trained by Palestinians. Although they were dismissed after two months, they had learned enough to begin their terrorist group, now called the RAF.

Organization

The best place to begin studying the RAF is within their organizational structure because it provides a foundation for understanding other facets of the group. The structure that evolved over the years was an organization of four levels: commando, resistance, sympathizer, and prison. The commando level included the hard-core, clandestine members who performed the most tactically difficult and risky acts. The resistance-level members were those who lived legal, open lives but carried out low-level, less risky and demanding terrorist acts in support of the commando level. It was from this level that the RAF recruited new commando members. Sympathizers supported the RAF with demonstrations and propaganda but were unwilling to become militant. The prison level comprised former commandos who had been arrested and put in prison where they continued the struggle.

The structure was basically an adaptation created by necessity when the original BMG members were arrested in June 1972. The group would have fallen apart had the leaders not worked through their attorneys to maintain direction from prison. They established a communication system and developed former supporters into the next generation of the RAF with the primary objective of getting the leaders out of prison. Some of the other supporters started carrying out smaller attacks in response to the actions of the prisoners or commandos with the intent to cause materiel damage instead of casualties, and the RAF members began to see these resistance members as an integral part of the strategy. However, the commando level always maintained a distance from the resistance level for security purposes. In 1991 the German police estimated that there were 12–20 commandos, and the total strength of the group was approximately 200–300 members. This organizational structure had a major impact on the types of operations the group undertook.

Operations

The RAF in its infancy was a small organization that answered only to its own whims. Until 1972 most of the group's operations were thefts and bank robberies. On 11 May 1972 the original RAF members began their first and only campaign with a bomb attack on the US Fifth Army Corps officers' mess in Frankfurt that killed one and injured 13. In rapid succession between then and 24 May, the group pipe bombed the Augsburg police headquarters, car bombed the Bavarian criminal investigation department in Munich, planted a bomb in a German High Court judge's car, set off three bombs in the Springer Publishing firm in Hamburg, and car bombed the European headquarters of the US Army in Heidelberg.

These attacks killed four and injured 59. The entire leadership of the group was arrested and imprisoned, and the campaign was disrupted. The next generation would be entirely different. As the RAF organizational structure evolved, different—but related—RAF operations were accomplished at each of its four levels. After its resurrection by the imprisoned leadership, the commando level began an operational campaign to obtain the release of the prisoners. The most sophisticated of these was the kidnapping of Dr. Hans-Martin Schleyer. As president of the Employers' Association of the Federal Republic of Germany and the Federation of German Industry, board member of Daimler-Benz, and personal friend of Chancellor Helmut Schmidt, Schleyer was a conspicuous capitalist target. The RAF nabbed Schleyer from an armed motorcade on 5 September 1977.

In coordination with their communiqué demanding the release of the RAF prisoners, on 13 October a Palestinian terrorist group member named "Martyr Halimeh" hijacked a Lufthansa airliner with 91 passengers. He flew the plane to Mogadishu, Somalia, and also demanded compliance with the RAF's demands. The German government refused to cave in and executed a counterterrorist operation that freed all the passengers and captured or killed all the hijackers. When the RAF leaders in prison learned this elaborate scheme had failed, they committed suicide. But the RAF commandos, insisting the prisoners had been murdered, killed Schleyer. This marked the end of the last major campaign of the RAF's career. From 1978 until 1991, the RAF struggled for its existence.

Able to muster only one or two attacks per year, the group relied on a parallel operations strategy to generate excitement among public supporters. All four levels activated simultaneously, and this resulted in (1) an assassination and communiqué by the commando level, (2) a hunger strike to the death by the prisoners, (3) low-level bombings by the resistance, and (4) protests and arson by the sympathizers. For example, in December 1984, about 30 RAF members in prison began a hunger strike that lasted until February 1985. During this period, there were about 60 terrorist strikes, one of which was the assassination of Ernst Zimmerman, chairman of a major industrial corporation. The other strikes were made in Germany, France, and Greece, which signaled another trend in RAF operations. On 15 January 1985 the RAF and a French group, Action Directe, announced in a joint five-page statement that they were setting up a united political-military front in Western Europe to oppose NATO employment and operations in Western Europe. Although the RAF tried a similar arrangement later with the Italian Red Brigades, neither arrangement amounted to much.

For the RAF, the 1980s were a struggle for viability. The overall record of the RAF is not terribly frightening as a threat to security. In the years 1972 to 1991, there were 24 commando-level attacks. Of these, 11 were directed at facilities and 13 at people. About 45 percent of the attacks were successful, but even many of the unsuccessful ones were audacious. The RAF did not shy away from attacking heavily defended targets, such as attempting six assassinations of heavily guarded individuals. In the entire period, a total of 23 people were killed and 100 injured by the commando-level attacks, including those in 1972.

Support

The RAF used various methods of materiel support necessary to maintain their two-decade war. The early group's actions resembled those of Marighella and the Tupamaros in that they tried to expropriate everything they needed from their enemies. They robbed banks to finance their activities and stole cars—BMWs were their trademark—to pull off the robberies. For their training, they attended Palestinian training camps in 1970. The PLO group al-Fatah also sold the RAF weapons. They obtained valuable support from East Germany. In 1980 the RAF met with the East Germans to discuss strategy and gain intelligence. In 1981 the East Germans trained three RAF members to operate rocket-propelled grenades.

Arrests in East Germany in 1990 uncovered that the RAF was receiving money, weapons, intelligence, and safe haven from their eastern brothers. Yet this materiel support could not guarantee the RAF's vitality. Maintaining the support of the public, or at least enough to continue recruitment, was the toughest part of the RAF's struggle. German intelligence officials estimated the number of sympathizers had been more than 1,000 in the 1970s, but by the mid-1980s the number had dropped to about 150. From this pool, it is difficult to maintain a steady stream of recruits. Struggle for support is indicative of the group's lack of ideological strength and resilience.

Motivation

The biggest weakness of the RAF was a profoundly unprofound ideology. The group seemed to be anti-everything: "There are thousands of unresolved problems that are crying out for a solution and that will lead all mankind into a catastrophe unless they are tackled soon and solved. All these problems sprang up as a result of the capitalist principle, according to which the only thing that counts is profit and power, and where people and nature play only a subordinate role." In the early years, this meant fighting the United States because of its involvement in Vietnam. After Vietnam the RAF had to look for another cause and latched onto the Palestinian struggle. But throughout the majority of its existence, the RAF was focused on the liberation and civil rights of its imprisoned members and continued a line of propaganda that the prisoners were being tortured and isolated. In 1992 German Justice Minister Klaus Kinkel put it more bluntly: "Without the prisoners, there would be no RAF."

Added to this, several of the group members, notably Baader, showed by their lifestyle that they were motivated as much by the sex and drugs that were loose and free in the group as by the save-the-world ideals. This haphazard mixture of aims severely diluted any Marxist-Leninist ideology the group may have used to reach its supporters. Even this Marxist-Leninist ideology was doomed. The fall of the Berlin Wall in 1989 took away the RAF's cross-border sanctuary, terminated support from all communist sources, and started the process of politically marginalizing the RAF. In the group's own words, "The collapse of the socialist states . . . has had a disastrous effect on the millions of people throughout the world, and now all those who are fighting for liberation all around the globe have to rely solely on themselves." But the "millions of people" were not willing to join the RAF in a struggle without the support of the socialist states. Two communiqués in 1992 set the stage for the dismantling of the RAF, and by 1998 they were completely disbanded.

The true RAF strategy was much different than the one that any group member may have recited during its existence. The organizational structure developed around the prisoners, with even the commandos usually following their lead. Their tendency was to try to get themselves out of jail or at least obtain access to each other in jail so they could communicate. These goals took priority over and diluted any higher calling. It is true that the group accomplished some impressive feats that, in quantity, could have caused NATO and the imperialist nations enough headaches to change policy. (This is the only possible mechanism for success.) But the RAF did not accomplish these in quantity. The main purpose of the operations was to maintain moral support from the public and materiel support from the socialist nations. The central theme of the RAF strategy was that of group maintenance—in Crenshaw's terms, they were an *organizational*-type group.

The label criminal may have even fit them better than terrorist, and the West German government's response to them reflected this. The Germans simply refused to negotiate with the RAF, most notably in the case of the combination Schleyer kidnapping-Lufthansa hijacking. The government kept the RAF in check by arresting and prosecuting its leaders—in June 1972 and November 1982 they arrested all the leaders. Although the group came back from these set- backs, they were never able to pose a serious threat to national security. When the Berlin Wall fell in 1989, there was no higher cause to drive them and no support to sustain them, so they expired.

Palestine Liberation Organization

Analyzing the PLO as a terrorist organization requires some explanation because many would object that the PLO is not and has never been a terrorist organization. Having evolved into the Palestinian Authority, which today is the governing body of a territory; it could now be considered a government. The PLO has always been an umbrella for many factions and groups, most of which have been terrorist in nature. But while the PLO was more than just these terrorist groups, it would have been nothing without them. The terrorist groups took control of the PLO, put it in the world public opinion limelight, and brought in enough recruits and sup- port to sustain its struggle toward their vision of a Palestinian-controlled state in the territory controlled by Israel. The PLO provided the framework and organizational structure within which these groups could claim a unified front toward a common goal, even if they had different methods for achieving that goal. In this respect, the PLO was no different than the IRA, which also had a central structure but had no real control over individual actions of its constituent groups.

The PLO should be viewed as an organization with a strategy that, from the beginning in 1964. included the use of terrorism through its constituent groups to achieve its ends. The British had promised the Palestinians they would become their own state after World War I. Instead, the Middle East was carved up and divided among the imperial powers and the Arab tribes. After World War II, the Jews who had flocked to the area managed to gain control of the state of Israel from the British through United Nations mediation (and after a terrorist campaign of their own). The Arabs attacked the Israelis but were defeated, and 500,000 Palestinians were forced to leave their homes and live in refugee camps in nearby areas, especially Lebanon. In these camps, the Palestinians built new lives and never gave up hope of eventually regaining their homes. They sent their children to get educated in Western universities, they used their education to set up successful businesses, and they prospered when merchant families in the unstable, oil-rich countries (Libya, Iraq, Iran, South Yemen, and Syria all underwent revolutions, but were rich from oil exports) hid their money in Lebanon. Then in 1964, Egypt's Gamal Abdel Nasser organized a Pan- Arabic convention that formed the PLO. But the formation of an organization could not assure the unity of the Palestinians.

Organization

The PLO was an umbrella organization for many other groups and was organized into three departments at the highest level: the Palestine National Council, the Executive Committee, and the Palestine National Fund (PNF). The Executive Committee was a group of 15 men, of whom Yasser Arafat was appointed chairman in January 1969, riding a wave of popularity due to his survival of a battle with the Israelis at Karamah. The PNF was eventually given total control of all the PLO's finances, although many of the groups' funds were directly from external sponsors who did not want their influence watered down by a common funding pot. The PLO attempted to develop unity through the Palestinian National Congress, of which there were 18 sessions between 1968 and 1990. But the amount of influence the PLO had over these groups was debatable, since each of them had its own internal organization, ideology, and support. The two main groups in the 1960s were Fatah and the Popular Front for the Liberation of Palestine (PFLP).

Yasser Arafat, who had started his career with the Muslim Brotherhood in Egypt, led the Fatah. When President Nasser destroyed the Brotherhood, Arafat moved elsewhere and formed Fatah. At the time of the PLO's formation, Fatah was already planning to begin military operations against the Israelis and thus gained the momentum which eventually made them the most powerful group within the PLO. George Habash formed the PFLP as a counterweight to Fatah. There were other factions, and many more would come later. The history of the PLO is one of continuous splits among splinter groups. The organization of the individual groups is not as important to the overall strategy of the PLO as the fact that the PLO was under the constant tension of having to try and integrate its own actions with those of the groups and who sometimes played along and sometimes did not. But their fate was ultimately tied to the fate of the PLO because of their common goal and the fact that the PLO was the organization that the rest of the world recognized as the authority over the smaller groups.

Motivation

The driving force behind the PLO and the only thing nominally holding the different factions moderately together was—as its name implies—the desire to liberate the Palestinians. In 1964 the resolution that initiated the PLO stated, "Palestinian people must play a part in liberating its country, and in achieving self-determination." Fatah under Arafat recognized the armed struggle as a transcendent cause requiring the organization to abandon all ideological and social divisions. The groups had ideological leanings. In 1974 Arafat admitted that Fatah realized the Palestinian struggle as one piece in the worldwide struggle against colonialism and imperialism. The PFLP was even farther to the left. In Marxist-Leninist style, the PFLP believed it would be a revolutionary party that could ignite a revolution (the liberation of Pales- tine from Israel) that would unite the entire Arab world. But it was the memories (and, among the youth, the tales) of the injustice and devastation of the exodus in the late 1940s—the hunger for their own land—that inspired the Palestinian people.

This is what basically motivated the PLO— most of the time. The Arab states had other goals and that complicated the PLO's organizational dynamics. They also had money and other forms of support that individual factions within the PLO needed. But in return for this support, these sponsors often spurred the groups to undertake operations against other Arab states or even other groups within the PLO. This often gave the illusion that the groups were simply fighting to maintain support from the Arab states. For example, the Lebanese civil war in 1975–76 experienced Palestinians fighting with the left-wing Lebanese against Syrians. In its aftermath, Anwar Sadat of Egypt made overtures to Israel and the United States to start a peace process. Iraq, dreaming of a pan-Arabic state under Iraqi control, hired Abu Nidal, a PLO terrorist group, to make strikes against moderate PLO members and against Syria, its political enemy. Thus, Fatah found itself fighting Iraq, other Palestinians, and Syria simultaneously.

In 1982 during the Israeli invasion of Lebanon, Fatah was expelled from Beirut by the Israelis, their refugee camps by the Christian Falange group, and the Tripoli area by the Syrians and the Lebanese Shiites, who were sponsored by Iran. The Palestinians and the Arab states had in common the desire to remove Israel from the lands occupied in the 1967 Six-day War. But the political dealings of the states got the PLO involved in operations that exacerbated the internecine nature of its groups. Nevertheless, the PLO found out along the way that they did not need the materiel support of the Arab states as much as they thought and found other ways to support themselves.

Support

Since the beginning, state support to the PLO has been unreliable. In 1971 only $40,000 of $10 million promised by Arab states was delivered to the PLO. This spurred the PLO to demonstrate, through spectacular feats of terrorism, that it still held credibility in the war against Israel. In 1975 the PLO made a tour of the Gulf States to coerce them into paying. Only Kuwait, Saudi Arabia, Morocco, and the United Arab Emirates could be counted on. The individual groups under the PLO umbrella received donations directly from the Arab states, who could then take advantage of the differing ideological leanings of the groups for their own purposes. Syria financed Saiqa and the PFLP General Command (PFLP-GC) to the amount of $50 to $100 million. At different times, Abu Nidal was hired by Syria, Iraq, and Libya to do their bidding, which included assassinations of PLO representatives in the late 1970s and an attempt on Arafat's life in 1974. Libya had made its debut into terrorism by stuffing $1 million into the PFLP's coffer in 1971.

Throughout the 1970s and 1980s, the PLO never received less than $100 million per year from the Arab states, and it usually received closer to $250 million. The problem was that their operating budget alone was more than $500 million by 1987. This is why the PLO had to turn to self-financing. Most of the efforts of the PLO and its groups in this endeavor were criminal. In the middle of the Lebanese civil war, 20 January 1976, the PLO teamed up with one of its enemies in the war, the Christian Militia, and the Mafia to pull off the largest bank robbery of all time. They robbed the British Bank of the Middle East for what was estimated at $100 million. 48 In 1972 the PFLP hijacked a Lufthansa plane and flew it to South Yemen where they were subsequently paid $5 million as ransom for the crew and the plane. The PFLP also ran a very profitable document forging business. In Lebanon—where the Palestinians essentially dictated the rules—robberies, looting, and pass-through taxes were commonplace. The PLO only made an effort to appear legal when it needed to—for political purposes.

However, it still needed to obtain the moral support of its target audiences. The PLO was as adept at communicating to these target audiences as it was at ignoring the opinions of its non-target audiences. In 1970 the PLO established Samed, or the Palestine Martyrs Work Society, under Arafat's Fatah. The organization's objectives were to develop skilled Palestinian workers, get them in jobs, and develop a thriving, self-sufficient economy that would allow Palestinians to continue the revolution. Samed was basically the economic arm of the PLO. It started by manufacturing basic necessities and expanded to become both a major institution with industrial, cinematography and informational, agricultural, and general commercial branches.

The PLO had a captive, motivated audience in the refugees. But it did not take their loyalty lightly. Besides Samed, the PLO also worked on instilling unity and loyalty to the cause in generations of Palestinians through a social welfare system that included free schooling, free medical care, and generous compensation to the families of anyone killed or injured in the fight against Israel. The PLO had no intention of losing the support of this target audience. Yet there was another target audience—the international community. For this type of communication, the PLO spoke with its terrorist operations.

Operations

The most famous and effective communications with the international community were those acts of international terrorism that vaulted the PLO into the limelight in the late 1960s and early 1970s. The PFLP, under Habash, believed terrorism was a necessary part of the armed struggle and, consequently, the PFLP took the lead in committing 15 acts of inter- national terrorism between 1968 and 1970. At this time, the Fatah acknowledged these acts as reprehensible and only later adopted such methods as desperation measures. The first PFLP incident was the hijacking of an Israeli El Al flight from Rome to Tel Aviv on 22 July 1968. The PFLP held the plane, its crew, and its passenger's hostage and demanded the release of Palestinian prisoners held by Israel. To its satisfaction, the PFLP found this was an extremely successful way not only to obtain this immediate goal but also to awaken the world to the Palestinian cause. The last of the 15 acts was to have different consequences. In early September 1970, the PFLP hijacked four planes, blew one of them up in Cairo, and blew the other three up at Dawson Field in Jordan in front of the television cameras that were filming the hostage negotiations.

Because of this act, the Jordanian Hashemite regime began a massacre of the Palestinians in Jordan and forced the PLO to relocate to Lebanon and spurred the Fatah to adopt more extreme measures out of anger and frustration. The Fatah secretly developed an organization called Black September to commemorate the month the massacre occurred. The most infamous act of this organization was the Munich Olympics kidnapping and murder of Israeli athletes. On 5 September 1972 eight terrorists killed two Israelis and kidnapped nine from their dormitory. They offered to exchange the hostages for 236 Palestinian prisoners in Israel and some RAF prisoners in Germany, and the hostages were taken to an air base to board an aircraft to Cairo. A rescue attempt by the West German police sparked a firefight, and the terrorists killed all nine hostages before the police could kill or capture the terrorists.

This terrible incident showed that even acts that fail to achieve the ostensible objectives could succeed strategically. Although the rest of the world perceived the terrorists as despicable, they also recognized them as a force with a serious cause. Palestinians acknowledged them as heroic defenders of this cause who were able to take incredible risks in its name. Most importantly, less than 18 months later, Arafat was invited to address the UN General Assembly, and the PLO was accorded special observer status. The PLO successfully used international terrorist operations to reach both its target audiences—the Palestinians and the world public. But these operations are only a small part of the spectrum of the PLO's military activities.

The majority of the PLO's military operations were more "conventional" guerrilla or terrorist operations or outright conventional warfare. Fatah began its operations against Israel in 1964 with border attacks that drew criticism from Arab governments. Because of this criticism, Fatah turned to sabotage attacks in an attempt to get the Israelis to go on the offensive.

Fatah's attacks probably contributed to the military developments that triggered the 1967 war. After the Six-day War, Fatah tried to secure strongholds along the Israeli border by attacking the Israeli settlements there but failed because the Israeli forces were too strong. However, when Arafat and Fatah (with substantial help from Jordan) successfully defended one of their bases at Karamah from a ferocious Israeli cross- border attack in March 1968, Arafat and the PLO became heroes to the Arab world.

Since then, the majority of the operations directed against Israel have been either hit-and-run attacks from across the border against Israeli transport or settlements, bombs, or shelling of Israeli settlements. The groups then turned to the international terrorism mentioned above. After the Yom Kippur War, the PLO groups, including PFLP, decided the hijackings had outlived their usefulness. As an acknowledged member of the world community, the PLO had to appear more moderate.

In addition, conflict in Lebanon would keep them busy for over a decade. In 1975 the Lebanese civil war kicked off, and in the period 1976–80, almost all of the attacks by the various PLO terrorist groups were against each other or against the traitor Egyptians. Sadat's 1977 trip to Israel and 1979 Camp David Accords added fuel to the fire, and the use of terrorism as statecraft was in full swing. The only real international terrorist acts during 1976–80 were those by Abu Nidal against Egyptian and PLO targets and a couple retaliations by Fatah. By the late 1970s, the PLO had built 36 up its military infrastructure, and by 1980 Fatah numbered more than 20,000 men.

When the Israelis invaded Lebanon in 1982, to put an end to the terrorist strikes they had been receiving from across the border, Arafat's Fatah was overcome by the weight of a large conventional attack. The PLO would never revisit its ways of the 1970s. The reality of the international environment forced the PLO to take a more political path. The Soviet Union had not helped the PLO at all, despite the PLO's left-leaning ideologies. Arafat began to see that the United States might be the key to any solution. To gain the good graces of the West, the PLO had to appear more moderate. Throughout the mid-1980s, Arafat walked a tightrope between trying to appear moderate to the West and appeasing the extreme factions inside his PLO. While he was officially denouncing terrorism, Fatah committed some terrorist acts, including financing the Palestine Liberation Front in the hijacking of the *Achille Lauro* in 1985. But Arafat was on a path to political resolution with Israel.

Even when the Palestinians in the occupied West Bank and Gaza Strip started an uprising called the Intifada in 1987, Arafat tried to play the peacekeeper. Rather than encouraging the popular revolt that he had wished for two decades earlier, he tried in vain to maintain the peace. But the Intifada accomplished much for the cause, as the West witnessed rock-throwing Palestinians fighting well-armed Israelis. World public opinion, the moderate stance of the PLO, and the active part of the United States led to the Oslo Agreement of 1993. The Oslo Agreement was not the end of the conflict. But it established a Palestinian state, with the former PLO, now the Palestinian Authority, as government. The PLO had come a long way toward achieving its goals. However, the goals changed—the original aim was to remove the Israeli state and get the 1967 land back. The Oslo Agreement did not do this. This shift in aims is indicative of the overall strategy of the PLO, if such a thing could be formulated.

The PLO was a politically motivated organization that used a number of coercive methods to gain its political aims. It was able to accommodate diverse groups under an umbrella organization. It developed a self-sufficient financial arm to provide for the welfare of its people. It used both legitimate and illegitimate methods to obtain the resources to take care of its people and defend itself. It did not rely on terrorism but was able to use terrorism to its advantage to gain worldwide recognition and support, while mounting more conventional military campaigns at the same time. The PLO was willing to compromise in the end to obtain an end state that was slightly short of its original aims, but one that was sufficient to put the PLO in power as a legitimate authority. All these are the signs that the ultimate strategy of the PLO (whether they knew it or not at any given time) was to obtain this legitimacy and power to govern its constituents using coercive methods where necessary.

The PLO's mechanism to accomplish this was raising its enemy's assessment of the costs involved in resisting its demands. Cross-border attacks would impose high blood and treasure costs on Israel, international terrorism would vault the PLO into the international limelight, and a moderate stance would convince the world (including the Israeli public) the PLO could be trusted. The result would be materiel, human, and political costs that Israel simply could not handle. It is not clear how this mechanism could have led to Israeli abandonment of its land, but the mechanism was sufficient to obtain a reasonable compromise.

The Israeli counterstrategies were most certainly not devised with compromise in mind. To the Israelis, the PLO constituted a national security threat. Mindful of their inability to absorb losses of territory and people, the Israelis have always had a distinctly offensive military doctrine, and the counterinsurgency campaign against the PLO was no exception. The Israelis have used a combination of regime targeting, selected air strikes, widespread artillery bombardments, limited land incursions, and fullscale combined operations. The Israeli security forces get much of the credit for the failure of the guerrilla campaigns of 1967. The Battle of Karamah in 1968 was an Israeli mechanized assault designed to wipe out one of Fatah's main bases in Jordan. It was swift and ferocious, but the Jordanians came to Fatah's rescue.

In 1978 Israel invaded again, Lebanon this time, an attack which was eventually halted by UN Security Council Resolution 425, which called on Israel to completely withdraw and allow UN forces to stabilize the region. The resolution did nothing for Israel's security. In 1981 Israel started shelling southern Lebanon in retaliation for the shelling of Israeli settlements. Then in 1982, Israel began Operation Peace for Galilee, an invasion of Lebanon with the declared intent to destroy the political and military infrastructure of the PLO. The invasion, led by Sharon, covered the planned 45 kilometers so quickly that the Israelis decided to press on to Beirut. However, they were unable to wipe out the PLO forces (although Arafat's Fatah fled the country), and in the process ignited resentment among the Shiites. Surgical air strikes were unable to protect the Israeli troops from terrorist harassment, and the Israelis had to pull back closer to the Israel border.

The Israeli dilemma is difficult and promises rewards for neither hard line nor soft. The troops dealt with the PLO from a position of insecurity throughout the entire struggle. Since the PLO's stated objective precluded the presence of an Israeli state, this was quite understandable. But they were facing an enemy that learned to use world public opinion very effectively, a skill the Israelis neglected. They never attempted a "hearts and minds" campaign and, consequently, missed opportunities to put the PLO on the defensive and also to make allies out of the Shiites in Lebanon. Instead, they have made bitter enemies. But they did enter into the peace process, signed the Oslo Agreement, and withdrew from disputed territory—possibly too little, too late. The PLO has become the Palestinian Authority, and Arafat won elections in 1996, but there is still no peace. The Islamic Hamas commands enough support, and the Palestinian Authority and Israel—enough distrust—that the Palestinian people are divided as to which way is the road to satisfaction.

Irish Republican Army

The foregoing cases provide good examples of the application of this study's analysis framework and process, but they do not completely define the nature of the old terrorism. While such a complete definition may be out of reach in this study, no discussion of modern terrorism is complete without some mention of the IRA. In much taxonomy, the IRA's struggle would be categorized with the PLO's because both are struggles for an ethnic nation. There are similarities, but a quick analysis of the IRA reveals many differences as well. Although the Irish conflict has cultural roots that extend back centuries, the struggle was rejuvenated in the late 1960s. This modern-day period began in 1969 when the Catholic civil rights campaign in Northern Ireland sparked violence. Since the formation of an Irish free state with British protection in Northern Ireland in 1921, the northern government had systematically reduced civil rights for Catholics living in the north.

In the 1960s, these Catholics started a major civil rights movement to improve housing and education. In January 1969 participants in a four-day civil rights march from Belfast to Derry were gassed and beaten. Then in August, at the annual Protestant Apprentice Boys celebration, violence erupted and sent Belfast and Londonderry up in flames. The British sent in the army to make peace. However, the army, under Gen Frank Kitson, tried to implement some of the measures that were successful in its Malayan emergency of 1948–60. This resulted in a security policy that was "repressive enough to continue the alienation of working-class Catholics but not repressive enough to actually defeat the Provisional IRA."

The army implemented internment, torture of prisoners, and house-to-house searches to try and control the situation. Then on 30 January 1972—"Bloody Sunday"—the Northern Ireland Civil Rights Association marched on Derry. Part of the crowd advanced on a British barricade, and violence broke out. The British paratroopers eventually opened fire, killing 13 and wounding 14 others. The events of 1969 through 1972 were enough to completely rejuvenate the IRA, inactive since 1962, and the war was on.

Motivation

The Irish conflict is a good example of Tololyan's culturally based struggle. The IRA has been described as "a dream working." The ideology of the movement is not analytical or political or even well-encapsulated, it is merely shared—"the perception assured by the dream." There is a political ideology espoused by Sinn Féin, but that is definitely not the ideology that has driven the movement. The IRA's training manual, "The Green Book," takes one small paragraph to mention that the objects of the movement are to establish a sovereign, Socialist Irish Republic, with civil rights for all and the Irish language as its official language.

The IRA's motivation defies intellectualism and appeals instead to the masses 39 who share the dream. The dream is a unified Ireland, and it requires sacrifice and struggle, not for vengeance against the evil Protestants, but for unity with misguided Irish. It is perpetuated through rituals, especially funerals that transform the dead into martyrs, rather than through indoctrination. Thus, the Irish acknowledged their problems stemming from the invasion of outsiders, passed down to them for generations in stories, and necessitating a constant struggle.

Operations

The struggle was violent. From 1969 through 1998, there were 3,289 killed (2,332 civilians) and 42,216 injured (27,238 civilians) as a result of the fighting. Although the IRA tries to avoid and then apologizes for casualties to innocents, these happen frequently. The IRA's tactics could have been designed by Mao or Sun Tzu: strike hard and disengage, mass again where the enemy least expects it, then strike again, always keeping him off guard. For example, on 27 August 1979 the IRA accomplished a spectacular double feat of terror. At Warrenpoint in Ireland, they set off a bomb that blew up a British military patrol truck, and then a second one where the soldiers took cover and the rescue helicopter was landing. This killed 18 soldiers. On the same day, they assassinated Lord Louis Mountbatten, on holiday in his boat off Mullaghmore.

Whether assassination or guerrilla warfare, it was always certain that the gun was the primary means of continuing the struggle—until 1981. In 1980–81, the IRA learned that communicating their cause could gain political headway. On their own initiative, 10 prisoners died from hunger strikes when the British refused to negotiate or concede to their demands. This brought attention to their cause from the Irish and from the world that the IRA command had not counted on and opened up a new battle- ground.

Sinn Féin got one of the hunger strikers, Bobby Sands, to run for Parliament. Sands was elected, and when he died, a Sinn Féin representative took his place. Since then the IRA and Sinn Féin have collaborated, although not without conflict, in a policy Gerry Adams laid out in 1977 as "the bullet and the ballot." The road was tough with internal dissension but it got them closer to peace and to their goal. The main problem with any policy in the IRA is the ability to enforce it throughout the organization.

Organization

The IRA organization has evolved, but the basic essentials have been again shaped by the struggle and Irish culture. In the early 1970s, the IRA was organized as a conventional army, with brigades that were given geographic responsibility in Ulster. These brigades were too large and easy for the British to penetrate. In 1977 the IRA adopted a cell structure, with limited contact among cells for security. These cells provided the desired security but also made it harder to coordinate operations.

The local commanders were the ones who decided when and where to act. This decision led to blunders, but it allowed the movement to keep unity, where tactical micromanagement would only have invited schism. The British estimated in 1984 there were about 300 hard-core members, plus several thousand sympathizers. There was a hierarchy to the organization: the Army Convention, Army Executive, Army Council, Chief of Staff Northern Command, and Chief of Staff Southern Command. But these positions did not carry with them the ability to control the cells. They mainly concentrated on marshaling the resources to continue the struggle.

Support

Throughout the years, marshaling the resources became a big business. Certainly the most highly publicized way the IRA obtained materiel resources was through the Irish Northern Aid (Noraid) that was established by Michael Flannery in 1969. Although Noraid contributed more than 50 percent of the IRA budget in the early 1970s and managed to set up major fund-raisers such as an annual fund-raiser dinner in New York, their support has waned over the years. This is because the British recognized that the United States was a major battleground in the moral support campaign. The British tried to counter the strong Irish lobby by playing on America's guilt for helping to finance and arm the perpetrators of atrocities.

For example, after the murder of Lord Mountbatten and the 18 British troops, the *Economist* spewed, "The killers were partly financed by citizens of the United States, and most informed Britons thought that the Carter administration's decision four weeks ago to delay arms sales to Ulster's police (so as to please some Irish American voters) would encourage the IRA into another murderous heave. This last effect was not merely forecastable, it was forecast." After this murder, the United States finally yielded to British pressure. The FBI set up a special squad just to interrupt the flow of cash and arms to the IRA. This resulted in a series of court cases in the 1980s that essentially took Noraid down. But the IRA was already evolving to a more self-sufficient method of support.

They started by forging tax-exempt certificates for building contractors in the early 1970s and eventually worked their way into the security business, the taxi business, and the nightclub business. The security business was a particularly devious one—the terrorists would approach a potential customer and offer security protection for a monthly payment. If the client refused, he was guaranteed to be involved in security incidents that convinced him he needed the protection. The IRA has basically been able to get its hands into any part of the market it wants, so it has not missed the Noraid money. Seemingly, it has not missed the moral support that Noraid represented in the United States.

The key to the IRA was always "the intensity of the faith and only incidentally the assets and even capacity of the underground." The IRA did not maintain the intensity of this faith forever. In the 1990s, the IRA switched from a primacy of the bullet to the primacy of the ballot. On Good Friday, 1998, the IRA signed an accord that settled for less than an independent, unified republic. Instead, they got political checks and balances on the Northern Irish Republic that they hope will eventually lead to a unified Irish Republic. Obviously, everyone was not satisfied—in October 2001 IRA members were arrested while working with terrorists in Columbia. The resulting outrage by the United States caused Sinn Féin to demand and receive a start to the disarmament process within the IRA.

Whether this was really the end of the IRA is another story. It is difficult to believe "the dream" that was kept alive for so long by violence could find resolution in a manner so devoid of drama. The reason this is so hard to believe is that the IRA's entire strategy to this point was one of maintaining a struggle. The IRA knew the dream of an independent, united Ireland was beyond its grasp. Even if it could force the British to leave, it would have to fight its Protestant brothers in Northern Ireland. Yet this dream still propelled its members. It propelled them to the point that they made themselves totally independent of outside support. Their operations were not spectacular—just a few killed here and there. Their organization kept its members to a life of isolation but exercised very little control over them. The key was always to maintain consensus, maintain the faith, and maintain the struggle.

The only mechanism for success was to simply outlast the enemy, imparting costs that the enemy could not handle. The IRA had the opposite problem that the RAF had—instead of too little focus, the IRA had too much. Ireland became a quagmire where an unstoppable force met an immovable object, which resulted in eternal tension. Exhausted by this process, the IRA switched to the political solution. But the process also confounded the British counterstrategy. The British search for an effective counterstrategy produced more lessons in what not to do than in what to do. In 1976 the British stopped trying to treat Ireland as a repeat of Malaya and turned to a policy of internal security where the Army played a supporting role to law enforcement. They ended internment and turned increasingly to the judicial process to prosecute the terrorists. However, the British Special Air Service still used harsh tactics that, at times, included killing rather than arresting the IRA.

Although they were effective at containing the IRA, it is probable that these tactics undermined the legitimacy of the British efforts and increased support for the IRA. The British also failed to recognize the fact that the Protestant paramilitaries were also terrorist groups. By responding only to the IRA and giving the Protestants latitude, the British allowed the Protestants to terrorize the Catholics, further legitimizing the IRA as the only protection the Catholics had. The other problem with British policy was a lack of cooperation between the politicians, the police, the army, and the Dublin government. Each saw its role in a different light and missed the effectiveness that could have been gained by cooperating to pass effective legislation, enforce the legislation, aim effective intelligence toward that enforcement, and patrol the north-south border.

There were fundamental differences among the old terrorist groups. The RAF's ideology centered around global revolution, where that of the IRA and the PLO were focused on territorial and nationalistic objectives. However, the RAF's organization was extremely limited by its focus on the imprisoned leaders. The RAF did not have the resources and leadership to link up with other groups who had similar goals. The IRA's organization was also isolated but very decentralized. Where the lower levels of the RAF took their cues from the prisoners, the lower levels of the IRA were fairly autonomous, which left its leadership to worry about forming a coherent strategy based on tactics that were out of that leadership's control. PLO leadership also had very little control over its constituent groups. The PLO played a key strategic role in managing both the materiel and moral support for the Palestinian cause. It arranged for funding from the Arab states and organized independent financial operations (legal and illegal).

Similarly, the IRA took donations from Noraid but eventually had to learn to support itself after the British won the propaganda war with the Americans. Both the PLO and the IRA benefited from solid moral support among their target audiences because of the historical roots of the struggles. The RAF, on the other hand, struggled for moral support. They obtained materiel support and sanctuary from East Germany and relied on the existence of the Soviet Union to prove their ideological relevance. When the Soviet Union dissolved, the group lost its ideological resilience. All the RAF's operations, consisting of parallel hunger strikes, bombings, kidnappings, and demonstrations, had to be aimed at developing moral support. The IRA and the PLO used operations to develop support as well—especially the PLO's dramatic hijackings. However, these two groups were also involved in a more guerilla-type war—targeting the enemy to wear him down and gain military advantage.

The PLO, at one time, had an army of almost 20,000 soldiers in Lebanon. It is difficult to say that old terrorism had any observable nature at all. The strategies of all these groups did, however, have something in common. Although each professed to be after an absolute victory, they were about outlasting the enemy to achieve political change. In the RAF's case, the strategy was more to ensure the survival of the terrorist group than to achieve any particular policy change, despite the group's stated aims. The PLO proved to be a political body willing to use terrorism to coerce and communicate and to compromise if necessary. The IRA was a stubborn, tunnel-vision group bent on carrying on a two-century-old conflict that had always been about violent struggle. But in the end, even they were worn down by the potential for political gain. In the background loomed the sponsorship of states, but in the world of the terrorist, the state became more of a nuisance than an aid. Unwilling to accept strings attached to the support they got from states, terrorist organizations developed their own resources.

This, of course, came too late to stop the debacle of Lebanon, where in the late 1970s and early 1980s it was difficult to determine if the terrorists were more of a threat to each other or the legitimate states. It also did not stop Libya from provoking violent confrontation with the United States in 1986. By 1987 state sponsorship amounted to about 2 percent of the PLO's budget, and 3 percent of the IRA's budget. The state support simply did not fit with their overall strategies. The states and the terrorist groups had in mind some sort of coercion to change the policies of another political body. Each hoped its enemy would see the costs of the current policies as too high and give in to the terrorist group's agenda.

The nature of old terrorism was that of coercion—threats to the policies of governments more than the security of its people. While all this was taking place, the beginnings of the new terrorism were already taking root. Samuel P. Huntington noted that while western cultures, styles, and habits were becoming increasingly popular among the masses of people in nonwestern countries, the elite of these nonwestern countries were becoming increasingly vocal about rejecting western values. This created conflict along the borders of what Huntington called the "fault lines between civilizations." Although not all civilizations have reacted violently, some have. "Islam has bloody borders."

3

The New Terrorism and the War on Terrorism

Those who slaughtered more than 3,000 persons on 9/11 and who, by their own admission, want nothing more than to do it again, constitute a clear and present danger to all people of good will everywhere in the world, not just the United States. Such acts are a pure example of naked aggression against innocent human life, a world-threatening evil that clearly requires the use of force to remove it. — "What We're Fighting For"

Five months after the 9/11 attacks on the World Trade Center (WTC) and the Pentagon, this carefully worded epigraph by 60 intellectuals summed up a position that most Americans could support. The letter that contained the statement acknowledged America's shortcomings yet rejected the notion that these shortcomings somehow gave justification to the terrorists that committed the attacks. It deftly pointed out the moral differences among the beliefs of terrorists, Americans, and mainstream Islamics. It represented a well-thought-out justification for the declaration of war on terrorism that the US government issued on 9/11.

Those who issued the original declaration of war were not given the luxury of the same five months to develop their rationale for the stand they took. At 0848 American

Airlines Flight 11, carrying 92 people from Boston to Los Angeles, crashed into the north tower of the WTC. Eighteen minutes later, United Airlines Flight 175, with 65 passengers on the same route, tore through the south tower. Then at about 0940, American Air- lines Flight 77, with 64 aboard from Dulles to Los Angeles, destroyed four of five rings in a section of the Pentagon. Meanwhile, United Airlines Flight 93, carrying 45 passengers from Newark to San Francisco, had crashed in Shanksville, Pennsylvania, where it had been heading in the direction of Washington. In the next hour, both towers of the WTC collapsed, burying thousands of victims with them. The immediate reaction of officials everywhere was volatile.

Gen Henry Shelton, chairman of the Joint Chiefs of Staff, promised, "I will tell you up front, I have no intention of discussing today what comes next, but make no mistake about it, your armed forces are ready." Other officials declared a state of "total war." The media instantly began to make comparisons that put the attacks into the same category as the conflicts in both world wars: "Just as Japan on 7 December 1941 destroyed America's long-standing belief in its ocean-guarded invulnerability, now 11 September 2001 joins that date to live in infamy."

Overseas, foreign diplomats also stoked the fire by declaring a new age of terrorism. Prime Minister Tony Blair promised Britain would stand "shoulder to shoulder" with America in fighting these mass terrorists, whom he called a "new evil in our world." Prime Minister Ariel Sharon of Israel declared, "This is a turning point in the international war on terrorism. This is a war between good and evil. The fight of the free world against the forces of darkness."

As US government officials were trying to deal with the disaster and its aftermath, the rest of the world was narrowing their policy options for them by declaring a state of war and even declaring the nature of that war. By the time the war cabinet met that night, there really were no policy options. Regardless of the initial inclinations of Ex-President George W. Bush's staff, the foregone conclusion was that the United States would be at war. While the events were unfolding, President Bush was aboard Air Force One for security. When the plane landed at Barksdale AFB, Louisiana, Bush said only that "the United States will hunt down and punish those responsible for these cowardly acts."

But by that evening, the tone had changed slightly: "America and our friends and allies join with all those who want peace and security in the world, and we stand together to win the war against terrorism." This statement, in peaceful times, could be taken to mean an ongoing struggle similar to that waged against drugs or crime—"war on drugs" or "war on crime"—but not that night. When told that the suspect, Osama bin Laden, was a global threat whose reach included about 60 countries, President Bush replied, "Let's pick them off one at a time."

Three days later, during a speech at the national funeral, Bush firmly planted the notion of a war with a foreseeable end: "This conflict was begun on the timing and terms of others," he said. "It will end in a way, and at an hour, of our choosing." In the furor of the world's shock at the devastation of 9/11, this could only mean total war against terrorism—whatever that means. The meaning of the statement war on terrorism is the subject of this study. A declaration of a war on terrorism (versus a war against a single terrorist group or an ongoing struggle against terrorism) is unprecedented, and as such it is a concept that cannot be grasped by referring to existing paradigms. Traditionally wars are declared on political entities, and terrorism is not that. Supposedly, one of the factors in declaring this type of war for the first time in history is the notion that there is a "new terrorism."

This notion implies that there was an "old terrorism," and that the nature of terrorism has changed so that today's terrorists must or should be defeated through total war rather than classic counter-terrorist measures. If that is the case, then lessons learned in the past may not be applicable to today's war.

If it is the case, the fact still remains that the United States is at war with terrorism, and as Carl von Clausewitz tells us, understanding the nature of the war is the first step in developing strategy. This study lends clarity to the war on terrorism and determines if there is a new terrorism by defining and comparing the nature of old terrorism with new terrorism. It considers whether the nature of terrorism (new or not) has implications for the American strategy in the war on terrorism and whether it can incorporate any of the old lessons.

Nature of Terrorism

The first, the supreme, the most far-reaching act of judgment that the statesman and commander have to make is to establish by [the nature of their motives and of the situations which give rise to them] the kind of war on which they are embarking; neither mistaking it for, nor trying to turn it into, something that is alien to its nature. Clausewitz's admonition determining the nature of a war points to the very issue that makes our declaration of a war on terrorism problematic. What is the nature of this war? Even before 9/11, terrorism experts were advocating a more proactive policy toward terrorism, while at the same time admitting that "the nature of the conflict is still to be defined."

There are precedents for using military force to combat terrorist groups. Certainly Great Britain and France have had experience with this, and there have been a number of South American countries that have had to resort to the armed forces to combat terrorism. But in each of these instances, the enemy was a particular group. The fact that the United States declared war on terrorism implies that there is a definable nature to a conflict against terrorism. It also implies that this nature has changed—that we are dealing with a new terrorism—since, in the past, experts have warned against escalation in counterterrorism.

This chapter challenges these two implications. It also briefly traces the history of terrorism to show that the changing nature of terrorism has added to the inability to define it, discusses the evolving view of a new terrorism and the characteristics that define it, and examines the problems that scholars have had in categorizing and defining terrorism as a phenomenon. This chapter presents a more practical way to analyze the nature of the war on terrorism:

To limit the scope to the enemy in this war, thereby limiting the potential that the war will grow beyond control. There is a real danger in misreading and overreacting to terrorism, a danger that is "not in terrorist acts per se, but in triggering off a wider and more dangerous armed conflict."

One danger in this wider conflict is, of course, that there may be more destruction and loss of human life due to the escalation than there ever would have been due to the terrorists themselves. However, there is an additional danger that the overwhelming use of force can actually be damaging to the society in general, possibly even aiding the terrorists' cause. This can best be understood by examining an actual example. The Tupamaros were a Uruguayan insurgent group whose movement to overturn the Uruguayan government lasted almost a decade and, though it ended in the group's destruction, had devastating effects on Uruguayan government and society.

In 1961 Raul Sendic unionized the sugarcane and sugar-beet cutters and marched on the capital, Montevideo, to demand land expropriation and redistribution. Imprisoned in the resulting riots, Sendic started the Tupamaro National Liberation Movement. The Tupamaros perceived the problems with the Uruguayan economy as stemming from the basic system of capitalism on which the economy was based. They claimed this system was doing nothing but making the rich richer and the poor poorer, while at the same time making Uruguay more indebted to imperialist nations such as the United States. The government was unwilling to solve these problems because the individuals running it were profiting from the existing system.

The Tupamaros wanted a Uruguay that was independent of the industrial nations, fiercely nationalistic, and operated by a socialistic government—not necessarily a strict copy of other Marxist- Leninist countries but tailored to Uruguay's particular conditions. Their strategy was to use violence—the very thing their government held most critical to the survival of its power monopoly—to seize power from the government. The Tupamaros planned to break down and demoralize the government forces through the selective use of violence in the city, to create a mass uprising of the people to take power, and to implement their ideological objectives. They sought to create a "power duality" where the Tupamaros would be immune to the government's power, and the people would see them as another, parallel source of power.

Their operations were chosen to create this condition. They tried to avoid indiscriminate killing and were "genuine idealists; some of the best of the young generation belonged to them." They coerced their enemies to finance their cause by stealing from sources that they recognized as supporters of the elite and explained, "The bourgeoisie's property is our natural fountain of resources and we have the right to expropriate it without compensation. [Our] revolution puts to use the surplus of the privileged."

The Tupamaros kidnapped officials they accused of corruption or wrongdoings (i.e., torturing prisoners) to blackmail the government and demonstrate their power.

To further intimidate, they bombed and killed other corrupt officials. In one case, the Tupamaros broke into an illegal loan company, took records, and forwarded them to a judge who convicted the company. This context in mind, it is clear the government's reaction was critically flawed. The government's policy in this struggle eventually led to the collapse of all democratic institutions in Uruguay. In the beginning, combating the Tupamaros was the job of the national police. President Jorge Pacheco Areco ruled with an iron hand and imposed wage freezes and press censorship in an effort to control the situation. In 1968 he gave himself emergency powers so he could quell demonstrations and silence opposition. When the policemen proved unable to handle their job, the president militarized them.

When the bankers struck in 1969, he militarized them. In 1970, during one month alone, he ordered extensive searches of more than 20,000 homes, many without warrants. In 1971, after the Tupamaros rescued more than 100 of their prisoners (and subsequently imposed a unilateral cease-fire for the elections), Pacheco ordered the armed forces to take charge of the entire operation. The army requested congress to declare a state of internal war and started a powerful, ruthless campaign that wiped the Tupamaros out. However, in the process the army also came face-to- face with corruption in the Uruguayan government (with the help of some prodding from the imprisoned Tupamaros). In 1973 the military seized power from President Pedro Bordaberry, and any pretense of democracy in the country was gone.

By many classic measures, the Tupamaros had lost the war—they were completely destroyed. The government had misjudged the nature of the war. It had fought a brutal war of attrition, as if the security of the state was at risk instead of the freedom of the people and the legitimacy of the government. To keep this from happening to our country, the United States needs to do a better job of determining the nature of the war it is fighting. One reason this is so difficult is that the term terrorism has been used to refer to many technically different phenomena throughout history. In fact, when trying to determine if there is a "new breed" of terrorist, one might question whether that is important because terrorism has changed so many times. Its origin is often traced (although not by the name terrorism) back as early as the Zealots of the first-century time period.

Later, the Assassins were a Persia-based group that spread throughout the Middle East in the eleventh through the thirteenth centuries. Although the group was driven by political aims on the strategic level—they were fighting the Crusaders—these killers seem to have been motivated by a millenarian vision, the notion that murder was a sacramental act of duty and the possibility of martyrdom. But when the term terror was first used, it referred to the efforts of the new government in France to suppress its enemies immediately following the revolution in the 1790s. In the mid-to-late nineteenth century, groups that are now labeled anarchists began using violence to try to overthrow governments they viewed as corrupt, especially in Russia. This represented a 180-degree shift in the nature of terrorism.

Some Marxists attempted to spread revolution through the use of terror following the Soviet revolution at the end of World War I. Following World War II, ethnic groups began to notice that campaigns of terrorism were sometimes effective at convincing colonial powers to abandon their colonies to self-rule. However, most writers agree that the 1960s really spawned the modern age of terrorism, and it is this modern age that is examined in this study. The youth of the sixties were reared by the conservative generation for whom World War II had been the formative years. Nurtured by the teachings of liberal or Marxist-minded university professors, these modern (as opposed to "new") terrorists rebelled against what they perceived as oppressive economic strategies and the abuse of the third world in the Cold War struggle. They introduced a new form of conflict that included the targeting of innocent civilians in hijackings, skyjackings, bombings, and kidnappings that grabbed headlines and made governments look powerless.

In this study, the terms old terrorism and new terrorism refer to the period between 1960 and the present. Yet even in this limited time period, defining the nature of a war on terrorism is a difficult task. One of the reasons the nature of a war on terrorism is elusive is that terrorism is a pejorative term that is used whenever it is convenient. It is a vaguely defined term. In general categories, we would have to begin with the fact that terrorism involves violence—the use of violence and the threat of more—by a certain group to instill terror in a certain population. It can be considered a form of warfare, such as conventional and guerrilla warfare. In more abstract terms, it can be considered a form of communication—a type of theater. Terrorists perform shocking acts to communicate a message to some target audience.

These categorizations have something to do with a means to achieving an end. But it is only used to describe one's enemies. Those who practice what others call terrorism claim their methods are necessary to accomplish a worthy cause. This is a distortion—the use of terrorist methods is recognizable and wrong. However, to combat terrorists it is useful to realize this is not a black-and-white issue in the minds of the entire world. Terrorists have a morality of their own. They believe they are fighting for a purpose worth the destruction they are causing. The nineteenth-century German anarchist Karl Heinzen proclaimed killing was justified by its very necessity— terrorists have no other way to achieve their aims. His point was that once governments had made killing acceptable, the only question in its justifiability was whether it would achieve its aims.

This is not to say that terrorists are the moral equivalent of law-abiding citizens. In war between states, the just-war tradition facilitates judging the justness of a war, and similar judgments can be made regarding terrorists' wars. Governments have sovereignty within their territory granted by the consent of the people. To merit violent action, an enemy must have vastly overstepped the accepted boundaries of its authority to determine rights in the common good of its citizens. Some judgment along this line would validate whether the terrorist cause is a moral one—whether the war is just (jus ad bellum) or if the means are just (jus in bello). Michael Walzer agrees that some past terrorists might be considered honorable in that they committed only "just" assassinations. He declares that after states introduced terror to war during the bombings of World War II, terrorists switched from assassinating responsible officials to targeting innocent civilians.

This action moved them into the category of violators of jus in bello, regardless of the justness of their cause. And no matter how just the cause, there is considerable doubt about whether the terrorism can really bring about lasting social change, even if the terrorists get their way. Resolution of the issue that a given terrorist group points to as the cause of its actions is not necessarily a cure for terrorism. It may seem that to develop a security strategy, the United States first needs to envision a desired societal end state and work towards that end state, instead of working for its own state interests. If the world could be rid of all the conditions that cause gaps between the haves and the have-nots, then there would be no reason to resort to terrorism. This goal is infeasible though admirable, and even if it were feasible, many writers disagree.

Walter Laqueur proposes that if everyone who claimed the right to autonomous rule could be given their own state, this would only increase the amount of conflict over borders and diasporas. He claims terrorism is least survivable in states with effective dictatorial regimes. Appeasement is not the answer.

The cause is not always the driving factor. Kachig Tololyan presents a convincing argument that political and psychological analysis of terrorism is meaningless without the corresponding analysis of the cultural milieu that gives them meaning. In his example of the Armenian culture, terrorism was the result not of ethnic repression but "the manifestation of a desire to give one's individual life an iconic centrality in the eyes of the com- munity, which professes to value certain forms of behavior articulated in narratives." It was not that the Armenians were repressed at present, but they were carrying on the fight because of stories and legends of their forefathers. Martha Crenshaw agrees that, although some groups—which she terms instrumental—use terrorist acts to achieve defined goals; others, termed organizational, use terrorism as a means to ensure survival of the group. For these groups, terrorism is simply a means to attract support and maintain viability. The groups offer incentives that require violent activity regardless of the cost, and the ideological purpose is only one of the incentives.

The fact that the cause is not the driving force does not mean it can be ignored. The cause or ideological purpose of a terrorist group may become an important battleground. In a terrorist group's struggle to be seen as a legitimate authority with legitimate power, the group must remain true to the cause. The strategy to defeat them must not add fuel to what may be the causal fire, or it will only make matters worse. The mind-set of those who live in states is often much different than that of those who consider themselves outside of states. While states are concerned with positions and interests, others may be driven by worldviews, and the two are bound to collide. The cause may indeed be an important pillar in the terrorists' strategy— terrorists and their audiences obviously believe they are in the right to intimidate by fighting against some kind of evil. Whether or not the cause is the driving factor, sensitivity to this cause is an important factor in maintaining the legitimacy to fight against terrorism—at least in the past. Writers since the late 1980s have been heralding the arrival of a change in the nature of terrorism that could nullify some of these principles.

Amir Taheri claimed the exportation of the fundamentalist Islamic revolution from Iran in 1979 had started the "new kind of terrorism." According to Taheri, while all terrorist movements in the past have been driven by political goals, these Islamic terrorists would be insulted if described as political. Their ultimate aim is the conversion of all mankind, by choice or by force, to the teachings of Muhammed. RAND Corporation analysts have come to broader conclusions. Brian Michael Jenkins, who in 1975 made the oft- quoted statement "terrorists want a lot of people watching and a lot of people listening, but not a lot of people dead," now advises a proactive strategy that includes military response and counters to possible spread of weapons of mass destruction (WMD).

In a 1999 study, RAND experts proposed that the new terrorism is marked by different motives, actors, sponsors, greater lethality, and a flatter, less hierarchical structure. Another RAND expert, Bruce Hoffman, points out that the ambition, coordination, security, and dedication necessary for 19 suicide bombers to pull off four suicide hijackings simultaneously and under total secrecy are unmatched in history. The fact that the hijackings killed more than 3,000 people adds to this factor.

He also points out that the planning for the 9/11 attack probably overlapped the execution of the November 1999 attack on the USS Cole in Aden harbor that points to the existence of a multitrack organizational capability. Laqueur, who formerly resisted categorizations, admitted that a new category of terrorist now exists—one with an apocalyptic vision, nationalist or racial elements, and access to WMD. Unlike Taheri most recent writers point to more than just the Iranian revolution as the facilitator of this new kind of terrorist. Christopher C. Harmon pointed out that the end of the Cold War may have terminated support from some former government sponsors of terror, but it also produced regional and domestic tensions that can now spawn terrorism.

Beau Grosscup proposed that the end of the Soviet Union's hold on these regions enabled these tensions to finally find violent expression. But he pointed out that it was the Gulf War in 1990–91 that thrust the new, post–Cold War terrorist, the militant Islamic terrorist, into the limelight. Despite the subtle differences, there is much support for the existence of a new terrorism. There are also signs that this is nothing more than a logical extension of past forms of terrorism. Terrorism has gone through so many transformations throughout history that it seems almost pointless to declare that there is a new terrorism. Indeed, Hoffman compares modern militant Islamic terrorism to the eleventh- and twelfth-century Assassins, also a radical Islamic sect. The Assassins not only believed violence as a form of struggle to vanquish their Christian enemies but also a ritual duty that was meant to cleanse the perpetrator and hasten the arrival of the new millennium.

Heinzen wrote of the desirability of acquiring WMD: "We need instruments of destruction which are of little use to the great masses of the barbarians when they are fighting a few lone individuals but which give a few lone individuals the terrifying power to threaten the safety of whole masses of barbarians." It is possible that some past terrorists would have been just as fanatical and lethal as current terrorists had they possessed the means. This is an important issue. To develop the proper strategy for an unprecedented war on terrorism, a strategist must know whether any of the lessons from past counterterrorism campaigns are applicable. This study determines whether there is a new terrorism by analyzing old and new terrorism in a consistent manner and begins with a good definition. Scholars have struggled with the issue of defining terrorism for decades, and they do not seem to have made much headway. In 1974 Jenkins defined it as "the threat of violence, individual acts of violence, or a campaign of violence designed primarily to instill fear."

He pointed out that the real target of terrorism is the people watching, not the victims of the attack, so that the object is not mass murder. Hoffman presents an admirable definition based on distinguishing terrorism from other forms of violence, such as guerrilla warfare, ordinary crime, and lunatic assassinations: "The deliberate creation and exploitation of fear through violence or the threat of violence in the pursuit of political change." Laqueur resists giving a definition, saying instead that ideally all studies of it would have a clear definition, but the lack of such a tool does not mean terrorism cannot be identified or studied.

He prefers interpretations of terrorism, of which his favorite is "the use of covert violence by a group for political ends," and admits it is usually directed against a government but can also be against an ethnic group, class, or party. Of course, those concerned with policy or law need a definition. The US State Department has used a consistent definition of terrorism since 1983, which is the definition contained in Title 22 of the US Code, section 2656f(d):

"Premeditated, politically motivated violence perpetrated against noncombatant targets by sub-national groups or clandestine agents, usually intended to influence an audience."

Here the term noncombatant is taken to include military personnel not on duty at the time of the attack. It should really include anyone not formally engaged in an armed conflict. These details cause disagreements over the definition of terrorism. But while most publications and authors struggle admirably to come up with a definition, what is really necessary to prosecute a war on terrorism is a clear conception of the enemy in this particular case. Given the trouble these scholars have had with the subject, an all-inclusive definition may be self-defeating. What is important is not mastery of the entire spectrum of terrorism but to point out the portion of the spectrum with which we are currently dealing. Since this study aims to inform American and allied decision makers in their development of strategy in the war on terrorism, it refines the nature of this particular war by studying statements by the Bush administration.

On 20 September, after the dust had settled from the initial statements in the aftermath of the 9/11 attacks, President Bush expounded on his view of the nature and aims of the war:

Our war on terror begins with al-Qaeda, but it does not end there. It will not end until every terrorist group of global reach has been found, stopped and defeated. These terrorists kill not merely to end lives, but to disrupt and end a way of life. With every atrocity, they hope that America grows fearful, retreating from the world and forsaking our friends. They stand against us, because we stand in their way. We are not deceived by their pretenses to piety. We have seen their kind before. They are the heirs of all the murderous ideologies of the twentieth century. By sacrificing human life to serve their radical visions—by abandoning every value except the will to power—they follow in the path of fascism, and Nazism, and totalitarianism. And they will follow that path all the way, to where it ends: in history's unmarked grave of discarded lies. Americans are asking: How will we fight and win this war?

We will direct every resource at our command—every means of diplomacy, every tool of intelligence, every instrument of law enforcement, every financial influence, and every necessary weapon of war—to the disruption and to the defeat of the global terror network. So the president had set out an extremely tough aim for the war—the defeat of every terrorist group of global reach. This action was a good morale boost for the public but was an extremely ambitious and ill-defined objective.

A joint statement by the United States and the European Union the same day echoed that the aim was to "eliminate international terrorism—its leaders, its actors, its networks. Those responsible for aiding, supporting or harboring the perpetrators, organizers and sponsors of these acts will be held accountable." The campaign in Afghanistan lent some clarification in that the United States used military force to augment diplomatic efforts, to freeze financial assets, and legal efforts by shutting down a government that would not cooperate in America's efforts to capture terrorists.

In January President Bush gave further guidance: "Our nation will continue to be steadfast and patient and persistent in the pursuit of two great objectives. First, we will shut down terrorist camps, disrupt terrorist plans, and bring terrorists to justice. And, second, we must prevent the terrorists and regimes who seek chemical, biological or nuclear weapons from threatening the United States and the world." In the same speech, he named North Korea, Iran, and Iraq to a special category called the "axis of evil" that could potentially supply terrorists with WMD. From this trail of statements, a number of things become clear. First, the United States considers terrorism a threat to its national security and its way of life. Bush declared that the terrorists had started a war against the United States and all who believe in its ideals to bring about the collapse of these societies. Second, this threat is great enough to warrant sending its military to a foreign country, where the United States does not have any appreciable interests, to fight a war. Third, the aim of the war is to eliminate all terrorist groups of global reach.

Bush implied terrorism is comparable to fascism, Nazism, and totalitarianism and would be rendered ineffective and un- desirable just like these ideologies had been. Fourth, the strategy for accomplishing this is to use the combined instruments of America's power to solidify all states in a worldwide coalition that gradually eliminates any support to terrorists, while simultaneously capturing and bringing to justice known terrorists. The war thus becomes one of a coalition of legitimate states defending the peace and security of their citizens against non state actors and their state allies who together threaten to disrupt that peace and security to impose some wide-reaching change. In pragmatic terms, this limits the scope of this study to those groups who have the ability to operate in the international arena and will therefore be acknowledged as a threat by enough of the coalition states to keep the coalition together.

This step is important in this study because of what it rules out, as much as anything. One common barrier to a global understanding of terrorism is the notion that "one man's terrorist is another man's freedom fighter." This is a false dichotomy because the term freedom fighter deals with the ends sought, while terrorism is a category of the means used. In any case, the type of terrorism being studied is narrowed to the enemies of legitimate governments, and especially the coalition in the US war on terrorism. Admittedly, this ignores the possibility that some current terrorists may have a legitimate grievance against a current government that they believe may have used terrorism to gain or solidify its position of power, as in the case of the Palestinians. This study does not examine terror used by a state to compel its own citizens to adopt its policies. It may not consider some indigenous terrorist groups that affect only a limited area, and thus are somebody else's problem.

It does not examine conventional warfare between equivalent political entities, where the participants are well identified and remain within established norms. The terrorists, by contrast, are usually not equivalent as political entities, are anonymous, and go well outside accepted norms of warfare. But so do guerrillas. Drawing a distinction between guerrilla warfare and terrorism as a form of war is not necessary in this type of analysis. Both are forms of insurgency or rebellion against authority—the difference is in the methods the insurgents use in each case. Bard O'Neill notes that guerrillas target "the government's armed forces, police, or their support units and, in some cases, key economic targets, rather than unarmed civilians."

But even he admits there are many grey areas and groups that use a combination of guerrilla and terrorist means. Laqueur puts a slightly different twist on the matter, insisting it is a straightforward matter to separate the guerrillas from the terrorists. He claims looking at the ultimate strategy should make the distinction. The guerrilla aims at "building up evergrowing military units and eventually an army, and establishing liberated zones in which an alternative government can be put up and propaganda openly conducted." Laqueur claims guerrillas have often used terrorist strategies, but the reverse is almost never true, because of the difficulties of creating safe havens in the urban setting. Here Laqueur reflects the positions of Mao Tsetung, who envisioned three phases of war: strategic defensive, stalemate, and strategic counteroffensive.

The purpose of guerrilla warfare, according to Mao, was to support regular warfare and to eventually become regular warfare. Part of this process was to "arouse the masses to arm themselves, and wage guerrilla warfare in co-ordination with the masses."

In other words, the guerrillas conduct a campaign to gain the people's support and new recruits. The guerrillas did not kill the civilians, they recruited the civilians. They concentrated on winning small military victories to secure one area at a time until they had control over enough area and enough support from the people to transition to a strategy of offensive conventional warfare. In Mao's type of warfare, the military would know they were involved in a conflict, albeit with an enemy they could not normally locate. There would not be a question of whether or not to fight the guerrillas militarily, as there is with terrorists. Thus, the technical distinction between terrorist and guerrilla is not as important in this war as the determination that the group is an insurgent, non state actor recognized as a threat to the security of a legitimate state and its citizens. However, labeling a group a terrorist rather than a guerrilla force may have strong implications in the propaganda war.

Determining the nature of a war on terrorism is a difficult but important task. The government of Uruguay proved that misreading the threat and, therefore, the war can lead to disaster for the government and the society. But the nature of terrorism has changed so much through the centuries that it cannot easily be defined. It is violence, a form of war, a strategy, a form of communication, a means to an end. But that end is not always readily discernible; therefore, even solving all the world's problems would not necessarily rid the world of terrorism. Nor is the cause always the driving force in terrorist groups. There is always a cause, and that cause cannot be ignored because it will form an important battleground. Although the nature of terrorism has changed throughout history, modern terrorism has increasingly involved acts that can be considered immoral: seemingly indiscriminate attacks against innocents for purposes that do not warrant this force.

The fundamentalist revolution and the end of the Cold War have created a world where radicals have an increasingly permissive environment for their extreme methods. The extreme nature of terrorism in the 1990s, culminating with the 9/11 attacks on the United States has caused many to warn of the arrival of a new terrorism. The United States has responded by declaring a war on this new terrorism.

But what does that mean? How can a state declare war on a form of warfare? The state must transform the war into a war against some political entity or entities. This war is a war of unequals in more ways than one. For the states involved, it has become a war to rid the world of a major threat to their security. The strategy is to simultaneously hunt down and punish terrorists while dividing the states of the world into two camps, with one eventually eliminating the other and thus cutting off all support for terrorism.

This strategy narrows the scope of terrorism to those groups that will simultaneously be acknowledged as threats to the security of (or at least not favored by) the entire coalition and leaves out some forms of terrorism, such as a state's repression of its citizens or indigenous terrorism where it only affects one state.

On the other hand, it eliminates some of the need to distinguish between some other categories, such as those who may have a legitimate cause and those who may technically be classified as guerrillas. But more importantly, it transforms the struggle into one of state powers defending their interests. This is a convenient way to enable the states to use their instruments of power against the terrorists, but is it wise? Has terrorism become a new phenomenon that warrants a war against it? Or is the US government totally misreading the nature of this war and condemning the effort to failure or even a disaster similar to but on a larger scale than the Uruguayan tragedy?

There is no doubt that the major distinguishing features of today's terrorism are the existence of militant Islamic groups throughout the world. In *Patterns of Global Terrorism*

1999, the US State Department mentions, "The primary terrorist threats to the United States emanate from two regions, South Asia and the Middle East. Supported by state sponsors, terrorists live in and operate out of areas in these regions with impunity."

The State Department lists the following groups as the primary threats from these two regions: the Hizb'Allah, HAMAS (an Arabic acronym for the Palestinian Covenant of the Islamic Resistance Movement), and Palestinian Islamic Jihad from the Middle East and "Usama Bin Ladin and a host of other terrorists loosely linked to Bin Ladin" in Afghanistan. In the descriptive list of Foreign Terrorist Organizations (FTO), 13 of the 41 groups have militant Islamic ideologies.

Although these groups share certain common characteristics, an in-depth look at any one of them would mask the true nature of the threat. The RAF tried to unite terrorist groups in Europe in a weak effort at global revolution. The IRA was only concerned with Ireland and thus cared little what the rest of the world did, except insofar as it affected their struggle. The PLO, on the other hand, had to attempt to unite all the Palestinian groups to have any chance at legitimately controlling Palestine. But none of these comes close to the scope of militant Islam.

Even Bin Laden's al-Qaeda group is just part of the system. As Yossef Bodansky put it, "Bin Laden has always been—and still is—part of a bigger system, a team player and a loyal comrade at arms. The terrorist operations in several parts of the world now attributed to Bin Laden were actually state-sponsored operations perpetrated by dedicated groups of Islamists." During the 1990s, militant Islamic groups crossed barriers that before had seemed impenetrable, such as Sunni-Shiite (the two biggest sects of Islam) and African-Arab-Asian barriers. As a result, a new transnational actor has emerged that has both state and private support but is eclectic and unpredictable.

Militant Islam

Violence is not new to the Islamic world. Three out of four of the caliphs who succeeded the prophet were assassinated because they were considered "weeds," or enemies of the faith. Systematic assassinations as a method of shaping the Islamic world probably had its beginning with Hassan Sabbah in the middle ages. Sabbah was a revolutionary who planned to take power from the Turkish Seljuk Dynasty. In 1090 he established a base at the fortress of Alamut in Rudbar, took over power, spread his propaganda throughout the countryside, and recruited fedayeen—those prepared to sacrifice their lives for Allah.

The fedayeen, who killed with poisoned daggers, became such heroes in Islam that their name has been carried into the twentieth century by the PLO and others. Sabbah indoctrinated his killers by giving them glimpses of paradise in special gardens where they were intoxicated by natural beauty and hashish, which grew in the fertile valleys of the Elburz mountain range. It was this practice that the group got their nickname hashasheen (smokers of hashish), which was later translated assassin. During the Crusades, Sabbah and his men turned their daggers against the Christians and infiltrated their camps on assassination missions that were often so obviously fatal that they could be considered suicide missions. However, there are great differences between the terrorism of the assassins and today's terrorism. The Muslim world is headed in a completely different direction today than it was in Sabbah's time. He fought to reform the faith but in the direction of progress.

During the amazingly rapid spread of Islam throughout the Byzantine and Persian empires, the Arab invaders—driven by their faith and the desire for conquest and booty—conquered mightily. But they did not impose conversion or any other constraints upon surrender. Instead, they opened themselves to the culture of the conquered lands by creating an atmosphere of relative freedom that really was tantamount to liberation from the harsh rule of the Byzantines and Persians.

Fereydoun Hoveyda called that action "a collective cultural suicide triggered mainly by the use of fundamentalism as an instrument of 'legitimacy' in the political race for power." Although the Arabs allowed the conquered peoples to continue with their lives, the Arabs assumed positions of power in the governments—positions the non-Arabs coveted.

To gain power over the Arabs, who claimed the Koran had been revealed to them, the non-Arabs had to become more Muslim than their Muslim teachers that set in motion a competition for orthodoxy that condemned creativity and science. Rulers, anxious to avoid being seen as "weeds" in the faith, allied themselves with the fundamentalist clerics and spread fundamentalism throughout the world of Islam. It was against this wave of fundamentalism that Sabbah fought. Militant backlashes have occurred in cycles throughout Islamic history since the twelfth century and whenever fundamentalists think modernization is threatening the faith. Today's militant Islamists may be part of such a cycle.

The twentieth-century backlash was created by the fact that the Muslim world, so long in isolation because of fundamentalism, has been penetrated and subjugated by the West in the last two centuries. The collapse of the Turkish Empire and subsequent redrawing of its borders by the imperialist powers after World War I culminated a process that probably started with Napoléon Bonaparte's arrival in Egypt in 1789. After the Great War, when British and French carved up most of the Ottoman Empire, western influence began to grow throughout the Muslim world. The Suez Canal Company provided about 90 percent of Egypt's foreign earnings and spawned cities around the canal that were westernized and extremely prosperous.

In one of these cities, Ismaili, in March 1928, Has- san al-Banna and six of his followers started the Muslim Brotherhood. Originally a peaceful teacher, Shaikh Hassan was influenced by King Fahd bin Abdul Aziz of Saudi Arabia and the fascists in Europe to choose a mantel of action rather than ideas. His plan banked on an Axis victory in World War II, combined with a heavy propaganda campaign, to bring down the government of Egypt. As the Axis defeat became apparent, he turned to terrorism in hopes of seizing power through a coup d'état. His fedayeen attacked cinemas, restaurants, hotels, inappropriately dressed women, and especially political leaders.

This terrorism did indeed shake up the country enough for a military coup in 1952. However, the brothers did not receive a share of the power. Colonel Nasser, apparently a former brother, became fearful of their power, turned toward socialism, and ordered a major crackdown on the Muslim Brotherhood. But the group did not die out—it provided fuel for the militant Islamic movement for decades. This fuel was sometimes in the form of trainees, disciples, and enemies. For example, the Sunni-Shiite gulf was the reason Shaikh Hassan could not work with Sayyed Mohammed Navab-Safavi, who later took Islamic terrorism to Iran to try to overthrow the Pahlavi Dynasty.

The group was eventually defeated, but not before they introduced a young mullah named Sayyed Ruhollah Khomeini to the power of militants connected with Islamic authority. Khomeini also developed strong ties to Mussa Sadr, a Shia cleric, who Iran sent to Lebanon in 1967. Iran needed to shore up support for the Shiite population there or lose all power to the Sunnis and Maronite Christians. Sadr organized the Shiites in Beirut, created a populist movement called Amal, and established ties with the PLO to train militants that would later aid Khomeini's revolution.

Thus, when Khomeini took power in Iran in 1979, he was well prepared to do what was necessary to hold and expand that power. Most sources cite 1982 as the year the Party of Allah, or Hizb'Allah, was created. Yet a group by that name already existed at the time, albeit in another form. In 1973, when Ayatollah Mahmoud Ghaffari was tortured to death in prison in Qom, he created the party with his last words. In 1979 Khomeini revived the name when he ordered all Islamic groups to band together in defense of the newly established government. At first they were nothing more than gangs in the streets throwing rocks and cans, but then Khomeini established training camps where children were sent as a precursor to service either in the cities or at the Iran-Iraq front.

In 1982 the Israelis invaded Lebancn to put an end to PLO guerrilla and terrorist attacks. Initially, the Shiites welcomed the Israelis. But when it began to look as if the Israeli presence might be- come permanent, Khomeini sent 500 members of his Hizb'Allah force (which at the time numbered about 20,000) to fight with and organize the Shiites in Lebanon. They became the Lebanese Hizb'Allah that fought the Israelis and terrorized the West in South Lebanon for the next two decades. While the Shiites were busy exporting their revolution, the Sunnis were building momentum of their own. The 1979 Soviet invasion of Afghanistan spurred Sunni Muslims from Saudi Arabia to issue a fatwa, or religious ruling, designating the war a holy war for which every Muslim was responsible. One of the Muslims who spread this word through his writings, Abdullah Azzam, set up an organization called *Makhtab al Khadimat*, the Office of Services, to finance the immigration of holy warriors from all over the Arab world.

He took on Bin Laden, a wealthy business partner, who helped finance the organization and run military affairs. In 1986 the two split up after a disagreement over the vision for the organization. Mr. Bin Laden wanted to train soldiers for a global jihad against the West, while Mr. Azzam wanted to focus on creating a Muslim state in Afghanistan and then expand. Bin Laden organized a group called al-Qaeda (the base) in 1988 and set up a training camp for Persian Gulf area Arabs. But Aghanistan was not the only hot area for Sunni Muslims in the late 1980s. The fight against Israel was also heating up. In 1987 Palestinians in the West Bank and Gaza Strip started a spontaneous uprising called the Intifada. During this uprising, a small nucleus of Muslim Brotherhood members banded together to form the group HAMAS. HAMAS aimed to emulate the Shia Hizb'Allah group in its struggle against Israel. HAMAS's zeal and fundamentalist leanings attracted Iran's attention, and in 1991 they obtained support from Tehran. This made it easier to reject Yasser Arafat's pleas for HAMAS to join forces with the PLO. HAMAS wanted victory through armed struggle, not appeasement.

In December 1992 Israel assured the group would gain international attention when it deported 415 HAMAS members and sympathizers to Lebanon, where they were homeless for months. The international community noticed, and the UN passed a special resolution (UN Resolution 799) in hopes of resolving the situation. HAMAS has since become feared for its extremist tactics, including suicide bombing missions in the West Bank and Gaza Strip areas. Another hotbed for Sunni Muslims was the Sudan. In 1989 middle- rank military officers seized the government of Sudan in a coup. With no unifying ethnicity, culture, or language, the leaders turned to a popular Muslim leader, Hassan al Turabi, to design the government. Turabi had established a Sudanese chapter of the Muslim Brotherhood in the 1960s, an organization that is now the National Islamic Front (NIF).

After the 1989 coup, he set about developing a state that would be unified by Islam, although a much more lenient, tolerant version than that of the fundamentalist Arab states. Here was an emerging Sunni Islamic state to match the Iranian state in its authority, if not its fundamentalist zeal. In 1991, in the wake of the Persian Gulf War, Sudan held a conference of militant Sunni organizations from 55 countries to organize an assault against the West in revenge for the war on Iraq. The big surprise was that Iran openly acknowledged the NIF as a legitimate Sunni Muslim organization and even supplied high-technology communication equipment to facilitate its operations in the future.

The Sunnis were completing a major consolidation with this big step. The Soviet withdrawal from Afghanistan in 1989 released thousands of trained Afghans who were militant Islamists with experience in the Afghan war. They went to Afghanistan in the late 1980s to get experience to use elsewhere. They had endured a final, unnecessary, bloody battle for Jalalabad that they viewed as a joint US-Pakistan setup, but they were now ready for action elsewhere. Bin Laden returned to Saudi Arabia a hero. However, it was not long before he clashed with the Saudi government. When the Saudis invited the US military onto its soil in 1990 to defend against the Iraqis, Bin Laden argued strenuously against the move. He offered to donate construction equipment and recruit Saudi Afghans for the defense. He warned that inviting infidels onto the sacred ground would desecrate the holy places and cost the Saudis their Islamic legitimacy.

This could have dire consequences for its position in the eyes of the militant Islamics. But the Saudi government ignored Bin Laden and eventually forced him and his family into exile in Sudan after the war. The Sunnis now had a Muslim state in the Sudan, two charismatic leaders in Turabi and Bin Laden, and unprecedented support from a Shia nation, Iran. A new, united militant Islamic movement was emerging.

Motivation

Muslims consider their faith predestined to animate

the entire planet. The difference between militants and less extreme Muslims is that the militants believe force is a necessary part of that predestination. Jihad was the force that created the Muslim empire, and jihad is exactly what many fundamentalists are calling for today. In Arabic, the word has several meanings, all of which are used in the Koran. It can mean effort, striving, or struggle, as in the obligation of a Muslim to live up to the stringent requirements of his religion. But militants focus on its connotation of holy war. And even though jihad is not an article of faith in the Koran, militants consider it a personal duty, as though it were a sixth pillar of the faith. The concept of holy war comes from some fundamental principles on which all Muslims agree. Islam's traditional view of existence is that the world is divided into two camps—the city of faith and the city of war. The city of faith, or *Dar al-Iman*, refers to all areas where Islam reigns supreme and its rules are obeyed. The city of war, or *Dar al-Harb*, refers to the rest of the world.

Relations between the two places cannot be anything but hostile, because Islam has to strive to eventually bring the whole world in line with the right path. As long as the two cities are easily recognizable and separated, there could be a truce, and conflict would occur only at the boundaries. However, this is not the case. Muslim society has been invaded by Western values and materialism, so even Muslims must be divided into the two cities. But the West is not the only culprit. Islam itself has always been divided. There are many sects, but the two largest, the Sunnis and the Shiites, comprise the vast majority of all Muslims.

Although these sects agree on most of the fundamental tenets of Islam, their differences are grave and ingrained by historical conflicts. From the dawn of Islam, its leadership was subject to violent struggle. Three of the four successors of the prophet Muhammed were assassinated, including Ali ibn Abi Taleb, the fourth caliph and the son-in-law of

Muhammed. Ali's murder gave birth to the split between the Shiites, who believed Ali as the rightful, divinely inspired successor to Muhammed, and the Sunnis, who believe no man since Muhammed has ever been a divine messenger from Allah. Shiites recognize 12 imams who were descendants of Muhammed and supposedly also endowed with his power of interpreting the Koran and thus revealing the truth. The twelfth imam disappeared as a child and, according to Shiites, went into occultation to reappear at any time.

This difference between the two sects, along with some other doctrinal disagreements, creates a schism that precludes the definition of a single city of faith, and thus there is constant conflict even within Islam itself. This difference between the two sects also dictates their respective views about government. Sunnis view the nation-state as a fact of life on this earth, to be accepted and used for the good of Islam. To a Sunni, the first order of business is to establish a government that is obedient to sharia, or Islamic law, and then use that government to expand the boundaries of the Muslim world. The Shiites, on the other hand, view government as an un-Islamic entity.

To a Shiite, the imam is the only legitimate ruler on earth. All government is therefore the property of the missing twelfth imam, and all Muslim clergy should avoid involvement in government, instead supporting all Islamic causes equally.

Shia clergy can tolerate rulers and advise them in keeping with the sharia, but cannot participate. Because of this, Shia writings have advocated Islamic government without specifying the details of how such a government would be run. Some Sunni writings, on the other hand, have gone into detail on how sharia should be applied to the administration of a state. Mawlana Abul Ala Mawdudi, a Pakistani Sunni theologian, laid out the specifics of how the people would elect a ruler of an Islamic state.

This ruler would be a "just despot," who would create a "monolithic institution that upholds one ideology, which is Islam, and uses all its enforcement agencies to ensure that Islamic principles are respected by everybody in all walks of life." Although the Shiites would shun this practice of laying out how a government should work, they would probably agree with the principles on which the Sunnis' ideal government was based. In practice, militant fundamentalists blur this line even further. Militants have little use for many of the doctrinal differences between the sects, preferring instead to stick to basics. Both Sunni and Shia fundamentalists insist that a spotless ruler run the government and that it strictly obey sharia. Khomeini, a Shiite, obviously had a different view of the clergy's involvement in government than the majority of Shiites.

The success of his revolution (and his military thugs) probably shielded him from criticism. Once in power, he went to great lengths to ensure the government was run in accordance with sharia. Khomeini thought that children were innocent and therefore better able to decide right from wrong. In view of this, he installed children as supervisors throughout his government, with the authority to blow the whistle on any untoward dealings they saw and even overrule important decisions. In the Sudan, Turabi talks of a moderate application of the sharia, but his government's record of punitive practice is a lot stricter than his propaganda. In the end, both Sunni and Shia militants are all aiming at the same thing—spreading Islam's power by whatever means necessary with the final aim of an entire world subject to the laws of Islam. The statements of the Islamic terrorist groups bear witness to this.

In a 1988 statement, the Hizb'Allah in Lebanon delineated their objectives:

- To eliminate the Americans, the French, and all other imperialists from Lebanon,

- To punish the Phalangists for all crimes against the Lebanese, and
- To permit the Lebanese to choose their own government.

However, the Hizb'Allah called on the Lebanese to choose Islam, which "alone, is capable of guaranteeing justice and liberty for all. Only an Islamic regime can stop any further tentative attempts of imperialistic infiltration into our country." The charter of HAMAS is more forthright. Although it also promises liberty for all people, it explains that "safety and security are possible only in the shadow of Islam, and recent and ancient history is the best witness to that effect." Furthermore, it warns that peaceful solutions are no longer possible: "Once the enemies usurp some of the Muslim lands, Jihad becomes an individual obligation for every Muslim."

Even though the charter admits the PLO is made up of its Palestinian fathers, brothers, and sons, it declares that until the PLO accepts Islam as its sole theology, HAMAS will not cooperate. But these two groups are focused mainly on the struggle with Israel. Osama bin Laden's vision is much more global, integrating all Islamic is- sues in a common struggle. In 1998 Bin Laden issued his third fatwa, an edict that religious authorities issue to guide followers on a particular issue and obliges them to take whatever actions it specifies. Bin Laden's 1998 fatwa claimed that the US occupation of Saudi Arabia, blockade of Iraq, and support of Israel in the Arab-Israeli struggle constituted a declaration of war on Allah.

Because of this, he proclaimed that it was every individual Muslim's duty "to kill Americans and plunder their money wherever and whenever they find it. We also call on Muslim ulema, leaders, youths, and soldiers to launch the raid on Satan's US troops and the devil's supporters allying with them and to displace those who are behind them so that they may learn a lesson." Bin Laden's 1996 and 1998 fatwa became the stated motivation for the 1996 bombings in Saudi Arabia (Riyadh and al Khobar Towers in Dhahran) and the 1998 bombing of the US embassies in Kenya and Tanzania, respectively. This highlights several important points about the looseness of the organizations involved and that Bin Laden's vision is a motivating force. Militant Islamists respond to his words with dedication given only to the highest authorities. He communicates a message that touches the hearts of a broad range of radical organizations, and they answer his calls.

However, lest the analysis indicate all operations are undertaken with the apocalyptic vision as their inspiration. Remember there are states and organizations involved, and these actors have interests. The states and organizations involved often act because they are in a struggle for legitimacy and power. When the United States entered Somalia in November 1992, Sudan and Iran held a conference in Khartoum to analyze the situation. A committee of intelligence officials from both countries proposed that humanitarian aid was a pretext to allow the Americans to strengthen their presence in the Gulf region. The Americans would gain control of the oil grid in Sudan, Somalia, Eritrea, and Yemen; install a pro-American government in Somalia; and enter the Sudan to wear down the Sudanese the way they were attempting to wear down the Iraqis. The committee assessed that the direct cause of this aggression was the failure of the Islamists to solve the Islamic and Arabic problems.

They decided on a long-run, joint Sudan-Iran effort to train and supply guerrilla fighters in Mogadishu and an immediate, indirect strike elsewhere—in Yemen. In the case of the 1998 bombings, the groups received Iranian and Sudanese support because it was in both nations' strategic interests: Sudan, because of its regional location and Iran, because of its desire to remain the most influential Islamic state in the region. At the same time, there was a surge of militant Islamic fever sweeping the Arab world. Even Egypt was publicly warning that it appeared the United States was pressuring Iraq to gain an opportunity to strike Iraq militarily. With anti-American rage at a high pitch, the militant organizations would have lost legitimacy had they not acted when they did. What emerges from this is a picture of militant Islam that is not a structured organization but certainly a movement that acts in a semi-coordinated way. Its followers are motivated by an ideology that crosses some historical- doctrine divides, but the leaders involved are also subject to organizational pressures based on identity and bureaucratic interests.

Organization

Because of the 9/11 attacks on the WTC, Bin Laden's group is thought of as the umbrella organization for all Islamic terrorism today. Most sources say the al-Qaeda was created in the late 1980s and has financed the training of more than 5,000 personnel from more than 50 countries worldwide. It is described as a loose network that holds together organizations such as Egyptian Islamic jihad, Algeria's Armed Islamic Group, HAMAS, Hizb'Allah, and various groups in Pakistan, Morocco, Libya, Tunisia, and the Philippines. Al-Qaeda was probably just a financial vehicle, starting as a network of charitable organizations that received donations and funneled them to militant Islamists. Militant Islamists trained by Bin Laden return to out- posts in countries around the world to perform in small cells that have at best indirect ties to al-Qaeda, including possible financing arrangements.

Many are veterans of the Soviet-Afghan war, and some are members of other rogue terrorist organizations. Bin Laden set up the financial networks and established propaganda organizations in London that could provide information on and explanations for militant Islamist operations without taking the blame. Now that the network is established, removal of any of its leaders would probably not debilitate the operations of its pieces. But Bin Laden gives the movement its overall direction. Along the way, he worked closely with the head of the Egyptian Islamic jihad, Ayman al-Zawahri. The two became the key personnel to organize, support, and direct operations in such places as Somalia and Bosnia. In June 1998, the two co-chaired a conference of 100 plus Islamists from organizations around the world and came up with a strategic plan of action for all who would be members of a worldwide front.

The front was named the World Islamic Front for jihad against Jews and Crusaders, and one of its first public documents, coauthored by Bin Laden and al-Zawahri, was the February 1998 fatwa. So Bin Laden's organization is an ideological umbrella called the World Islamic Front, which includes loose alliances to many militant Islamic organizations and a complex support network called al-Qaeda, which trains and supports small cells throughout the world. But, as extensive as Bin Laden's influence is, there is more to the movement than just him. The militant Islamic movement is, to a large extent, state-sponsored so the organizational picture includes influential ties to Iran, Sudan, and Pakistan. Many militants in countries other than Iran and Sudan view their own governments as corrupt because they are not strictly obedient to the sharia.

They look to Iran and Sudan for guidance since these two were successful in developing governments based on Islam. Iran's dominance over the movement was unquestioned during the 1980s, when it was the sole bastion of Islamic government. But Iran is cautious about its use of terrorism, even more so since Khomeini's death in 1989. It often acts through clandestine agents who issue no proclamations or by supporting other groups like Hizb' Allah or HAMAS, who take all the credit for the operations.

Iran is interested in maintaining its legitimacy as a state but also retaining the ability to pressure and shock the world. It extends its influence and pressure through its embassies and through the deployment of its Revolutionary Guards, or Pasdaran, who train militants abroad. It employs the Iranian Ministry of Intelligence and Internal Security to terrorize counterrevolutionaries at home and abroad and supplies aid to schools and mosques abroad through charity funds that can be used to funnel funds to militants.

After the coup in Sudan, Iran supplied support to them like parents taking children under their wings. But in the mid-1990s, as Iran's terrorist operations started to draw unwanted attention to Tehran, Iran started to realize the potential of the Sunni militant movement. It organized Hizb'Allah International under a committee of three leaders: Imad Mughaniyah of Lebanese Hizb'Allah's Special Operations Command, Ahmad Salah of the Egyptian Islamic Jihad (al- Zawahri's group), and Osama bin Laden. In this way, Iran tried to deflect attention and show deference to the idea of a unified movement, while still harnessing the authority it felt it rightly deserved. At the same time, the Sudan was attempting to shore up its own influence over the Sunni movement. Turabi established the first real Sunni Islamist organization, the Popular International Organization with a representative from each of the 50 countries where Islamic struggles were taking place. But in a conference in Tehran in 1991, Turabi saw how far behind the Shiites his organization was, despite its zeal.

Iran built up the Sudan with weapons, know-how, and money, but the real progress happened when Turabi got Bin Laden to work for him. Sudan was struggling after the Bank of Credit and Commerce International (BCCI) in London, its biggest financial cover, was closed. In exchange for land and business contacts in the Sudan, Bin Laden organized a support network that financed militant groups and acted as covers for them. The end result was called the Islamist International and its military wing, the Armed Islamic Movement (AIM), which is now a Khartoum-headquartered umbrella for Sunni militant groups. Bin Laden has departed Sudan, but AIM still spearheads militant Islamic groups, most of whom are former Afghans. Bin Laden's 1996 departure from the Sudan, necessitated because of pressure from Saudi Arabia, ushered Pakistan into the spotlight.

Pakistan had considerable influence in the world of militant Islam because of its support of activities in Afghanistan. Following the Soviet withdrawal, the Pakistanis, through their Inter-Service Intelligence (ISI), built up the Taliban with weapons and training to fill the power vacuum and avoid a collapse of Afghanistan.

With the ISI's help, the Taliban defeated warlords and rogue tribes to secure Pakistan's access to the major road system from the Indian Ocean to Central Asia. The Taliban and ISI maintained training camps where Afghans could freely move about and train for operations in their home countries. When Bin Laden arrived in the spring of 1996, the Taliban eagerly welcomed him. Pakistan, on the other hand, was more wary of its standing in the world community.

The ISI had the Taliban put him on loose house arrest until Saudi Arabia denied that it wanted Bin Laden extradited. He was elevated to the position of emir, in charge of Afghanistan's terrorism-supporting activities. The struggle for influence in the militant Islamic movement does not end with Bin Laden and the states—it also includes some of the larger, established terrorist groups. For example, HAMAS has evolved into an organization with interests of its own. It has a seemingly hierarchical structure, built around cells, villages, and sub-districts. But it is also well-represented in the Palestinian social arena through departments of education and community services.

HAMAS has also gotten entrenched in the political realities of its struggle. It now realizes that to attain its two divergent goals—that of a complete Islamic state in Palestine with no concessions to Israel and that of a community that lives in peace and harmony—it may have to give in some face-saving way. Groups such as HAMAS and Hizb'Allah need and accept the support of state sponsors and Bin Laden, but it is difficult to imagine them being controlled by this support. Rather, it is more probable that sponsors could use the groups as a rheostat—the introduction of more resources would spark additional activity, but on terms chosen by the groups and possibly in line with existing fatwa from legitimate Islamic leaders. The organizational structure that emerges from this analysis of the militant Islamic movement is admittedly amorphous but no less a reality. Yet the semiautonomous pieces are bound together more tightly than any terrorist organizations in the past. The RAF failed miserably to unite Communist insurgent organizations in Europe.

The PLO had the same troubles uniting its factions for the struggle against Israel—and they were all focused on the same, very limited regional objective. The Islamic movement is no *Brady Bunch* either—Islam still has internal struggles. But the militant Islamic movement has succeeded in building a loose, global hub and spoke type network. Iran, Sudan, Pakistan, and Bin Laden vie for control of the "hub of Islam." The outlying spokes can act autonomously but in concert because of their shared vision as elucidated by the fatwas of its leaders. Furthermore, when it is necessary, the spokes have the benefit of support from the hub.

Support

Financing a terrorist organization is a tough job, but it is easier when you are rich. Bin Laden inherited a sum estimated at $300 million from his father, the late construction magnate Muhammad bin Laden. His enemies, including the Saudis and the Americans, have attacked this nest egg, yet he still has a considerable portfolio of investments in everything from construction to banks to agriculture. It was this money that originally allowed him to contribute to the development of the Mujahideen Services Bureau, which imported thousands of Arabs to Afghanistan and trained them in Pakistan and Afghanistan to fight the Soviets. He also imported heavy construction equipment to build roads, tunnels, storage de- pots, and hospitals in Afghanistan's mountainous terrain. But these tasks were relatively easy compared to his later feats. In Afghanistan there was a single fight to support. Bin Laden's biggest contribution to materially supporting the militant Islamic movement is his establishment of the financing network that hides and invests the money and funnels it to the militants.

His first effort at this began soon after his move to the Sudan. Officials of the Bank of England closed down the BCCI, which Arab states and terrorist organizations used to launder money and finance weapons deals. Officials of the BCCI kept sparse, if any, records, and embezzled money as payment for their services. Turabi and the Muslim Brotherhood were using this bank heavily to build up their own banking system, on the way to becoming an independent sponsor of Islamist groups. The closing of the bank left them stranded, so they called on their new visitor, Osama Bin Laden. He set up emergency collateral using his money and that of some wealthy supporters, then went to work setting up a financial network to move money through legitimate businesses already owned by wealthy members of a group he called the Brotherhood Group.

He upgraded this structure in the late 1990s to a more global network that is even harder to trace—a "highly complex, tangled, and multilayered organizational network that spreads throughout the world and in which bin Laden's name does not appear at all." His payment for the work there was in the form of business opportunities in the Sudan, including construction of an airport and highway and ownership of a bank, an import-export firm, and several farms. Of course, money must be funneled into this network to sustain it. One of the ways this happens is through one of the pillars of Islam: alms giving. Wealthy donors give money to Islamic organizations, many of which are part of Bin Laden's network or give directly to terrorist organizations.

Islamic states, including Saudi Arabia, Iran, Sudan, and Pakistan, also give to these Islamic organizations, either knowingly or unknowingly supporting Bin Laden. Another way money finds its way into Bin Laden's coffers is from drug trafficking. Afghanistan has a large opium crop that al-Qaeda militants help export for use in manufacturing heroine and morphine. Not only does this make the network rich but also adds to the degradation of the West by feeding their addictions—a double bonus. Money is only one of the important resources the militant Islamic movement needs. US officials estimate training camps that Bin Laden established in Afghanistan alone have been responsible for training more than 20,000 militants from all over the world. Based on the materials found in caves, the training camps were highly professional and capable of handling soldiers with extremely diverse language and cultural differences.

Apparently, Bin Laden has even developed contacts for training HAMAS and Hizb' Allah in some of these camps. When the training camps in the Sudan, Pakistan, Lebanon, and Iran are included, it is clear that the movement can train a large quantity of militants in a very professional way. Another important role supporters played was arranging the logistics for operations. In 1993 when Sudan and Iran decided to strike at Yemen as a statement against the

American buildup in Somalia, Bin Laden's job was to round up Yemenite Afghans to conduct the operation, recruit Sheikh Tariq al-Fakli to leave his London exile and take charge of the operation, and transfer the money to banks in Yemen. Meanwhile, Iran and Sudan were training and arming forces for the eventual clash in Mogadishu. Bin Laden also moved 3,000 of his Yemenite Afghans there with heavy weapons in time for the Mogadishu operation.

He smuggled guerrilla warfare experts and heavy equipment into Mogadishu by plane and boat and established a headquarters from which the experts could direct the fighting. This type of cooperative support has continued through the present. Recently, Iran has found indirect ways to help Bin Laden. During the war on the Taliban and al-Qaeda in Afghanistan, Iran opened its borders to escaping Afghans, which allowed them to immigrate to other countries in the Middle East and Africa. Although there is no doubt that hostility exists between the different militant Islamic factions and states, all involved benefit from the increased moral support that the appearance of solidarity brings. This is because there are two target audiences from which moral sup- port is needed. The first is the world of donors who support the Islamic organizations that funnel money to the militants.

The second is the pool of possible militants who may be convinced to support the militant agendas if they perceive the agendas are genuinely inspired. In neither case does the target audience include Westerners. As Edgar O'Ballance put it, "Such fundamentalism can only operate in Islamic countries where a moderate Muslim population is available for conversion, and it does not seek—nor would it have any chance of success if it did, as universal Islam has little appeal to Westerners—a proselytising mission amongst non- Muslims." As Bin Laden put it, "The Western regimes and the government of the United States of America bear the blame for what might happen. If their people do not wish to be harmed inside their very own countries, they should seek to elect governments that are truly representative of them and that can protect their interests."

Thus, those who propose the main purpose of their terrorist operations is to instill terror in the hearts of the potential victims are off the mark. The victims are not part of the real target audience. To appeal to donors who provide cash support, the Islamists have full-time propaganda operations. The objective with this target audience is to appear ideologically (in this case, religiously) legitimate. To this end, Bin Laden made several trips to London, where he purchased property and set up organizations to act as fronts for the various Islamist groups. The most authoritative of these was the Liberation Party, run by Sheikh Omar Bakri. Throughout the 1990s these organizations, which had plausible deniability of any involvement in operations, could provide accurate data and explanations that would satisfy the Muslim intellectuals.

At the same time, the charitable organizations spend large sums of money distributing food, medical services, education, work, religious services, and housing. This combination of acceptable intellectual justification and charitable service helps to keep the Islamists legitimate even to moderate Muslims. To appeal to the pool of potential militants, the Islamists need to show strength and sacrifice—the tougher the message, the better.

The attraction for this target audience seems to be the notion that the cause is an inspired one, since so many are willing to die fighting the evil city of war for it. When the United States responded to the 1998 bombings with a cruise missile attack, Bin Laden's popularity soared. As the *New York Times* put it, "Attacking Mr. Bin Laden with missiles gave him the status of a state—a nation unto himself, as an intelligence official said—in a war with America." Victory over the Americans in Somalia gave the Islamists a huge propaganda tool, which Bin Laden flaunted in a 1998 interview: "They had thought that the Americans were like the Russians, so they trained and prepared. They were stunned when they discovered how low the morale of the American soldier...was our boys were shocked by the low morale of the American soldier and they realized that the American soldier was just a paper tiger." As long as there is dramatic action against the evil West, especially the United States and Israel, this target audience gives support whether it sees the actors as victims or as heroes. The key is dramatic action, which is most effectively achieved through terrorist operations.

Operations

This analysis considers mostly operations against the United States and Israel. However, many operations against governments that are sympathetic to the West, such as Egypt and Saudi Arabia, have been part of the same strategy. Bin Laden's energy has been directed mostly at Saudi Arabia from the moment it invited Americans onto its sacred soil until Bin Laden helped the Islamists triumph over the United States in Somalia. It is a Muslim's duty to identify those who deviate from the sharia and to punish them or pressure them to reform.

Of course, this is also a way for militants to maintain legitimacy in the eyes of the faithful. Either way, it is a fact of life with militant Islam. During the 1980s, the Sunnis were busy fighting the Afghan war while the Shiites were fighting the battles of Lebanon. Hizb'Allah carried out numerous hijackings, kidnappings, and assassinations aimed at Israeli and Western targets throughout the 1980s, but perhaps the most disturbing development was that of the suicide bomber. Hussein Mousawi, a breakaway Amal commander, and Imad Moughniyeh, the Hizb'Allah operations director, led the development of this devastatingly effective terrorist tactic. On 18 April 1983,

Moughniyeh's men (who called their group Jihad al-Islami, but were effectively working with Hizb'Allah) drove a van with about 440 pounds of explosives into the American embassy in Beirut, killing 63 and injuring 120.

On 23 October 1983, Hizb'Allah suicide bombers simultaneously truck-bombed French and American bases in Beirut, which caused 300 deaths (including 241 US Marines) and many more injuries. Here was something new. When the IRA killed 18 British soldiers and Lord Mountbatten in a single day, that was the Irish group's biggest strike, and they aimed it at parties they held responsible for their plight. The PLO directed their hijackings at innocent people, but tried not to kill them—instead using them to gain political advantage. But here were people who cared so little for life that they would kill themselves along with all the innocent people they could. Today, the militant Islamic movement has kept this as one of its trademarks.

But the movement has proved to be capable of more than terrorism. During Operation Anaconda in Afghanistan in 2002, the United States uncovered documents that showed that the training camps prepared militant Islamists in diverse skill sets via a multilevel training program: "Implicit in the split levels of training was the Islamic groups' understanding of the need for different sets of skills to fight on several, simultaneous fronts: along trench lines against the Northern Alliance in Afghanistan; against armor or helicopter assaults from conventional foes in Chechnya; as bands of foot-mobile insurgents in Kashmir, Central Asia or the Philippines; and as classic terrorists quietly embedded in cities in the Middle East, Africa, the former Soviet Union and the West."

This training had its roots in the 1980s, when the Afghans had been trained to fight the Soviets in many different ways. As the Americans arrived on Somali soil in

1993, Iran and Sudan thought it was the perfect opportunity to put these skills into practice again. While training and supplying the Somalis, they ordered an indirect strike on en route American troops in Yemen. This strike was merely an attempt to make a statement quickly—although the strike was a tactical failure, it was sufficient to express the Islamists' rage at the American presence.

Meanwhile, the Islamists were building up forces in Mogadishu. Al-Zawahri led the operation to ambush the US rangers on 3 October 1993 that led to the withdrawal of the American troops. First, he got Mohammed Farrah Aideed, the local warlord the troops were pursuing, to leak a tip that hung two of his aids out for the Americans to pick up. Then, using Afghans trained by Iranians and Iraqis, he set up an ambush that downed three American helicopters and trapped soldiers in Mogadishu for the night under intense fire. Although the helicopters were most likely downed by Aideed's men, they used weapons modifications and techniques taught by the Islamists. The resulting withdrawal was a major victory for the Islamists, who would later set up similar operations to oppose the UN forces in Bosnia after the Dayton Accords and the Russians in Chechnya.

The militant Islamists, far from being strictly terrorists, would use whatever techniques or methods suited their purpose at the time. Terrorist operations were, however, usually the chosen modus operandi. On 13 November 1995, Saudi Afghans bombed the Military Cooperation Building in Riyadh, Saudi Arabia, a military training center operated by the United States for the Saudis. The operation was professionally planned. A special van had been cleaned of all identification. A sophisticated timing device controlled the bomb with remote control backup. The timing was perfect—at 1140 hours Americans were eating lunch in the snack bar. To top it off, a second, antipersonnel bomb exploded in the parking lot, which killed some of those who came to help. On 25 June 1996, an even more complicated job was accomplished at the Khobar Towers complex, a facility that was used to house American airmen in Dhahran, Saudi Arabia.

A combination of Saudi Afghans, Iranian intelligence officials, Hizb'Allah terrorists, and Syrian experts performed preparations for months to plan the job and smuggle the explosives, incendiaries, and electronics into the country. They constructed a sophisticated, shaped-charge, fuel-oil incendiary bomb on site in a stolen tanker truck, which they parked outside a security fence, well within the powerful bomb's range of the barracks. The bomb took off an entire side of a four-story building, killing 19 and wounding 515. Two years later, on 7 August 1998, militant Islamists blew up American embassies in Nairobi, Kenya, and Dares Salaam, Tanzania, on the eighth anniversary of the American deployment to Saudi Arabia to fight Iraq. The simultaneous explosions were both vehicle bombs, and the operation involved smuggling in experts and parts and assembling the bombs on site. Yet each team had knowledge only of its own operation.

This time, about 300 people were killed and 5,100 injured. Two years later, 12 October 2000, Yemeni Islamists performed a suicide mission in an explosive-laden refueling boat that blew a gaping hole in the USS *Cole* that killed 17 and injured 39. Yemeni officials had less than two week's notice that the *Cole* would make the stop, pointing to a highly proficient, flexible, and possibly indigenous capability. These are just the headliner missions. There are plenty of other examples. The bombing of the WTC, numerous attacks in Egypt, the Philippines, and Saudi Arabia, and numerous failed attacks can be traced to militant Islamists who are tied together in one way or another—usually through Bin Laden. Palestinian groups started conducting suicide operations in 1994, and now groups such as HAMAS say the suicide bombers are their most effective weapon against the overwhelming Israeli military forces.

Taken in the context of these operations, the attacks of 9/11 were typical, though extreme, in their characteristics. The operatives had been living in the United States for up to seven years, mostly using their names. The pilots trained at American flight schools. One attended an Air Force professional military school. Each probably knew only a limited amount of information on the overall operation. Thus, some of the operatives were probably living in the United States, in isolation, watching the operations in Kenya and Tanzania and the bombing of the USS *Cole* and awaiting their chance. The planners meticulously laid out the details to get the operatives through security and aboard the right flights at the right times so the geographically separated attacks would occur almost simultaneously. The new part was the substitution of the fuel-filled aircraft for sophisticated bombs— a deviously creative combination of hijacking and suicide bombing.

When taken together, this analysis shows a disturbing picture of the nature of the new terrorism. The Iranian revolution set the stage for this phenomenon. Khomeini's message—that the only good government was the sharia, and it was every Muslim's duty to spread this revolution, by force if necessary—was the basic fuel for the fire. But it was not until the Sudan became an Islamic state, the Afghans returned from the war with the Soviets, and Saudi Arabia asked for US help in defending against Iraq that the movement truly gained momentum. Finding itself the lone superpower in the world, the United States had to take action in the unstable Middle East and Africa for its own security. The resultant meddling played right into the Islamists' portrayal of the United States as the "Great Satan" bent on destroying Islam.

Despite the traditional Sunni-Shiite gulf, the militant Islamic movement developed into a pseudo-united organization. The organization has a hub consisting of Iran and Sudan and Bin Laden's World Front for jihad against Jews and Crusaders. It also has spokes, which are the militant groups that now have access to resources from the hub (through the al-Qaeda network and training camps in numerous countries) and to some extent take direction via their fatwas. And the organization is global—but not universal. The target audience does not include those who are in the city of war, as the message is not conducive to converting them—only conquering them. The message is conveyed by the operations of the militant Islamic movement, which do not aim at coercion but victory. Where possible, the militants confront the West's military. Where necessary, they simply kill its infidel citizens. All four factors in the analysis, therefore, add up to a strategy of violent worldwide insurgency by confrontation.

The mechanism for success is that violence on the militant Islamists' terms will lead to strength in their movement and weakness in the West. This happens in two ways. First, terrorist attacks and attacks on the American military (such as the USS *Cole* and the rangers in Somalia) show the militants' ability to weaken the paper tiger (i.e., the West). Second, these attacks provoke violent reactions from the West that the militants can characterize as attacks on Islam. In these two ways, the movement's strength will increase until Islam finally confronts the West from a position of military strength and overpower it. Then the whole world will be ruled by sharia. The mechanism is flawed in that the Muslim world is slipping farther behind the West in social, economic, and military strength. But the elegance is that all the Islamists have to do for now is survive. Counterstrategies in the past have aided the Islamists' cause.

To appeal to their target audiences, the Islamists need to maintain their Islamic legitimacy, and they need to appear strong. The latter can be accomplished by surviving an attack by a powerful enemy, but defeating this enemy in military confrontation is even better. Neither the Soviet Union nor the United States knew the enemy they were facing in Afghanistan or Somalia, respectively. But the fact that the militant Islamists were able to defeat both of these superpowers significantly bolstered the movement. The United States responded to the 1998 embassy bombings by launching cruise missiles at the Ahawar Kili terrorist camp in Khost, Afghanistan, and a pharmaceutical plant in Khartoum, Sudan. The Clinton administration had intelligence indicating there would be a meeting of top Bin Laden officials at the Afghanistan camp, and they suspected the Sudan plant of developing chemical weapons.

Though Bin Laden did nothing but survive the attacks, he still gained hero status because of them. The Israelis have tried both appeasement and destruction. In June 2000 the Israeli army pulled out of the Lebanese territory it had occupied since the 1982 invasion. Although this could be seen as admitting defeat by the Hizb' Allah, it allowed the Israelis to withdraw to a "morally defensible position, from which they'd be better able to fight if the need arose." Again, the Hizb'Allah are harassing the Israelis across the border.

The all-out military offensive the Israelis launched, in the West Bank at the end of March, appears to have increased the number of volunteers for martyrdom among young militant Islamists. The conundrum is that this makes it appear there is no way to defeat the terrorists but to destroy them—all of them. In short, win a total war against terrorism. But how can victory ever be claimed in that type of war, whose aim is the total destruction of clandestine units throughout the world? If victory is claimed and there is another terrorist act, the victor's reputation is destroyed. If victory is never claimed, it is damaged just the same. Is this really the only way?

It would seem that the United States embarked upon a war whose aim is the total destruction of all terrorist groups of global reach. But contemplating the end state of this type of war should give policymakers pause. Even if one could imagine a world where no terrorism existed, where all terrorist groups had been destroyed, and where terrorism as a strategy had been shown ineffective so no new groups would emerge, it is difficult to imagine having the operational ability to accomplish destruction in the first place. Such an operation, "would involve simultaneous strikes against al-Qaeda's network in dozens of countries, as well as strikes against manufacturing and storage facilities for weapons of mass destruction in countries that might be willing to share them with al-Qaeda. The strikes could include attacks against the leaders of some of these countries."

This war on terrorism is a war between a coalition of states and an opposing insurgency that poses a threat to the national security of that coalition. That is the most useful way to analyze terrorism in this context because terrorism is not a phenomenon that can easily be defined. It is a strategy, or a means to an end—an end that is not always readily discernible. Defeating terrorism is not a matter of solving social problems or even distinguishing between right and wrong, although injustice, right or wrong will form a major battlefield in the war. Defeating terrorism is a matter of national security. The fundamentalist revolution and the end of the Cold War have created a world where radicals have an increasingly permissive environment for their extreme methods. The extreme nature of terrorism in the 1990s, culminated with the attacks on the United States on 9/11, has caused many to warn of the arrival of a new terrorism.

The United States has responded by declaring a war on this new terrorism. Defining the problem as a national security threat to states narrows the scope of terrorism to those groups that will simultaneously be acknowledged as threats to the security of the entire coalition. This leaves out some forms of terrorism, like a state's repression of its own citizens and indigenous terrorism that only affects a limited area. It also eliminates some of the need to distinguish between some other categories, such as those who may have a legitimate cause and those who may technically be classified as guerrillas. The war becomes one of states against a global insurgency.

The appropriateness of this point of view depends on whether the nature of the threat warrants it. Defining the nature of the threat requires detailed analysis of the strategy upon which the terrorist groups are staking their hopes of success. This study develops a framework that is a hybrid of those used by several terrorist experts, which consists of four primary factors: operations-lethality, motivation, support, and organization. The second and more difficult step was the subjective process of determining the mechanism by which these four factors could possibly translate into success for the terrorist group. The two steps, taken together, emphasize the terrorist group's strategy—a strategy that the group may or may not be able to articulate among themselves.

This process, therefore, transforms an operational analysis into the strategic threat posed by a group. Only when this strategy has been assessed can the true nature of the threat be determined, and only then can appropriate counterstrategies be developed. With this type of analysis, it is possible to compare the nature of old terrorism and new terrorism in a meaningful way. One of the big differences is the congruency—or lack thereof—of all four factors. The RAF had a vision of worldwide revolution, but its organization and support revealed that its strategy was built around ensuring the survival of the group.

Whenever the group needed an adrenaline shot, it combined hunger strikes by the prisoners, bombing by the commandos, and demonstrations by the sympathizers to provide a spark. But the viability of the group's Leninist-

Marxist revolutionary vision was dependent on the existence of a mother state that could provide the political base for the revolution. When the Soviet Union dissolved, the group faded away. The PLO proved to be a political body willing to use terrorism to coerce and communicate, capable of developing a large army and willing to compromise if necessary. The simplicity of its cause gave it a huge support base and made it resilient enough to withstand the Israeli invasion of Lebanon in 1982. But the diversity of the groups that belonged to the PLO forced Arafat to be a chameleon, striving for progress through compromise. This compromise led to the Oslo Agreement, but that appears to be far from the end. In the latter part of the 1990s, Arafat came under intense pressure from groups such as HAMAS, for whom compromise was unacceptable.

At this writing, Arafat is a prisoner in his own headquarters building in Ramallah, an acknowledged terrorist but still an important player in the peace process. The IRA was a stubborn, tunnel-versioned group bent on carrying on a two-century-old conflict that had always been about violent struggle. Its loose organization seemed to add to its effectiveness—the authority of the local commanders ensured the primacy of the bullet over the ballot, and Sinn Féin was mainly afforded the role of postoperative apologist, rather than strategist. But the IRA's vision for a united Ireland seemed to be incongruent with its moral support base, which did not include part of that same Ireland. The IRA was also forced to compromise and reverse the primacy to the ballot.

The tenuous peace from the Good Friday Accord continues today. The mechanisms are difficult to categorize, due to the incongruence. Additionally, during this period, state sponsorship loomed in the background, but in the world of the terrorist, the state became more of a nuisance than an aid. Unwilling to accept the strings attached to the support they got from states, terrorist organizations developed their own resources. The state support simply did not fit with their overall strategies. The mechanisms of both the states and the terrorist groups were based on some sort of coercion to change the policies of another political body. Groups such as the IRA posed only internal security threats in their own countries. The RAF theoretically aimed at being a worldwide national security threat, but given the weakness in its organization and support, posed an internal security threat as well.

The PLO arguably posed (and continues to pose) a national security threat to the existence of Israel, which could be destabilizing to the region. There are many insurgent groups in the world today whose strategies resemble this type of coercion. Many of these do not pose a security threat to the world's states and are, therefore, not the enemy in the war on terrorism. The militant Islamic movement is not focused on coercion and poses a much broader security threat. It is focused on world domination by force. The Iranian Revolution, the Soviet-Afghanistan war, the emergence of the Sudanese Islamic state, and the Persian Gulf War all contributed to the rise of a global movement. The strategy of the movement is congruent in all four factors. Its motivation is an extreme form of fundamentalist Islam that promises the domination of the world by Islam—through force, if necessary. Its organization is global, uniting nations and sects that have never worked well together. The hub and spoke network provides support for the militant groups while allowing them autonomy and security, yet their devotion ensures they follow strategic direction in the form of fatwa.

The materiel support for the movement comes through this al-Qaeda network from both private and state sponsors. The movement does not worry about moral support from anyone who disagrees with its methods because in theory they will be overcome in the end, unless they convert. It does, however, take pains to explain its actions to the Islamic elite to maintain legitimacy. The movement is capable of accomplishing operations over a spectrum of violent measures, including conventional warfare, guerrilla warfare, and terrorism. Its members are willing to die for the cause—intentionally, if necessary. It takes little imagination to envision a scenario where the group would use WMD. The biological attacks in the United States after 9/11 may have been such a scenario.

All four factors are congruent and are appropriate for the same mechanism. The mechanism is that of a global insurgency. Like Mao, the militant Islamists envision being able to concentrate force in a limited time and space to perform tactical actions on their terms. Unlike Mao, the militant Islamists do not care about the support of the people who are victimized because these people are not the target population (unless the attacks occur in a Muslim country). Each of these actions that is successful weakens the enemy to a small extent because it shows the government is not strong enough to protect its citizens. This also makes the Islamists appear as heroes in the eyes of their target population. Counterattacks by the government can also make the Islamists look like heroes, as long as they survive the attacks. In this way, the movement theoretically builds up strength by surviving, shoring up Muslim support, and striking until it can eventually fight from a position of strength.

The difference between old terrorism and new terrorism is the congruency of the operational factors in forming a strategy. There are differences between the old and the new in each of the four areas, but none of these by themselves warrant an unprecedented counterstrategy such as the current war. There are also similarities. Militant Islam's motivation is vaguely similar to that of the RAF because its aim is world revolution. Its organization is vaguely similar to that of the PLO in that it is a loose and sometimes internecine conglomeration of diverse groups.

Its moral support requirements are also vaguely similar to those of the PLO since its target audience is not in the population where its operations occur. The real difference is that for the militant Islamic movement, the strategy is a coherent one, where all four operational areas—motivation, organization, support, and operations—are congruent because they point to the same mechanism: global insurgency that gradually builds strength for a final takeover of the world. This is the nature of the war on which we are embarked.

Implications

Today's terrorism is significantly different than the terrorism of the last few decades that suggests a new counterstrategy. The enemy is not a single group whose aims are focused on a limited political objective. This is why limited strikes such as the cruise missile strikes on Afghanistan and Sudan failed. It is why military campaigns that were not backed up by the resolve to succeed (e.g., the campaign against Aided in Somalia) did more damage than good. It is why Israel, which is focused only on its own survival, cannot possibly make progress alone regardless how forceful its actions. The threat from today's terrorism is different. But since there are limited similarities with old terrorism in the four operational areas, there may be lessons from past efforts against terrorism that can be incorporated into this war. The RAF may have taught us a lesson about dealing with ideologies of worldwide revolution: This type of ideology alone is not enough to sustain a global revolution.

Without an organization and support that are also worldwide, the RAF needed to point to a powerful state (the Soviet Union) whose existence validated the ideology. When this state disappeared, the ideology was discredited. The Soviet Union was not conquered; it was beaten in the arena of ideologies. Had the United States conquered the

Soviet Union militarily, there is no guarantee the same effect would have been achieved. On the contrary, this may have fueled the fire of such revolutionary groups as the RAF to continue indefinitely. This lesson only applies to the current conflict if there is some way to discredit the militant Islamic ideology of world domination by showing that the ideology has failed in the states where it took hold. This failure should not be measured by the standard of living of the people in the states but by the adherence of the governments to sharia. The ideologies espoused by Khomeini and Turabi represent deviations from several accepted tenets of fundamental Islam.

Khomeini's assertion that Islamic clergy should participate in the government was a departure from the beliefs of many Shiites. Turabi's moderate application of sharia could be considered offensive to many fundamentalist Muslims. Certainly, Islamic clerics would not condone many of the ruthless methods used by both men and by the Taliban in Afghanistan. Therefore, the information war must be a major front in this war. The Israel-PLO struggle revealed several lessons about dealing with a loose organization of diverse-minded groups. The Israelis tried several different strategies, including diplomacy, invasion, surgical strikes, and regime targeting. The invasion of 1982 was extremely effective militarily, but when the Israelis continued after achieving their initial, limited goals, they created another enemy in the Hizb'Allah.

Surgical strikes and regime targeting have been of limited use because there are no targets that are valuable enough to cause the collapse of the entire organization. Diplomacy has at times seemed successful, as in 1993 with the Oslo Accord. However, militant Islamic groups who will not accept compromise have attacked Arafat because of the political nature of his strategy. This is how the conflict in the Middle East has become inextricably linked to the global conflict. Israel cannot defeat the security threat it faces on its own. If Arafat could be isolated and protected from groups like HAMAS, Israel would be able to deal with him diplomatically. These groups are part of the global insurgency in the militant Islamic movement and cannot tolerate the existence of the state of Israel in the midst of the Holy Land.

This is a place where the frontiers of Islam meet the frontiers of the West. The only hope of solving the problem is to find a way to isolate and destroy the terrorist groups while still recognizing the legitimacy of the cause of the Palestinian people.

Again, the information war is a major part of this effort. The British struggle against the IRA can teach lessons about the coordinated use of different national instruments. The IRA as a movement bears little resemblance to the militant Islamic movement, except that it was forced to develop a covert support system with overt fronts to finance itself without relying on outside help. The British counterstrategy treated the legal and military aspects of the fight as separate, compartmented operations, and as a result lost any hope of synergy between the two.

The war on terrorism is even more complicated because there are multiple fronts—military, economic, legal, political, information—and also a coalition of multiple states involved. A lack of cooperation among states could lead to the loss of opportunities to arrest important suspects. More importantly, if the United States is perceived as fighting the war alone, it will lose a major battle on the legitimacy front. This would add credibility to the Islamists' claims that the United States is the Great Satan, which is out to get Muslims. The important task is to develop a strategy in this war that incorporates only the lessons from the past that have been adjusted for the nature of this war. The nature of war is the world's states fighting against a global insurgency—the strategy should keep this in mind at all times.

The main strategy must be developed to defeat the insurgency's strategy and not to prosecute war in a certain manner just because that is the way the states normally operate. The way to accomplish this is to develop strategy using the analysis framework by working backward from the insurgency's strategy mechanism to the four operational factors and by developing an effective counter that is congruent at every level. The strategy of the militant Islamists is to gradually dominate the world by conversion and force and to build up support from militants through tactical successes and survival, while maintaining legitimacy in the eyes of fundamentalist Muslims. That is what the counterstrategy should be designed to defeat. The coalition's mechanism of defeat inspires the growth of the coalition until, in the end, the materiel and moral support for the militant Islamic movement are gone.

Any small groups that exist are isolated from the hub of Islam, and—or, possibly because—the militant ideology is discredited as being un-Islamic. The organization of the coalition will be ad hoc. Forums such as the United Nations can be used to shore up support in the court of world public opinion, but the majority of the effort will consist of behind the scenes diplomatic overtures to ensure solidarity of the coalition. Unfortunately, this may involve giving up the ability to call all the strategic shots. The important thing is to maintain the coalition's solidarity while disrupting the insurgency's already loose organizational solidarity. It is not necessary to stick to an arbitrary definition of terrorism to determine the enemy. Instead, the enemy is any organization that is seen as a threat to the security of the coalition.

For example, it is possible to acknowledge the legitimacy of the Palestinian cause and the security of the state of Israel yet condemn the extreme methods used in pursuit of each. It is also necessary to identify those groups that are acting outside the bounds of legitimacy, such as

HAMAS and Palestinian Islamic Jihad, and combine efforts with the two legitimate authorities in the region, the Israeli government and the Palestinian Authority. Even though Oslo is as good as dead and Arafat is an acknowledged terrorist, keeping him on the side of the coalition would do the most good for the coalition. One good example of this coalition-building is the Bush administration's successful courtship of the Pakistanis prior to Operation Enduring Freedom in Afghanistan. This amounted to "asking Pakistan to help destroy what its intelligence service had helped create and maintain: the Taliban." Yet Pakistan's Pervez Musharraf supported the United States fully in each of its seven ultimatums. This was a strategic victory that took a notch out of the hub of the militant Islamic movement, and it shows the type of organization the coalition will have.

Besides coordinating strategic activities, the coalition governments will need to develop the capability to coordinate operational-level activities as well. For instance, there must be legal methods for any country to aid another in its pursuit of known, declared terrorists in the latter's territory. This will require that each state involved has an organization with a single authority that can cross bureaucratic lines to make resources available as a team in support of the war on terrorism. Each state's committee for the war on terrorism should have knowledge of the state's operations on each front to coordinate them among the coalition states.

The motivation of the coalition is the peace, security, and prosperity of the states involved. Secretary of Defense Donald H. Rumsfeld outlined this in ordinary terms in a February interview: "The ultimate victory in this war is when everyone who wants to can do what everyone of us did today, and that is get up, let your children go to school, go out of the house and not in fear, stand here on a sidewalk and not worry about a truck bomb driving into us." However, this statement portrays a war of total elimination of terrorism itself, which is a long-term—and probably infeasible, although admirable—goal for a continuous conflict, such as the war on drugs or the war on crime. When the Bush administration outlined its intentions to eliminate all terrorist groups of global reach, it shaped the war in a different light. As Michael Howard put it, "To declare that one is at war is immediately to create a war psychosis that may be totally counterproductive for the objective being sought. It arouses an immediate expectation, and demand, for spectacular military action against some easily identifiable adversary, preferably a hostile state—action leading to decisive results.

In the initial strategy discussions at Camp David, Deputy Defense Secretary Paul Wolfowitz pushed hard for including Iraq in the initial phase of the war, while the opportunity to strike was hot. The media also took up this cry in some places. The problem with this is that it feeds right into the insurgency's motivation. Arab and Muslim public opinion of Americans turned venomous when the United States bombed Iraq for noncooperation in the UN weapons inspection in December 1998, and there is a high probability it would again. The United States and the coalition need to avoid aiding the militant Islamists in polarizing the world into the city of faith and the city of war. Instead of making the enemy states un-Islamic, this would make them look more legitimately Islamic.

The strategy must take into consideration coalition materiel and moral support and insurgent materiel and moral support. The coalition obviously has a major advantage in the area of materiel support. The terrorists cannot match the resources of the coalition states, even with state support from the rogue states. Coalition resources will only be available as long as the governments dedicate the resources to the effort. For the United States, the declaration of war in the wake of the devastation of 9/11 provided all the impetus needed to gain support from Congress, which guaranteed the support of the American people. As the war drags on, this moral support may be harder to obtain. As conditions in the Middle East heated up at the end of March 2002, American analysts were already questioning Bush's ability to keep up what they called a good-versus-evil view of the war on terrorism. While the coalition is worrying about keeping its materiel and moral support going, it must attack the insurgency's support as well. Difficult as it is to attack the materiel support, there have already been successes—161 coalition countries have combined to block $104.8 million of terrorist assets.

Another, more dramatic way to separate the militant groups from materiel support is to eliminate or deter the groups' state sponsorship. The war in Afghanistan was undoubtedly a big step, as it eliminated a major training ground and a major portion of the global network. The US-led force took pains to avoid making this war a moral support victory for the insurgency. Obtaining Pakistan's support and concentrating on humanitarian aid were a huge part of that plan. This revealed to the world the fact that the Taliban, who claimed to be a fundamentalist Islamic organization, were unworthy of the authority they took from the government of Afghanistan. For Muslims, to side with the Taliban was to admit corruption as a part of Islam. A big part of the moral support front depends on how well the coalition plans its operations. The coalition operations need to be aimed at defeating the insurgency while denying it moral victories. Obviously, homeland defense is a big part of this, as long as it does not go so far as to erode the freedoms that are essential to our way of life. How to conduct offensive operations is not quite as obvious. The military can be a big part of these operations, as in Afghanistan, but the operations have to be guaranteed successes with limited objectives.

If the operation fails, the insurgents claim a major victory. If the operation is tactically successful but falls short of its strategic goal and the insurgents survive, the insurgents also claim victory. But if the coalition forces are seemingly able to accomplish any mission they undertake, they retain the appearance of strength even if the insurgents survive. For example, in Afghanistan, had the objective been to transform the state of Afghanistan into a state that is hostile to terrorism, the objectives would have been met before Operation Anaconda began. The operation could have been avoided, and even though some enemy soldiers would have survived in caves, they would have been insignificant—and acknowledged as such. If, however, the objective is to round up and capture or kill all enemy soldiers, any enemy troops that escape represent a significant moral victory for the insurgency.

If there are other objectives that are important enough to warrant the operation, then state them. For example, perhaps the intelligence that was gained from the caves was worth the risk of putting soldiers down to go in after it. Perhaps the sheer act of intimidation that comes from being able to kill them wherever they go is the object. The important thing is to limit the objectives to those having strategic effects. This may mean that the armed forces play a supporting role to other instruments of power. The US armed forces may be placed in the position where they must provide intelligence to civil law enforcement officials from other countries. American space assets, airborne reconnaissance assets, and Special Forces may be particularly well suited to these tasks. The Air Force may be used extensively to provide humanitarian assistance and supply of foreign and covert agents.

Army and Marine ground forces may spend a lot of time doing peacekeeping while law enforcement officials perform the direct actions involved in apprehending the enemy in situations where it is appropriate for this kind of action. These are missions that can have strategic effects. As Maj Gen David Deptula, author of the air strategies in the wars in the Persian Gulf and Afghanistan, put it, "The biggest piece of this war could very well be the information piece." It may be that there are few opportunities for the armed forces to be used in a destructive manner as they were in Afghanistan. But in Afghanistan, the American forces fought on the side of an insurgency against an authority. In this scenario, even in a small war, a conventional force can be successful using regular tactics.

This principle applied in Bosnia in 1995 and Kosovo in 1999 as well. It also applied in North Vietnam after the Easter Offensive of 1972, during Linebacker I and II. However, in Vietnam before 1968, the United States tried to use conventional force (especially an airpower strategy of conventional targeting) against an insurgent force and was not successful on the strategic level. The Israelis have shown the same tendency by using conventional force against the PLO in Lebanon, which gave them tactical, even operational success but was a strategic failure. They drove the PLO out of Lebanon, but gained a new enemy in the Hizb'Allah, and merely forced the PLO to relocate. When there is an opportunity to eliminate a dangerous resource that could potentially be used by the insurgency, such as WMD in the hands of a state that has ties to terrorists, conventional war-fighting operations may be appropriate. But this should only happen when the conditions have been set so that the actions will be decisive and legitimate in the eyes of the coalition.

As Pericles warned the Athenians 2,433 years ago, "I have many other reasons to hope for a favorable outcome, if you can consent not to combine schemes of fresh conquest with the conduct of the war, and will abstain from willfully involving yourselves in other dangers; indeed, I am more afraid of our own blunders than of the enemy's devices." This war is a war of states protecting their security from a global insurgency that does not have the strength to do major damage to them at this time. The insurgency's strategy relies on the hope that Allah will eventually honor their efforts by making them strong enough to overpower the evil city of war, and the entire world will be run according to his will. In the interim, they must work from a point of weakness. That very weakness is to their advantage since they do not need to accomplish much to gain support. Survival is sometimes enough.

However, limited victories are even better. The strategy that will defeat them depends on gradually growing a coalition that cuts off materiel and moral support for militant groups that will then be isolated and illegitimate in the eyes of Islam. This will take cooperation among the states of the coalition and among these states's instruments of power. It will not lead to a classical, decisive victory that eliminates terrorism, but to a long struggle that marginalizes the insurgents and makes terrorism an undesirable strategy for all others. The coalition must maintain its own moral support in the form of public opinion, which assures materiel support for the war from the governments. It must also cut off materiel support to the insurgents without increasing the moral support to them.

This may mean that decisive action by the armed forces is not the chosen venue of action most of the time. The armed forces may be more useful performing indirect operations that have strategic effects on the information front. All use of force (civil or military) should be decisive and limited in its objectives so that the objectives are achieved as effortlessly as possible. When it is necessary to use conventional war-fighting operations, the conditions should be set so that the actions are seen as legitimate in the eyes of the coalition. This is a war that can be lost more easily than it can be won. American leadership is essential, but leadership implies someone to lead, and in this war, those who are following may make all the difference.

4

In the New Age of Prevention

We are entering a new age of preventive war. The emergence of mass-scale suicide terrorism, the proliferation of weapons of mass destruction, and the loosing of rogue states from Cold War constraints are leading nations—and not just the United States—to embrace the temptations of preventive military action. The official rhetoric, in Washington and elsewhere, is couched in the more acceptable language of preemption, but there can be no mistaking the growing acceptance of preventive uses of force. While this is in some ways an understandable, and perhaps even inevitable, development, it is one that threatens to undermine coordinated attempts to battle terrorists and contain rogue states, and will render the United Nations even more irrelevant in coping with such threats than it already is.

If we are in fact reaching the end of an era dominated by traditional notions of deterrence and facing the rise of a new age of prevention, then it is imperative to consider how this situation came about and, more importantly, how to govern the use of force in such a dramatically changed world. Otherwise, it is too easy to envision a future where nations simply resort to raw self-help with little pretense of order and even less possibility for international institutions to bind the international community with a sense of common purpose. In turn, the anarchy that is the fundamental condition of international life will become more dominant than at any time since the collapse of the League of Nations and undermine international cooperation at the very moments when it will be needed most.

Of course, preventive war, violent intervention in the affairs of sovereign states, and forced regime change (all of which can be described more generally as discretionary uses of military force) are not new. While in the modern era these have largely been considered unsavory and even illegal tools of statecraft, nations have resorted to their use when their leaders believed their interests dictated it, such as Imperial Japan's preventive attack on the U.S. fleet at Pearl Harbor in 1941.

Likewise, it was an undeniable reality of the Cold War that the United States and the Soviet Union breached the sovereignty of other states and even effected violent regime change in their spheres of influence as a means of policing and expanding their respective coalitions. Still, the international community during the Cold War strongly professed adherence to a norm against such actions, a presumption so powerful that even the two mightiest nations on earth felt the need to show their respect for it in principle even when they disregarded it in practice. Both Moscow and Washington dressed their actions in veils of legitimacy regarding "fraternal assistance" and "self-defense," even as they crushed rebellions and removed hostile governments.

But they never sank (at least publicly) to the moral poverty of the ancient Athenians on the island of Melos during the Peloponnesian War. The Athenians told the militarily helpless Melians (whom they would later massacre) that there was no need to trifle with arguments about justice or rights. Rather, they insisted that Melos must submit to Athenian rule because it was the nature of things that "the strong do what they can and the weak suffer what they must." Moscow or Washington could have easily dictated similar terms to the targets of their interventions but instead clothed their actions in legalistic language that ironically honored the norm against discretionary uses of force even as it was being violated.

The idea that the world is shifting away from these Cold War norms toward a greater acceptance of discretionary uses of force may seem an odd claim given the international fury directed at the policies of the Bush administration, which are fundamentally preventive in nature despite attempts to portray them otherwise. The "Bush Doctrine" was enunciated in the 2002 National Security Strategy of the United States of America, which describes a strategy of prevention with such unapologetic candor that some critics have derided it as little more than a barely veiled justification for the creation of an American empire in which any state or actor resisting U.S. hegemony would suffer Washington's wrath. The 2003 American-led invasion of Iraq—the Bush Doctrine in action—served to confirm the worst fears of the administration's critics, as American forces rolled into Baghdad after the expiration of the president's ultimatum that the Iraqi regime, in effect, either surrender or be destroyed. The Americans, it seemed, had arrived at Melos ... via Baghdad.

And yet, as two American scholars recently noted, despite often hyperbolic criticism of the invasion of Iraq, "a mounting body of evidence suggests that a significant number of states are beginning to embrace the Bush Doctrine's underlying logic of 'preemption,' which seems a great deal like preventive war, despite their initial hostility to the Bush Doctrine and continuing widespread opposition to the [2003] Iraq war." This is a puzzle that needs explaining. Are other states seizing on the American example out of opportunism, or even just self-defense? This is a central accusation of critics who have charged that for many reasons, U.S. policies will "invite imitation and emulation, and get it."

To claim, however, that the United States (or any other nation, for that matter) is leading a change in international norms is to confuse cause and effect. Analyses that trace these developments to U.S. policies after 2001 cannot explain striking changes in beliefs about the use of force on the part of other actors in the international community over the past decade. These changes are characterized by the rejection of traditional notions of absolute state sovereignty, a steep erosion of faith in the concept of deterrence, growing concern over the spread of weapons of mass destruction (WMD), and the demonstrated potential of catastrophic terrorism. While the terrorist attacks against the United States in September 2001 spurred a greater acceptance of preventive violence, the preconditions for the overturning of old notions about force and the emergence of new norms regarding prevention were in place long before the first airliner ever struck the Twin Towers.

It is true, however, that this collapse of previous norms and the transition to a new age has accelerated and become more obvious since 9/11. Political scientist Stephen Krasner warns that if a series of nuclear terrorist attacks were to strike three or four cities concurrently in the developed world, "conventional rules of sovereignty would be abandoned overnight," and preventive strikes, including "full-scale preventive wars" without even the pretense of United Nations approval would become accepted practices. Krasner is correct, but the flaw in his prediction is timing: much of what he sees happening in the future is happening now. New norms are already emerging, even if new rules to govern them have not yet coalesced.

These changes are due to the cumulative and corrosive effects of a series of frightening, even sickening, events that have been inexorably altering the way the world thinks about security. Since the Cold War's end, and particularly in the past few years, we have seen a parade of atrocities: in London and Madrid, bombings of public transport; in the Middle East, beheadings broadcast on the Internet; in Russia, mass hostage takings in a hospital, a theater, and even an elementary school in the small town of Beslan (which resulted in a botched rescue and the butchering of scores of Russian schoolchildren). These outrages followed a decade immediately after the Cold War darkened by campaigns of rape, ethnic cleansing, and even genocide in Europe and Africa. The nuclear clock, once slowed by the Cold War's end, has been set ticking again by the North Korean nuclear program, as well as by the evident intention of Iran's extremist mullahs to become members of the nuclear club.

It is small wonder that peoples and leaders in many nations show greater unwillingness to tolerate risk in a world seemingly threatened by outright barbarism. Successive atrocities have strained their patience with states or groups that seem to respect neither law nor custom, nor basic human decency, as well as with international institutions that appear impotent at best and obstructionist at worst. If these frustrations deepen, in the future international order may well be secured not by laws or institutions or even by "coalitions of the willing," but rather (in the words of a British general) by "coalitions of the exasperated." How did we get to this point, and where do we go from here?

Humanitarian Intervention

The belief that the international community or its members could resort to force even if it meant breaching the sovereignty of a recognized state did not originate as a response to terrorists or proliferators after September 2001. Rather, the foundations for the new age of prevention can be found in the failures of the international system of the

1990s. As the Cold War waned, the superpower coalitions began to disengage from involvement in the affairs of smaller nations, often leaving instability and uncertainty in their wake. As the threat of nuclear war receded, civil war, mass rape, starvation, and genocide came to the fore. The collapse of order and the human suffering it engendered repeatedly challenged the international system. The performance of the United Nations in this period was dismal even by the reckoning of its supporters, and its failures were bound to have a profound impact.

The two most important cases in point were the 1994 genocide in Rwanda and the attempted genocide in Kosovo five years later. In Rwanda, the world organization's paralysis—induced in no small part by the initial unwillingness of U.S. and British officials even to speak the word "genocide," lest it trigger a costly and risky obligation to intervene—cost thousands upon thousands of lives, and raised fundamental questions about its capacity to deal with such challenges. When genocide loomed in Kosovo, the United States and its NATO allies (to some degree chastened by their failure to stop the carnage in Rwanda) did not wait until it was too late, and acted without the Security Council's approval rather than risk a Russian veto.

In 1999, Secretary General Kofi Annan acknowledged the damage done by these crises. After Kosovo in particular, he evidently sensed that important members of the international community might have crossed a threshold. Annan bowed to new realities by embracing (within carefully defined limits) the principle that states could at times interfere in the internal affairs of others: "This developing international norm in favor of intervention to protect civilians from wholesale slaughter will no doubt continue to pose profound challenges to the international community.... But it is an evolution we should welcome." Such a norm, Annan admitted, could even be a deterrent: "If States bent on criminal behavior know that frontiers are not the absolute defense and if they know that the Security Council will take action to halt crimes against humanity, they will not embark on such a course of action in expectation of sovereign impunity."

Ironically, some NATO nations agreed to participate in the Kosovo operation only because they regarded it as a tolerable exception to existing international norms. But the translation of this "exception" into a norm in itself became more evident two years later, when the Canadian-sponsored International Commission on Intervention and State Sovereignty published its report.

The authors went even further than Annan, declaring that the international community not only could act during humanitarian disasters, but that it had a positive responsibility to do so. The commission's co-chair, former Australian foreign minister Gareth Evans, later alluded to the soul-searching that produces such changes in norms, noting that it "took us most of [the 1990s] to re-learn that war can be a progressive cause: that in some circumstances, threatened genocide conspicuous among them, military intervention is not merely defensible, but a compelling obligation."

The commission (composed of a dozen noted political and intellectual figures from around the world) argued that this "responsibility to protect" is "an emerging international norm, or guiding principle of behavior for the international community of states," and that over time it could even become customary international law.

And in a prescient warning, the commission noted that the repeated inability of the United Nations to act effectively, coupled with successful interventions outside of its auspices, would eventually erode its stature and credibility. The emergence of this new norm of intervention led some to the further conclusion that if sovereignty can be violated to stop the murder of thousands, it can also be violated to prevent such disasters—including terror attacks.

For example, Lee Feinstein (a former Clinton administration State Department official) and the Princeton legal scholar Anne-Marie Slaughter have argued for a "duty to prevent" as a corollary to the "duty to protect." They claim there is nothing "radical" in such a proposal, which "simply extrapolates from recent developments in the law of intervention for humanitarian purposes—an area in which over the course of the 1990s old rules proved counterproductive at best, murderous at worst."

Proliferation and Prevention

By the end of the 1990s, it was clear that humans wielding machetes and machine guns were more likely to inflict mass death than intercontinental nuclear missiles. But even as the threat of global nuclear war faded, new fears grew about the uncontrolled spread of nuclear arms in a world unmoored from the paradoxical security of the Cold War's strategic nuclear standoff (and from previously strict Soviet control of nuclear technology and components among its friends and clients). Like the debate on intervention, reconsideration of the problem of proliferation gained a new momentum after 9/11, but thinkers and policymakers had begun to grapple with these changes well before.

The question of coercive nonproliferation, for example, long predates current debates. In 1993, the historian Marc Trachtenberg wrote:

> The idea that the international community has a right to intervene, Albeit in exceptional cases, in the internal affairs of independent states—that sovereignty is in important ways limited by the existence of an international community—has suddenly become widely accepted. In particular,

> it is now often argued that the world community has a right to prevent countries like Iraq, Libya, and North Korea from developing Nuclear capabilities—by force if necessary, many would add.

A year earlier, MIT professor John Deutsch (who was later appointed CIA director under President Clinton) advocated serving notice to would-be proliferators that they could well face the possibility of "multilateral, and in exceptional cases, unilateral military action." In 1995, the foreign policy analyst Michael Mandelbaum made essentially the same point, warning that stopping the spread of nuclear weapons to places like Iraq and North Korea "may ultimately require destroying those states' nuclear programs by force." He also noted that such actions would require the American public to embrace the concept of preventive war, which it had never been asked to do, and that the "next Hiroshima"—that is, a nuclear attack on U.S. territory—"could create in American public opinion a consensus in favor of preventive war to keep the bomb out of the hands of rogue states." For many Americans, it seems, the deaths of nearly three thousand people in a single day of terrorist attacks were enough to qualify as Mandelbaum's "next Hiroshima."

Debates related to, but not directly centered on, preventive war increased in intensity in the late 1990s, as Saddam Hussein's continued defiance of U.N. arms inspectors raised fears that he had reconstituted his WMD programs. In 1998, President Clinton gave a speech that just as easily could have been given by George W. Bush in 2003:

> Now, let's imagine the future. What if [Saddam Hussein] fails to comply, and we fail to act, or we take some ambiguous third route which gives him yet more opportunities to develop this program of

> weapons of mass destruction and continue to press for the release of the sanctions and continue to ignore the solemn commitments that he made? Well, he will conclude that the international community has lost its will. He will then conclude that he can go right on and do more to rebuild an arsenal of devastating destruction. And some day, some way, I guarantee you, he'll use the arsenal. And I think every one of you who's really worked on this for any length of time believes that, too.

For a variety of reasons, notably domestic political troubles and disarray in the Security Council, Clinton never carried out this implied threat. Nonetheless, in a bipartisan vote, Congress passed, and Clinton signed, the 1998 Iraq Liberation Act, which made it "the policy of the United States to support efforts to remove the regime headed by Saddam Hussein from power in Iraq and to promote the emergence of a democratic government to replace that regime." (The act, however, only "supported" such efforts by the Iraqi opposition and was notably silent on the question of the use of American force.)

In all this, however, there was little in the way of a systematic examination of the question of preventive war in general, as concern centered specifically on the nagging problem of Saddam Hussein. The fact that removing Saddam would have constituted a preventive war was elided because the war would have been justified as enforcing U.N. mandates and not as the preventive removal of a direct threat to the United States or its allies. A more thorough analysis of the question would occur only after one of the most destructive terrorist attacks in history.

The Impact of 9/11

Before 2001, terrorism was viewed (at least in the United States) as largely a police matter rather than as an international security issue. As former secretary of state George Shultz later recalled, during the 1980s "we didn't really understand what motivated the terrorists or what they were out to do." In part, this was because the non-state nature of terrorist organizations did not fit into the state-centric image of the world held by policymakers, who viewed international relations as a matter between states; terrorism, by contrast, was viewed as a criminal act perpetrated by individuals.

This changed with al-Qaeda's attacks on New York and Washington in 2001. In the space of minutes, terrorism changed from a law enforcement problem to an issue of war and peace. America's European allies apparently agreed: at a NATO meeting the day after September 11, NATO representatives invoked Article 5 of the Atlantic Charter, declaring that the attack against the United States was an attack on all members of the alliance. This was a dramatic statement, as Article 5 was originally meant to be triggered in the event of a Soviet invasion and had never before been implemented.

The perception of terrorism as a new kind of threat began to coalesce quickly, not least because September 11 was preceded by ever bolder terrorist attacks, most of which were the product of movements like al-Qaeda. These included the first attempt to bring down the World Trade Center in 1993, the car bombings of U.S. embassies in Africa in 1998, the failed plan to blow up Los Angeles International airport in 1999, the suicide attack against the USS Cole in Yemen in 2000, an Algerian terrorist hijacking meant to crash an airliner into the Eiffel Tower in 1994, and a 1999 plot to bomb Jewish neighborhoods in Canada. With 9/11, however, terrorism finally came to be seen not as a disorganized series of horrible criminal acts, but as a coherent means of warfare, "the method of choice," as George Shultz has put it, "of an extensive, internationally connected ideological movement dedicated to the destruction of our international system of cooperation and progress."

Treating terrorism as a protracted war rather than an international law enforcement issue has deep ramifications. It implies that the mechanisms of law enforcement, with their lengthy procedures and unavoidable risks that criminals might somehow go free, are unacceptable given the magnitude of the potential destruction. This in turn pushes aside the presumption of innocence in favor of a risk-minimizing assumption that rogue regimes and terrorists intend to do harm and will in fact do so unless stopped. British Prime Minister Tony Blair expressed a common view a year after the Iraq invasion:

> From September 11th on, I could see the threat plainly. Here were terrorists prepared to bring about Armageddon.... And my judgment then and now is that the risk of this new global terrorism and its interaction with states or organizations or individuals proliferating WMD, is one I simply am not prepared to run. This is not a time to err on the side of caution; not a time to weigh the risks to an infinite balance; not a time for the cynicism of the worldly wise who favor playing it long. Their worldly wise cynicism is actually at best naivete and at worst dereliction.

This unwillingness to tolerate risk underlies debates about future strategies, as it pits traditional notions of deterrence against calls for a more active defense.

Fading Faith in Deterrence

The emergence of large-scale suicide terrorism is a challenge to entrenched beliefs about deterrence and rationality in international conflict. Coupled with the reckless and defiant attitude of potential rogue proliferators, some argue that it is now pointless—or worse—to speak of traditional notions of deterrence. "It is dangerous," the

Georgetown political scientist Robert Lieber wrote in 2002 with regard to Iraq, "to rely on assumptions about containment and deterrence developed in response to a very different set of circumstances that prevailed between the United States and the Soviet Union during the four decades of the cold war." Other analysts as well have noted that in many nations classical notions of deterrence and retaliation are "increasingly disparaged and renounced."

The debate over whether to strike terrorists preventively has thus become intertwined with a parallel debate about what to do about rogue nuclear forces, and in particular whether it is acceptable to engage in preventive attacks to neutralize them. These concerns converge in the question of whether to wage preventive war against regimes that may serve as the nexus between terrorist organizations and weapons of mass destruction, which was the primary U.S. argument for invading Iraq.

Faced with enemies schooled in a culture of martyrdom, or regimes led by delusional leaders, it is not difficult to see why assumptions of rationality—the very cornerstone of deterrence—no longer persuade. Some call for abandoning the concept, which critics contend is based on ethnocentrically Western notions of rationality and reasonableness, whereas likely enemies may operate under the influence of distorted information (or other unpredictable influences, like drugs) and may value transcendental goals more than their own lives. These concerns are closely tied to claims that the world now faces a qualitatively new kind of danger in leaders and organizations prone to high-risk strategies and whose willingness to kill indiscriminately means that the only prudent course regarding their attempts to gain WMD is to assume that "possession equals use," and therefore to act against them as soon as possible.

A related objection is that trusting in deterrence against rogue states and terrorists may come down only to trusting in the sanity of a single person. While the president of the United States and the secretary general of the Soviet Communist Party could both trigger mind-boggling levels of nuclear destruction, each side had bureaucratic and military checks in place to ensure that a single madman could not initiate an apocalypse. Do such checks exist in North Korea to restrain a leader described by some who have met him as a "vain, paranoid, cognac-guzzling hypochondriac?" Would a nuclear-armed Saddam Hussein have been any less reckless than the one who rained Scuds on Israel? Osama bin Laden did not hesitate to murder over three thousand people in a day; would he be more reluctant to kill three million?

No one really knows, and uncertainty makes preventive action seem more attractive than trusting in the reason, sanity, or values of a particular leader. Finally, because terrorists and rogues are fundamentally opponents of the international status quo, they do not have a vested interest in its stability. Indeed, they may actually seek to create crises rather than to resolve them, springing surprises and making daring moves in an effort to alter or transform the system, as North Korea did with its sudden and risky announcement that it had acquired nuclear weapons, or as al-Qaeda did with its surprise attack on 9/11.

This unreliability and unpredictability provides a strong incentive to strike preventively rather than to trust in deterrence, or in unverifiable agreements, or in negotiation and diplomacy—a path particularly discredited by long years of duplicitous and cynical Iraqi and North Korean behavior—and especially in the unproven deterrability of terrorists who believe that engaging in mass murder and instigating a global religious war will secure them an eternity in paradise.

Perspectives on Preemption and Prevention

Eroding faith in deterrence and a movement toward more unilateral preemptive or preventive policies spreads with each successive atrocity. As the American scholars Peter Dombrowski and Rodger Payne put it, "In the wake of the horrible 9/11, Madrid, and Beslan terrorist attacks, national leaders are more and more declaring their disinterest in absorbing such strikes and then finding and prosecuting the perpetrators after the fact." The French analyst Francois Heisbourg noted in 2003 that "there are signs that preemption can and has already begun to be incorporated into other countries' national defense strategies."

Despite the row between the United States and some of its allies over Iraq, many European states (if not necessarily their populations) supported the U.S.-led invasion. This may reflect the fact that, in the words of one European observer in 2003, they "have gone through a thought process very similar to Washington's," concluding that pre-9/11 security strategies are simply outdated. Tony Blair's 2004 speech on the anniversary of Operation Iraqi Freedom is representative of this sea change: "Already, before September 11th the world's view of the justification of military action had been changing....

For me, before September 11th, I was already reaching for a different philosophy in international relations from a traditional one that has held sway since the treaty of Westphalia in 1648; namely that a country's internal affairs are for it [to decide] and you don't interfere unless it threatens you, or breaches a treaty, or triggers an obligation of alliance." This "different philosophy" according to Blair, rejects deterrence and containment precisely on the grounds that "terrorists have no intention of being contained," and that "states that proliferate or acquire WMD illegally are doing so precisely to avoid containment."

Likewise, even as its members split over the Iraq war only weeks earlier, the European Union in June 2003 released its "Basic Principles for an EU Strategy against Proliferation of Weapons of Mass Destruction," a document that echoed the anxieties expressed by Washington, London, and other members of the eventual "coalition of the willing" that supported the invasion of Iraq. Weapons of mass destruction, the report notes, "are different from other weapons not only because of their capacity to cause death on a large scale but also because they could destabilize the international system," which, of course, is exactly what the leaders of rogue states or terrorists would hope they would do. And although the EU document understandably privileges nonviolent solutions to such threats, when "these measures (including political dialogue and diplomatic pressure) have failed, coercive measures under Chapter VII of the UN Charter and international law (sanctions, selective or global, interceptions of shipments and, as appropriate, the use of force) could be envisioned."

The French government released its own defense White Paper, symbolically dated September 11, 2002, at about the same time the U.S. National Security Strategy was being released in Washington. The French defense minister noted that the new peace in Europe did little to protect France against new, asymmetric threats. This in itself is scarcely remarkable; what is noteworthy is the proposed response:

> Outside our borders, within the framework of prevention and projection-action, we must be able to identify and prevent threats as soon as possible. Within this framework, possible preemptive action is not out of the question, where an explicit and confirmed threat has been recognized. This determination and the improvement of long range strike capabilities should constitute a deterrent threat for our potential aggressors, especially as transnational terrorist networks develop and organize outside our territory, in areas not governed by states, and

even at times with the help of enemy states.... Prevention is the first step in the implementation of our defense strategy, for which the options are grounded in the appearance of the asymmetric threat phenomenon.

While the French use of the term "prevention" also includes the use of "preventive" diplomacy and other means, the document clearly shows an increased interest in anticipatory and discretionary action. Indeed, the language of the White Paper was so blunt that the French government quickly had to go on record to deny that it had abandoned nuclear deterrence in favor of preventive nuclear strikes against rogue nuclear arsenals.

Even the Vatican changed its position in 2004. The late Pope John Paul II's foreign minister, Archbishop Giovanni Lajolo, in response to a question on this issue, said, "Certainly there is the need for prompt intervention [under U.N. auspices], indeed prevention of acts of terrorism," an answer that at the time represented a shift in the Holy See's previously firm position against discretionary military action.

Australian prime minister John Howard has observed: "It stands to reason that if you believe that somebody was going to launch an attack on your country, either of a conventional kind or a terrorist kind, and you had a capacity to stop it and there was no alternative other than to use that capacity, then of course you would have to use it." His government has also called for the U.N. Charter to be changed to permit "preemptive" action against terrorists, although Canberra's staunch support for the U.S. action against Iraq—Australia was one of only four nations to contribute military forces—suggests that its understanding of "preemption" is similar to the rather loose American interpretation of the term. It is a position that reflects mainstream Australian sentiment since 9/11, especially after the deaths of dozens of Australians in the 2002 al-Qaeda terror attack in Bali.

The Japanese face a particular problem due to their proximity to an openly hostile rogue proliferator, and this has raised serious questions at least of preemption, if not prevention. In response to a question from a Japanese legislator about North Korea, Shigeru Ishiba, director of the Japan Defense Agency, said in January 2003: "If North Korea expresses the intention of turning Tokyo into a sea of fire and if it begins preparations [to attack], for instance by fueling [its missiles], we will consider [North Korea] is initiating [a military attack]...." Foreign Minister Yoriko Kawaguchi, present at the same meeting, agreed. Ishiba later stressed that Japan's "Peace Constitution" did not require complete docility in the face of danger: "Just to be on the receiving end of the attack is not what our constitution had in mind.... Just to wait for another country's attack and lose thousands and tens of thousands of people, that is not what the constitution assumes." Ishiba reiterated this point a month after his initial comments, saying that it would be too late to act if North Korean missiles were already on their way, and that preemption would be "a self-defense measure."

Ishiba later backed away from these statements, saying that Japan would not use its own forces against North Korea, but would rely on U.S. forces to strike back in the event of hostilities. The debate continues, and as a 2003 analysis pointed out, there are many in Japan arguing for "jettisoning military minimalism"; more important, such figures "are no longer considered extremists or militarists and, in some cases, include senior officials who, in earlier times, would have been fired for their lack of caution." In any case, the Japanese unwillingness to trust the mercurial North Korean regime illustrates how the line between preemption and prevention will be blurred in coming years, as threatened populations show a growing unease with traditional definitions of preemption that require them to wait for unambiguous signs of attack before responding.

Russia has repeatedly reserved the right to engage in both preemptive and preventive action. These claims initially came in the form of a draft Russian defense doctrine published in October 2003 and subsequent statements made by Defense Minister Sergei Ivanov, which were quickly dubbed the Ivanov Doctrine. Ivanov said that Russia could use preventive military force in cases where a threat is "visible, clear, and unavoidable," and represents "an attempt to limit Russia's access to regions that are essential to its survival, or those that are important from an economic or financial point of view," which certainly opened a considerably broad range of possibilities.

This raised Western eyebrows, and Ivanov later tried to clarify the Russian position at a meeting with NATO defense ministers, implying that Russia's primary concern was not U.S. missiles five thousand miles away, but terrorists and rogues nearer to its own borders. "The doctrine," he said, "does not specify any preventive nuclear strikes, it merely implies that Russia retains the right to use military might for prevention, CIS [Commonwealth of Independent States] countries included." After the Beslan tragedy in September 2004, Russian officials became more strident. Gen. Yuri Baluevsky, chief of the Russian General Staff, declared: "As for carrying out preventive strikes against terrorist bases ... we will take all measures to liquidate terrorist bases in any region of the world." A few days later, President Vladimir Putin affirmed that Russia was "seriously preparing to act preventively against terrorists."

The rationale, as Russian security analyst Andrei Piontkovsky has argued—essentially echoing Tony Blair's position—is that terrorists cannot be deterred or contained as those concepts have traditionally been applied, and therefore "can only be counteracted with preventive measures." Russian diplomatic and military officials continue to insist that Russia absolutely opposes unilateral actions without U.N. sanction, but this seems hard to square with statements about what Russia believes are its rights regarding terrorists in neighboring states. It is unclear if Moscow has embraced a preventive strategy to the degree Washington has, especially given its relatively poor capacity to project conventional power, but its pronouncements emphasize the Kremlin's insistence on the possibility of action against sources of instability in former Soviet republics.

France, Great Britain, the United States, and the Russian Federation have all shown an interest in preventive action (although to judge by their diplomatic activities, the French and Russian positions seem to be that such actions might be acceptable only so long as it is not the United States engaging in them). The position of the fifth permanent member of the Security Council is less clear. China did not support, but did not veto, the authorization of the use of force against Iraq in 1990, nor did Beijing make a serious attempt to head off war between the United States and Iraq in 2003. Indeed, an editorial in one of China's official newspapers in September 2002 warned Baghdad about "the last chance for Saddam Hussein to deprive the Americans of a legal case against himself," and two months later China voted for Security Council Resolution 1441, which was intended, however unsuccessfully, as a last warning of impending but unspecified "serious consequences" should Saddam fail to cooperate with U.N. arms inspectors.

Like other authoritarian states, however, China is allergic to any possibility of interference in its domestic affairs and remains a determined champion—as repressive regimes tend to be—of a strict understanding of sovereignty. Beijing strongly opposed NATO'S action against Serbia, for example, objecting on the grounds that foreign forces had entered a domestic dispute, that NATO had bypassed the United Nations, and that military force had been used to further NATO'S ends. This represented a more general division between the democracies and authoritarian states, as the Chinese position was supported by the states whose leaders were no doubt able to imagine themselves one day in Serbian president Slobodan Milosevic's shoes.

Since 2001, Beijing has been supportive of the general idea of a global war on terror, but most likely because it is embroiled in its own struggle with Muslim Uighur separatists in western China. The Chinese, like the Russians in their war with the Chechens, no doubt anticipate some insulation from human rights charges if they appear cooperative in a common fight against terrorism, but it is unlikely that they will explicitly accept a new norm of prevention, even if at some point they end up practicing it themselves on their western borders.

In 2003, Kofi Annan, once more trying to keep the United Nations ahead of the innovations put forward by its members, created the High Level Panel on Threats, Challenges, and Change, which released its findings in late 2004. "The Panel's report," Dombrowski and Payne dryly note, "offers room for a meaningful discussion between the United States and other UN member states, in large part because it accepts the central claim of the Bush administration that there are circumstances when preventive action is justified." Of course, the report's authors (drawn from a wide range of member states) insist that such action can occur only with the blessing of the Security Council.

Although "preliminary indications suggest that there is a long way to go before the membership in general accepts the entire report," current objections amount to little more than haggling over the document's details rather than its central conceptions.

The more crippling flaw is that the report ducks the larger question of how to govern preventive use of force.

Its authors sternly reject any redefinition of the charter or the role of the Security Council, a stubborn but not unexpected honoring of tradition that practically guarantees that the report will become a dead letter, while the United Nations is pushed even further to the sidelines.

The Role of the U.N.

As new threats grow and traditional notions of deterrence collapse, many of the most capable states in the international system are moving toward strategies of preventive action. The most pressing question for the international community is not whether to accept this development—it will soon be upon us whether we like it or not—but how to govern it. What are the possible futures in an age of prevention, and what can be done to avert anarchy?

The most worrisome possibility would be the rapid abandonment of international institutions by states strong enough to act on behalf of most of the international community without the consent of the rest. In such a world, the preventive use of force would be essentially ungoverned and ungovernable. It is also an outcome that most resembles the present, in which powerful nations, either alone or with ad hoc coalitions, act to keep international order, stop proliferators, change odious regimes, and extinguish genocidal conflicts. In the long term, this would be the least stable alternative, because threats to the status quo would likely be dealt with only erratically by the major powers, which would organize the equivalent of international posses and take selective action depending on the interests and beliefs of the coalition of the moment.

This outcome represents a world in which international institutions have lost any ability to control the use of force. Are there other options? The most important question in this regard is whether the new age of prevention will be governed by the United Nations or some other institution, or even by a new set of arrangements.

A renaissance of the United Nations as it is currently constituted is unlikely, not least because the perception that the organization is dysfunctional, or at the least outdated, is now commonplace. This is not a view limited to traditionally skeptical Americans; as Canadian scholar Irving Brecher has written, the United Nations "can be particularly proud of its socio-economic achievements" but "has, in general, performed abysmally on the political, diplomatic, and military fronts." Andrei Piontkovsky dismisses the United Nations and the Security Council: "Who indeed, will ... define whether the preventive strike is legitimate, and the extent of its validity [regarding] the actual threat? The Security Council? Has the Security Council ever defined anything?" (Piontkovsky's alternative is to have the G-8 step in to decide such matters, which guarantees the participation of the industrial democracies of three continents—while also, of course, ensuring a place at the table for the Russian Federation.) The British historian Robert Skidelsky has pointed out that "the UN system was not set up to deal with the problems posed by rogue and failed states."

And a decade ago, Stanley Hoffmann wrote that the organization "is simply not equipped to deal with collapsing states or with rulers who systematically violate human rights. Nor does the United Nations seem any better prepared today to cope with the additional problems of mass terrorism and accelerating WMD proliferation. Defenders might argue that the United Nations itself is not really the problem, but rather the unwillingness of the major powers to use it, with American and British reticence during the Rwandan genocide an indicting example. The United Nations, such reasoning goes, is perfectly capable of taking action against the unholy trinity of humanitarian disaster, proliferation, and terrorism, if only the most privileged states in the Security Council resolve to do so.

This requires leadership, and critics of U.S. foreign policy in particular might describe many of the various disasters of the 1990s not as failures of the United Nations, but as failures of American leadership and imagination. "The task," says Gareth Evans, "is not to find alternatives to the Security Council as a source of authority, but to make the Security Council work better than it has." But the bottom line is that those who wish to salvage a role for the current system find themselves supporting the United Nations mostly from a lack of anywhere better to go. As the American legal scholar Anthony Arend has put it, "Policymakers could declare the UN Charter framework dead," and admit that "charter law is no longer authoritative and controlling." But to do so, even if it would be "the most intellectually honest approach," would only bring about a situation in which "many states would rejoice at the funeral and take advantage of such a lawless regime," and so the system remains the arbiter of force not by choice, but by default.

One remedy to this problem would be not to abandon the United Nations, but to work around it. Stanley Hoffmann has proposed a two-step process for ratifying interventions against clearly "evil" regimes that reinforces a moral order in which decisions about employing force would be made not by a legalistic body like the United Nations, but by an organization based on shared democratic and liberal values. In Hoffmann's alternative, the first resort in any proposed intervention would be the Security Council. But if the Security Council demurs or is paralyzed, Hoffmann proposes a recourse to a new body, which he calls the Association of Democratic Nations. This would be composed of NATO members and "Asian, African, and Latin American liberal democracies, such as India, South Africa, and Chile, as well as Australia and New Zealand. Only liberal democracies would be admitted as members. If such an association approved a collective intervention to change a regime, it would report its reasons and its decisions to the secretary-general of the UN, and could proceed to act."

Hoffmann's plan is interesting in many respects, but first and foremost because, unlike purely procedural solutions, it addresses the fundamental flaw at the heart of the United Nations: its membership. There is no way around the reality that the current international order embodied in the United Nations is one in which brutal autocracies can and do thwart the efforts of advanced democracies—and indeed do so even while subjecting the ambassadors of those democracies to grating, high-minded speeches about human rights and international justice. Little wonder that when procedural rigging by some of these nations torpedoed a vote in late 2004 to condemn human rights violations in Sudan's Darfur region, U.S. ambassador John Danforth said with frustration: "One wonders about the utility of the General Assembly on days like this." Such shameful moments have produced a kind of international case of cognitive dissonance, in which the admirable goals of institutions like the United Nations cannot be squared with a feeling that the inmates may be running the asylum.

A world in which Libya chairs the Human Rights Commission, for example, is a world that makes little sense to many people. (Nor will things improve any time soon, with such champions of liberty as Sudan, Zimbabwe, and China taking their seats there in 2005.) During the Cold War, such bizarre arrangements could be dismissed as harmless opera bouffe in the halls of an essentially powerless organization. But in an age where states like Libya, or worse, now demand that decisions about the use of force against terrorists and madmen must be made collectively, the humor is decidedly lost.

The central dilemma here is that it is inherently illogical to expect democratic nations and their authoritarian enemies to have a shared vision of international community. Dictators cannot be expected to support the overthrow of dangerous dictators any more than regimes run by religious extremists can be expected to approve violations of national sovereignty aimed at the elimination of terrorist groups that share their ideology. As Hoffmann has rightly noted, "Too many states among UN members have bloody domestic records, and they can be expected to block any proposal for a forcible collective intervention to change a regime."

If the United Nations cannot bring itself to condemn even the horrors of Darfur because such "naming and shaming" can be stopped by reprehensible regimes eager to escape such censure themselves, how can it be expected to exercise actual force against such regimes in the future? During the 1994 genocide in Rwanda, one of the rotating seats in the Security Council was held by ... Rwanda. (There was no move to expel it.) During the 2003 deliberations about Saddam Hussein's repeated defiance of the council's demands, another of the rotating seats was held by Syria, itself a Baathist dictatorship like Iraq. If the Security Council must contend with such regimes in its midst, how can it ever be expected to govern the international system in a way that will reassure other nations and convince them to forgo their right to self-help?

The United Nations cannot be salvaged as the arbiter of discretionary force in an age of prevention without significant reform to both its structure and its charter. And salvaged it should be: despite a history of severe, sometimes even buffoonish missteps by its leaders, the organization seeks noble ends and retains a distinct legitimacy in the eyes of many around the world. Soldiers have died in its service, attempting to save the innocent and to keep peace and order in corners of the earth that would otherwise have been left to their unhappy fates. To create an alternative institution in competition with it, such as Hoffmann's notional Association of Democratic Nations (or the actual Community of Democracies founded by over a hundred nations in 2000), would only complicate matters, as each member of the new institution would in effect be redefining the original U.N. Charter and their obligations to it, and placing themselves and the remaining U.N. loyalists on a collision course.

How, then, can these contradictions be reconciled so that the United Nations can function effectively as an instrument that can instill fear in, and act against, genocidal dictators, aggressive rogues, and suicidal terrorists? Strict interpretations of international law and of the U.N. Charter no longer have much force or appeal. Worse, attempts to corral violence under a legalistic U.N. regime will only increase the tendency for states and their leaders to think in terms of their own security and values rather than loyalty to a universal institution, a "perverse effect," as the legal scholar Michael Glennon calls it, of the "effort to force a legalist use-of-force system on a world that is not ready for it...."

The reason the world is not ready for a universalist legal order regarding the use of force is that the world is not populated by universally legalist regimes, and that realization points to a difficult, even radical answer.

Embracing Democratic Exceptionalism

Much ink has been spilled in recent years over the question of whether democracies are inherently less aggressive (at least against each other) than other kinds of regimes. Whether spreading democracy can stop terrorism or bring international peace is not the issue here; the more important question, given the obstinacy of dictatorships when it comes to efforts to keep a just and humane peace among nations, is whether terrorism, genocide, and other such threats can be stopped by anything but democracies. While the democracies have much to answer for, recent history nonetheless confirms that illiberal regimes cannot be counted on to act against threats to a liberal order. Accordingly, the membership and the procedures of the Security Council must be changed. What follows is a proposal to that end.

The conceptual foundation of this reform would consist of jettisoning years of hypocrisy and embracing democratic exceptionalism. This means going beyond utilitarian arguments about the inherent peacefulness of democracies, and establishing a principle that they are fundamentally better systems of government that by moral right are empowered to make decisions for the sake of the international community that despotisms may not. This would merely codify what Marc Trachtenberg identified over a decade ago as a "long-term historical trend...toward increasing recognition of the right of the civilized world to uphold certain standards of behavior—that states, for example, should not be free to massacre their own citizens or allow their territory to serve as a base for piracy or terrorism." This would amount to an assertion of democratic supremacy: that regimes chosen by, and accountable to, their own people have rights in the international system that other kinds of regimes do not. No longer would a Canada or Norway or Japan have to justify itself to a Cuba or Burma or Iran, a situation that has long defied common sense and offends even a rudimentary sense of justice.

The structural expression of this affirmation of the supremacy of democracy would be to close the membership of the Security Council to illiberal regimes—that is, to states whose leaders govern by coercion, are unaccountable to their own people, and who suppress basic human freedoms. Such a restructuring would amount to a declaration that regimes that violate human rights, threaten international order, and seek ever more lethal technologies will no longer be welcomed in deliberations about whether to use force against regimes that consistently violate human rights, threaten international order, and seek ever more lethal technologies. There is a reason that felons cannot vote or sit on juries, and this jurisprudential principle should now be applied in the international community as well. While this could be derided as discriminatory, the Security Council—with its permanent and unaccountable Big Five—is already inherently and structurally discriminatory. The existence of the veto in particular "makes nonsensical the Charter's organizing principle of sovereign equality."

Accordingly, concurrent with this reform of the Security Council's membership, the veto as it is currently practiced should be abolished. Irving Brecher rightly argues that the structure of the Security Council and the veto are now outdated, and that in an age of rogues and terrorists, "decisions on war and peace are too important to be left to the whims, threats, or machinations of any single member-state."

The Security Council veto is not necessarily any worse an idea than the veto in a domestic presidential system. It slows intemperate action and allows the five permanent members the ability to act with less fear of being overtaken by resolutions of hostile intent. But it is an absolute veto and cannot be overturned. In a body whose rotating members may include some of the world's worst regimes at any given moment, this is wise. But if the Security Council were restructured to admit only liberal regimes (perhaps by vote of established democracies that mutually recognize and accept each other as such), it might be possible to create a mechanism by which a supermajority of the council could defeat the veto of one member. This might be a way out of the paralysis in which the council constantly finds itself, and could open the way for greater unanimity in its decisions.

This would help make powerful democracies, including the United States, more inclined to think of the United

Nations as the first resort in times of danger, since its decisions would be the product of deliberation among states like themselves that they would be more likely to trust. No great power will ever abide by a decision it finds utterly unacceptable, but where there is room for compromise, the moral force of a preponderance of voting democracies might have more influence than a five-way chess game among the veto-holders. And while there may always be conflicts with prickly powers like France, disagreements between France and the United States are at least arguments between allies that have each sacrificed lives for the defense of liberty and have earned a greater right to decide questions of international order than thuggish states like Syria or North Korea.

I realize that any radical proposal for reform is unlikely to succeed because of the tautology of the veto (that is, any proposed changes in the nature of the Security Council and the veto will, of course, be vetoed). But what I propose is possible if the United States and the major powers of the world agree to change the charter—and threaten unilaterally to revise their own understanding of their right to self-defense if their demands are not met.

That is, the United States and other countries advocating reform would have to demand that the United Nations change or henceforth issues of international security will be settled outside of New York. America and other like-minded nations might retain their U.N. membership, but they would refuse even to go through the motions of submitting proposed military actions to the Security Council. (This might even be popular: a recent German Marshall Fund study of European and American attitudes toward the use of force found that Americans by a significant majority value the approval of their main allies more than that of the United Nations, or even NATO, while almost as many Europeans would accept the approval of their chief allies as they would the blessing of the United

Nations as sufficient legitimization for action.) The democratic great powers would withdraw into a twenty-first-century version of the Concert of Europe, with U.N. bureaucrats left to supervise things like literacy and child vaccination programs on whatever budget wealthier states wished to afford them.

The most obvious impediment to this idea can be summed up in five words: the People's Republic of China. How can any such reform take place when the world's largest dictatorship holds a permanent seat in what should be a conclave of democracies? There is no easy answer to this question. The first step would be to defang the veto: if the United States, Britain, France, and even Russia were to agree to limits on the veto, Beijing might see this as a development that it had no choice but to accept. But even this assumes that Russia and France—which exercise diplomatic power in the council far in excess of their actual military or economic capacity only because of their absolute veto—would agree to accept a new, democratically sustained veto. (Britain, it could be argued, "punches above its weight" in international affairs, not because of its veto but because of its unique relationship with the United States and greater willingness to employ its military forces.)

But France and Russia should be reminded that their systems of domestic government, like America's, contain similar veto override mechanisms, and it is at least possible that they might accept that their interests would be less threatened by a chamber composed only of liberal democracies whose voters would be no more unpredictable or emotional than their own. Here, the United States would have to exercise the boldest kind of leadership. A stated American willingness to abide by such a reformed veto would create palpable pressure on China and other states to follow suit, not only because it would represent Washington's stunning departure from 40 years of precedent, but because it would show an American acceptance of new rules that could actually constrain the use of U.S. power.

One optimistic sign is that China has not opposed what appears to be a recent tendency for the Security Council to act in favor of democracy, as the American legal scholar John Owen has noted:

> Is a norm arising calling for the extirpation of illiberal government wherever it is found? Such a norm, of course, would lead to continuous interventions around the world. But so long as China remains illiberal, the Security Council will not adopt that norm. Instead, it seems to have adopted a more limited norm opposing the forcible overthrow of liberal government. The Council is leaving established authoritarian States alone, but acting to restore liberal government where it has been illegally removed.

China may not be opposing this trend because there appears to be a "grandfather clause" for existing dictatorships and, indeed, an assurance that the democracies in a reformed United Nations will not embark on a democratization crusade might be necessary. However, there is no reason for the democracies to accept a retroactive absolution of current U.N. members when it comes to Security Council membership (or, for that matter, seats on committees on human rights or nonproliferation).

In the end, if the other major powers insist on change—another significant assumption, since it would require Russia and France to oppose China, which neither nation has shown itself inclined to do—Beijing would have the choice of accepting its seat in a reformed Security Council or opting out of the U.N. system entirely. If the world's largest country in terms of population withdraws, it could be a mortal blow to the U.N. Charter. But if China defected alone, it could also be the beginning of a long period in which China returned to its pre-1971 status as something of a pariah state. Neither alternative is a happy one, but neither is worse than the collapse of order that will come without reform.

The potentially irresolvable problem of China aside, there are numerous other diplomatic objections that might be raised about redefining U.N. membership and basing it on the nature of regimes, rather than on their mere existence as states. On a purely practical level, the symbolism of closing the Security Council to illiberal states means offending some American friends like Pakistan that are providing significant support—at the moment, anyway—in the struggle against terrorism. (Uzbekistan, for example, recently decided it has heard enough U.S. criticism of its authoritarian ways and now wants the American base there vacated by 2006.) Likewise, drawing a clear line between democracies and dictatorships will be difficult to do, and risks alienating nations in transition. More alarming is that such exceptionalism in the Security Council could end up widening the gulf between the democracies and the countries they hope to shepherd away from authoritarianism.

But the fact is that the United States and its major allies already practice discrimination in organizations like the G-8, NATO, and even the European Union (just ask Russia or Turkey). In these institutions, the democracies have taken the stand that they should take in the United Nations: to join us in our discussions about administering the global economy and the global peace, you must represent a regime that is like ours. This not only enhances the moral clarity and political coherence of these organizations, it also provides a powerful incentive to the nations that wish to join them. It could be argued, for example, that Russia has not slid further back toward repression, and is not a more illiberal regime, precisely because it wants to keep its place in the G-8, just as other states would hope to maintain their right to sit in a new Security Council.

A second answer to charges of discrimination might be to ask: So what?

At what point do the nations that have created and sustain the liberal international order cease apologizing for insisting on the right to take measures for the stability of that order without having to suffer the presence of the enemies of that same order in their deliberations? Or as George Shultz put it: "If you are one of these criminals in charge of a state, you no longer should expect to be allowed to be inside the system at the same time that you are a deadly enemy of it."

None of this is to deny the historical sins, blunders, and even crimes the democracies have committed in the past century in establishing the international system as it exists today. But acknowledging, for example, that Belgium and Japan were once cruel colonial powers does not logically lead to the conclusion that they therefore and in perpetuity, no matter what atonement they make, have no better moral right to intervene against genocidaires or to destroy terrorist training camps than the countries that actually produce or support such threats. Nor is the system perfect; the age of prevention should not be a pretext for ensuring the hegemony of a small circle of powers by crushing all challenges to the status quo. But hypothetical fears of imperialism should not be the argument for inaction in the face of tangible dangers.

One final and more immediate objection to all this is that it is irrelevant, because the age of prevention has not arrived and never will. Neither the United States nor its allies, critics will object, have the unlimited capability—or more importantly, the will—to engage in a series of wars to right the world's many wrongs. In the wake of the costs of the ongoing conflict in Iraq, why assume that citizens of the democracies will continue to take up the burdens of preventive action even if the United Nations is changed to allow it? Washington and London, in particular, have been reminded that regime change is a messy, even sordid, business (as it was, for example, in Haiti a decade ago), and it is an open question how many more such complicated operations the American and British publics will approve.

There is no way to tell what level of threat will be required to trigger American public support for another intervention somewhere in the world. As of this writing, a majority of Americans disapprove of President Bush's handling of the war, but the current state of affairs in Iraq probably says little about what measures they might countenance if al-Qaeda once again burrows into a ruling regime as it did in Afghanistan, or if a bizarre leader like Kim Jong Il were to make imprudent or risky threats to use nuclear weapons against American territory.

But to ask if the democracies will support more operations like Iraq is to ask the wrong question. Regime change would doubtless be the very rarest kind of military action in the age of prevention. Totalitarian states like Baathist Iraq, which due to their inability to reform peacefully are likelier candidates for regime change when they become a threat beyond their borders or begin the massive extermination of innocents, are few and far between. Rather, the more common incidents will involve smaller-scale operations resembling the Israeli raid on an Iraqi nuclear reactor in 1981, or the use of covert operations, commandos, or other specialized forces in strikes like the attack on al-Qaeda operatives in Yemen in 2002. (Anne-Marie Slaughter, for one, has called for reforms that would allow the United Nations to issue death warrants against dangerous dictators rather than punish innocent civilians in wars to remove them.)

Even larger operations will not require investments the size of Operation Iraqi Freedom; the commanding general of the U.N. force in Rwanda at the height of the genocide asked for only 5,000 troops. Likewise, dousing the civil war in Somalia in the early 1990s—a temporary victory, to be sure, and one that unraveled for political, rather than military reasons—took less than 40,000 soldiers. None of this is to say that any of these actions can be accomplished without complications, unintended consequences, or the deaths of innocent civilians. Friction and confusion are immutable characteristics of military conflict. And without question, it should never be assumed that wars to topple governments, whether on a humanitarian basis or as a preventive campaign against a dangerous regime, will be without risks.

But the fact remains that more limited preventive actions or even smaller preventive wars, meant to achieve specific goals (such as destruction of a weapons site or elimination of a terrorist facility) rather than fullscale occupations, are well within the capabilities of the developed democracies, especially if they act together, and can be conducted without undue strain on their societies or their economies. The need to undertake a mission the size of that in Iraq or even Afghanistan will (it is hoped) be rare; in any case, if such actions are undertaken with the approval of a reformed United Nations they might well attract a larger multilateral force that will share the burden.

In the end, objections to reforming the Security Council or the United Nations as a whole risk becoming moot, because they are already being overtaken by events. The wars in Iraq and Afghanistan, and the subsequent occupations, were in fact actions taken by coalitions of democracies in order to topple hideous governments and place their populations under de facto trusteeships until elections could be held to create freely chosen (if not yet completely independent) governments in both of them.

In Afghanistan, the United States issued an ultimatum to a Neanderthalic regime that was not recognized by the rest of the world (save for Pakistan, which created it), and when the ultimatum expired, the regime was removed and the country put under the administration of a multinational force. In Iraq, the United States, Britain, and their allies made a calculation that the regime in Baghdad had finally become an intolerable threat and again, after an ultimatum, they removed it by force. They have since administered the affairs of Iraq—not always competently, to be sure—with the U.S. coalition the guardian of the Iraqi state until it could be handed to leaders chosen by the Iraqi people. Neither Iraq nor Afghanistan was ever officially called a "trusteeship" or "protectorate," but if we are to call things by their right name, that is what they were.

Critics may well object that it is pure arrogance to declare certain governments incompetent or dangerous, and then to attack their territory or even remove their leaders. But such objections will not stop the great powers from doing so again when they think they must. It might be better simply to abandon all pretense and accept the reality that there are states that either cannot, or will not, administer their own affairs in a way that is not a danger to their own people or to others. When they must be reckoned with by force, as some of them necessarily will be, such actions should be exercised within the constraints of, and as much as possible subject to, the requirements of a reformed Security Council.

The essential point is that unless the iron tautology of the veto is broken and the composition of the Security Council changed in a way that reflects the growing wave of global democratization, the United Nations will be doomed, at least as an arbiter of the use of force. If states are going to act on notions of rights and justice in going to war—whether to alleviate suffering or to prevent aggression, terrorism, or other disasters—international organizations must be constituted by members who believe that they have the moral standing to levy judgment on each other. They also must be able to act in concert, and no matter how much unseemly hissing and catcalling may sometimes take place between democracies, there is an essential bond of trust between them that makes this cooperation possible.

This kind of trust will be essential to governing the use of force in an age of prevention, because without it, the temptation to self-help will become almost irresistible, especially as the formal institutions of international order become increasingly divorced from how international order is actually maintained. Michael Glennon has put it best in comparing the two "universes" of conflict resolution in the modern world and his description is worth considering at length:

> In one universe a de jure regime continues the traditional pacific dispute settlement process established by the charter .... In the other universe is a de facto system. It is a geopolitical regime over which the strong preside. It bears little resemblance to the formal regime of the Charter. Its ordering principle is not consent but power. Its rules are made not by students' international law journals but by NATO activation orders and the Pentagon's rules of engagement. Its membership is selective. Its participants are the like-minded states of NATO and other Western democracies ... [that] by and large trust one another because they share the same values. They support the jaw-jawing of the de facto regime because they recognize that when pacific dispute settlement fails, it is they who will have to do the heavy lifting: When international order is threatened ...they are the ones to restore it.

This de facto order exists because the regimes in it realize their democratic and humanistic values cannot be served by international institutions that are infested by some of the worst enemies of democracy and humanity. It is time at least to acknowledge, if not solve, this problem.

The Next Step

The dilemma of preventive war is here to stay. There are still too many places that stand apart from civilization—where human rights are not respected, where dictators who answer to no one rule with the whip of violence and intimidation, where fanatics brew plots against the international status quo and seek the weapons that could bring them to fruition. Too many "states" are little better than criminal enterprises, ethnic killing zones, and havens for terrorists and other barbarians. They are threats both to their own people and to international order. The Westphalian notion of sovereignty has already been breached by the necessity for humanitarian intervention, and now the international community must take the next step and legitimize action not only to prevent terrible regimes from annihilating their own people, but also to coordinate preventive action against such regimes when they seek to undermine international order.

Current international norms and legal statutes are outdated, with international institutions consequently incapacitated in the face of these new dangers. Changes—legal, institutional, normative—are necessary, and given the dangers of the new century, a dramatic reinterpretation of traditional notions of sovereignty and of the traditional prohibitions on the use of force may not be such a bad thing after all.

The alternative is a world where international order will depend only on the willingness of powerful states to secure it, either alone or together. At first glance, this might seem an arrangement that favors the interests of the United States, the most powerful nation the world has ever seen. But it cannot be in America's interest, or anyone else's, to live in a world where order, to say nothing of justice, is administered in an anarchic environment where firm alliances against civilization's common enemies break down into temporary marriages of convenience. Such improvised arrangements will solve problems only fitfully, and probably only once they reach crisis proportions. No matter how noble their intentions, if powerful states take it upon themselves to act (whether alone or in packs) to extinguish potential dangers, they run the risk not only of reprising the arrogant sins of ancient Athens but also of coming into conflict with each other, with catastrophic results.

5

Violence and Brutality in the Age of Terrorism

What will future historians call this time in which we are living? Everyday, national and international headlines tell us about acts of terrorism and atrocity that lead to unimaginable human suffering and the death of thousands across the globe. Suicide bombers are killing thousands and injuring countless more. Terrorist activities result in a loss of human life that is staggering. Additionally, there is famine and hunger, genocide, widespread disease, human enslavement, and children abused, orphaned, left without medical care, or pressed into hard labor and combat. How do you cope with it?

As I write this piece, the radio broadcasts daily news about the war Afghanistan and Iraq, the tensions between Pakistan and India, Israel and Palestine, the genocide in Darfore, and famine in Niger. Did you know that there are over 50 armed conflicts going on around the world? How do you cope with it? I realize the world has always been like this. Wars have always existed, bringing death and trauma to millions. What makes our age different is the media coverage. In the past 50 years, war and human slaughter is something we watch from our sofas in the evening. We read about it over the morning coffee. We hear about it on the radio on our morning commute. Despite technological advances, we are as helpless as our forebears to stem the tide of death and suffering on a massive scale. How do you cope with it?

On New Year's Eve, 1999, the world celebrated the new Millennium. Like nave children, we thought that putting a different number in front of the years would somehow usher in a golden age of enlightenment—The Age of Aquarius September 11, 2001 dashed our hopes.

I'm not a politician, or a diplomat, or a policy-maker. I am a mental health counselor, working with people who want to make sense of their lives. From where I sit, anxiety is running rampant in our population. Every week I talk with clients gripped by irrational, inexplicable fears—afraid to leave the house, afraid to go to sleep at night, afraid to drive to work. Anxiety and panic disorder are becoming epidemic. The symptoms are sudden and frequent onsets of rapid heartbeat, difficulty breathing, dizziness, tension—all signs of intense fear yet, the symptoms occur in the absence of any real danger. Huge numbers of people seek relief through self-medication with illegal drugs, cigarettes, alcohol, and food. They use these self-destructive habits just to make it through the day. The appalling rate of obesity in this country is ample evidence that food is the addiction of choice.

Strangely, no one seems to be making a connection between this epidemic of anxiety and the daily witnessing of global violence, atrocity, and human suffering. Doesn't anyone think these two things might be related?

In 2002, I published an interview in Anchor Point magazine with Ed and Maryanne Reese, two psychotherapists in Florida who have been at the forefront of research on Post- Traumatic Stress Disorder, in partnership with Dr. Charles Figley of the Psycho-Social Stress Research Program at Florida State University. They theorize that the publicity surrounding acts of terrorism and violence over the past decade is re-igniting trauma-related emotions in people who, sometime in their lives, have been traumatized in one way or another.

This group of people could include Viet Nam and Gulf War veterans, crime victims, and survivors of abuse, auto accidents, and traumatic injury. An article by Mary Sykes Wylie in the July-August 1996 issue of the Family Therapy Network magazine states that an estimated one-half to three-quarters of the general population in the United States has been exposed to an event that's severe enough to result in diagnosable Post-Traumatic Stress Disorder. This could mean that a large percentage of people, exposed to violence via the media, are re-experiencing their own residual fears and anxiety from their personal past. However, they don't understand the origin of these emotions, so they associate the emotions with everyday, innocuous activities such as getting up in the morning, driving to work, and going to sleep at night.

To complicate matters, most people, including physicians, simply do not realize that post-trauma psychotherapy can be brief, effective and reliable. So instead of recommending therapy, physicians prescribe mood-altering drugs. We are the most over-medicated nation on earth, and we are spending billions on anti-depressants, anti-anxiety drugs, and sleeping pills, just to function normally. How it this normal? Drugs help to stabilize the worst symptoms, but they don't teach people how to cope, how to think, and how to manage their own emotions.

I don't claim to have the answers to the world's woes, but I can tell you this. Among my clients whose lives are wracked with anxiety and panic, I have observed one of three deficits. These deficits are People, Purpose, and Peace. I have come to believe that these three factors are the essence of resilience and the ability to maintain equanimity in the

Age of Terrorism. People: I believe it is essential for each of us to develop and maintain a safety net of loving, caring relationships with friends and family. To do so requires emotional intelligence and a strong sense of self-esteem.

Purpose: Without a sense of purpose, life seems directionless. An overriding sense of purpose gives meaning to life and will sustain you in the face of loss. Purpose gives people the strength to go on living and planning for tomorrow.

Peace: I believe it is necessary for everyone to have a spiritual practice and a system of faith that allows inner peace and provides an emotional refuge in the face of chaos. These three elements, People, Purpose, and Peace can provide the foundation for the values and decisions that guide our daily actions in these times.

This is all I can offer and it is a humble palliative, I know. Modern life poses a dilemma. How do we detach from the reports of violence and mayhem enough that we can get on with our daily lives, yet stay engaged enough to have opinions—to feel outrage, instead of apathy; to call for action, instead of looking the other way. We must continue to condemn violence, brutality and terrorism. The democratic nations of the world can no longer respond with passivity. The U.S. and its allies are the only hope for millions who live in fear and suffering. In the meantime, please take care of yourselves. I ask everyone who reads this article to cultivate and maintain loving relationships based on dignity, equality, mutual respect and responsibility, find a clear sense of purpose and pursue it daily, and discover a source of inner peace in your lives. How do you cope with it? That's how.

A war Against Terror

It is widely recognized that we have entered a new era of warfare. With horrible poignancy, on September 11, 2001 terrorism announced that it had come of age. No longer are wars waged between symmetrical powers—state versus state. Now we are immersed in asymmetrical warfare, where states face non-state enemies who are palpably post-modern: transnational, decentralized, more closely resembling a fog or that mythic beast with multiple and multiplying heads, the hydra, than the traditional more or less well-defined and (at least potentially) containable national enemy. Moreover, this hydra is one given particularly to living amongst and preying upon civilians. In other words, as the smoldering ruins of Ground Zero reminded us, this is an enemy who does not respect the traditional moral parameters of warfare.

The response to this new kind of enemy—the "global war on terror"—has been no less remarkable for the novel directions it has taken warfare. Consider, for example, the strategy of "shock and awe," with its stated aim of inflicting the psychological equivalent of the bombing of Hiroshima and Nagasaki on the enemy population; the policy of pre-emptive war as outlined in the US National Security Strategy of 2002; the illegitimacy of neutrality as implied in President Bush's address to a joint session of Congress on September 20, 2001: "Either you are with us, or you are with the terrorists"; the collapse of the international principle of national sovereignty and self-determination as the enemy is pursued across national boundaries around the globe; or the softening of international conventions on war as enemy combatants (and in many cases, civilians) are stripped of the protections of the Geneva Conventions and imprisoned under brutal conditions, often after being "disappeared" to clandestine locations inaccessible to the likes of the Red Cross through the process of abduction called "extraordinary rendition."

And these are only some of the characteristics of this new manner of waging war. No doubt, much is happening about which we know nothing, given that this form of warfare involves not only more conventional, visible campaigns like those in Afghanistan and Iraq, but also "ghost wars," fought covertly in ways such that, as President Bush said, we will not know that they have begun or ended. Accompanying this recognition is the suspicion that these developments have finally rendered the just war tradition obsolete, irrelevant, impossible. In these changed circumstances, the traditional criteria just do not seem to fit. The global war on terror and the demands of waging it successfully defy such antiquated notions like legitimate authority, last resort, and the possibility of distinguishing between combatant and non-combatant.

Put more starkly, are we not now in a perpetual (color-coded) "supreme emergency," to use Michael Walzer's well-known concept, one that does not permit us the luxury of the moral purity or "clean hands" that the just war tradition, in more amenable times, afforded? Or, to echo the logic some have used in defense of suspending key protections of the Bill of Rights, surely the just war tradition is not a "suicide pact," rigidly binding us to a code of conduct in the face of a vicious enemy that does not share our moral vision of war? Or as the US administration's briefs suggest, does not the "military necessity" of crushing the evil of terrorism overrule the binding character of just war criteria?

The challenges presented to the just war tradition by the current situation are real. For example, as warfare shifts from the nation-state model to conflict with and between non-state actors, the criterion of legitimate authority, which has traditionally conferred the power to wage war upon heads of state, is called into question. Likewise, the current situation appears to many to render the criterion of "last resort" obsolete. After all, it is argued, when facing a purely evil, irrational, nihilistic enemy like a terrorist movement, war becomes the only possible means of response. In a similar manner, many proponents of the war against terror note the difficulty both in identifying what the successful end of such a war would look like and how to measure the probability of its attainment. Consequently they have effectively replaced this criterion with what might be called a "sincere hope for success."

Lastly, the difficulties the current situation presents for the criterion of non-combatant immunity are obvious. The predominantly civilian context of this war has led some to suggest that the civilian/military distinction may disappear altogether and that prohibitions on practices like torture are anachronistic. Although the challenges are real, the shadow of suspicion cast over the just war tradition by the current situation is itself not a novel development. The tradition has consistently faced questions concerning its viability since at least the advent of nuclear weapons. Furthermore, public perception notwithstanding neither is the changed context of terrorism and the global war on terror unprecedented.

The just war tradition arose and came into its own before the advent of nation-states. Indeed, it was precisely the variegated threats posed by decentralized bodies of fighting men in the high middle ages—brigands, mercenaries, pirates, and even feudal lords themselves—that prompted the just war tradition to further limit the scope of justified violence by narrowing legitimate authority and enhancing non-combatant immunity. So, if neither the question put to the tradition, nor the circumstances that currently prompt such a question, are new, then why the generalized sense that the just war tradition is perilously close to being eclipsed? Certainly there is some truth in the claims of those who suggest that the crisis is brought on by certain crypto-pacifist distortions of the tradition that effectively make it impossible to satisfy the criteria.

There are, for example, those who assert that any civilian deaths render a war unjust or that there can always be one more intervention before last resort. Likewise, there is certainly some truth in the claims of those who suggest that the mere invocation of the tradition's language is not a sign of the tradition's health but conversely a sign of its brokenness. After all, realists and their public relations apparatus are not above cynically and pragmatically using (parts of) the tradition on behalf of agendas that do not in fact cohere with the tradition. Yet, these distortions and manipulations are not the essence of the tradition's perceived problem. However these and similar misuses of the tradition contribute to the sense of crisis, they do not get to the heart of the matter. For the tradition's difficulties run deeper than its mere manipulation.

The challenge faced by the tradition stems from conflicting accounts of the tradition's end or purpose. The source of the tradition's difficulties is found in two very different accounts of the end of the just war tradition. This is to say, the difficulty facing the tradition stems from how one answers the question, "what is the just war tradition for?" What is its function? What end, what community, does it serve? The prevailing answer is that the just war tradition first and foremost serves the state. It is widely accepted that the just war tradition is a theory of statecraft. Typically this means that it is principally concerned with defining the moral responsibilities of states and the politicians who manage them. In its extreme form, the church and all non-politicians are effectively stripped of any legitimate role in just war deliberations on the grounds that the just war tradition is a public policy tool that belongs solely to public policy makers, with the church relegated to the sidelines as a sort of moral values cheerleader.

In its more popular form, on display in countless editorials and essays and heard from not a few pulpits and lecterns, the just war tradition becomes a casuistic checklist dusted off on the eve of conflict by which a state's war-making is evaluated by anyone and everyone. It is just war understood as a theory of statecraft, a public policy instrument for politicians, that finds itself under particular duress in an age of terror. Consider, for example, the challenges that confront the criterion of legitimate authority. As a theory of statecraft, the just war tradition presupposes the existence of states and of a relation between them. Accordingly, many have interpreted legitimate authority as restricting licit wars to those between states. Hence the difficulty in an asymmetrical situation. When one is facing a non-state actor like Al Quaeda, the traditional criterion of legitimate authority, geared as it is toward states, appears to be rendered obsolete.

This problem, however, is not insurmountable. Some have simply turned this difficulty into an opportunity. The Bush administration, for example, declared that Taliban fighters were not legally entitled to the protections afforded by the laws of war on the grounds that they were members of a non- or failed state. In other words, facing a non-state enemy relinquishes one—in a manner reminiscent of the medieval treatment of infidels—from the constraints of a just war ethic that might otherwise apply. In this way, the tradition does not so much collapse under the weight of changed circumstances as it is interpreted in a permissive manner. The just war tradition delineates those conditions under which limits apply; in the absence of those conditions—in this case in the absence of a legitimate state—the limits do not apply and so a just warrior is free to do what needs to be done.

Others have responded by reinterpreting the criterion to include at least some non-state actors within its purview. Thus, some non-state entities are legitimate targets (and, one assumes, initiators) of a just war because they effectively function like states, it is said. Such a reinterpretation is not particularly farfetched or inappropriate. After all, the tradition itself has slowly been moving in a similar direction as it has carved out a small space for just revolutions. There is another dimension to the challenge faced by the criterion of legitimate authority understood in terms of statecraft that is worth mentioning. It has been suggested that the kind of war that the global war on terror must be if it is to be effective requires such secrecy that no state could publicly make the case for the justness of a given war, with the result that its authority to wage war could never in fact be legitimated. Consequently, the public could not decide one way or the other about the justice, and so their participation in, a given war.

What is noteworthy about this argument is what it does not say. It does not claim that the just war tradition is irrelevant, obsolete or impossible. Rather, it argues that the just war tradition is in effect with full force and that the global war on terror fails to measure up and so just warriors may refuse to fight—not because they are secret pacifists, but because they are just warriors who take the tradition seriously. What conclusions can be drawn from this brief consideration of how just war as statecraft is challenged by current circumstances, and the three very different responses to those challenges? None of the responses concede that the just war tradition is in fact broken, although in at least two cases the tradition's survival depends on its being significantly modified and in the third case it issues in a paralyzing agnosticism about contemporary warfare.

Although only one criterion was examined, consideration of other aspects of just war as statecraft would reveal a similar fate. Just war as statecraft survives the crises effected by the changed circumstances of terrorism and a global war against terror, but only by means of significant adjustments that finally may not put the suspicion to rest that the just war tradition is on its last leg. Thus just war as statecraft survives (so far) with a limp. There is, however, another and older response to the question of the proper function or end of the just war tradition, a different account of what just war is good for. And unlike the preceding answer, this one is not thrown into turmoil by the changed circumstances of terror and a global war against a terrorist organization, perhaps because it is a far more demanding discipline than a politician's policy checklist.

This alternative answer begins with the church. Before there were modern nation states and a modern just war theory, there was just war as an ensemble of practices that were part and parcel of the discipline of Christian discipleship. And contrary to the claims of many prominent contemporary interpreters of the just war tradition, the medieval just war tradition as a form of Christian discipleship was not a theory of statecraft. Rather it is first and foremost an ecclesial discipline, the end of which is the edification of the body of Christ and the equipping of the saints as a witness to God's kingdom where a just peace rules the day.

Now, it must be quickly added that this does not mean that the just war tradition so construed and practiced has nothing to say to the governing authorities. To the contrary, it remains an account of governance—which is the kernel of truth in the arguments of proponents of just war as "statecraft." Insofar as it is part of an account of governance, just war as discipleship may or may not entail statecraft. Whether it does depends upon the particular form governance takes in any given epoch, which, in any case always includes more than states because it must include the church. The tradition remains a vision of political ends and the ordering of human community. The shift from public policy checklist to ecclesial discipline means, however, that the primary community to which the tradition speaks is the church and that the guidance the tradition rightly and necessarily offers secular governing authorities in the form of public policy advice and so forth arises out of that primary community and as an expression of that principal end.

As a Christian practice, the just war tradition is deeply implicated in the character of ecclesial communities. The just war tradition only makes theological sense as an expression of the character of ecclesial communities that are concerned daily with justice and loving our near and distant neighbors, as we raise families, interact with friends, encounter strangers, serve the poor and needy, work and worship. In other words, as a form of Christian discipleship the just war tradition is an extension or expression of those virtues that consistently characterize the Christian life, in peacetime as well as war. Which means that embodying the just war tradition entails much more than pulling out a social statement with its checklist of criteria on the eve of a state's military mobilization. Rather it about inhabits certain virtues—like justice and courage and temperance and prudence—something graciously made possible through the church's liturgy and preaching and teaching and practices of discipleship.

Thus, the challenge before a people who would be just warriors today is not that of figuring out how the present circumstances alter the checklist or nullify the criteria. The challenge instead is the perpetual one of establishing and sustaining those habits and institutions that make the virtuous life possible in season and out, in times of peace as well as war, even in a time of terror and asymmetrical warfare.

To appreciate the difference that approaching the just war tradition as an ecclesial practice that revolves around the character of a community and virtues instead of a public policy checklist makes, consider how just as Christian discipleship war explicates just cause, right intent, and noncombatant immunity. In particular, it is worth noting how it is able to address features of the contemporary situation that create problems for just war as statecraft.

As part of a theory of statecraft, the criterion of just cause has encountered particular difficulties when faced with terror. This is because statecraft holds as sacrosanct the concepts of national sovereignty and self-determination.

These concepts make intervention difficult and as a result just cause has been reduced to self-defense. As a matter of statecraft, the only just cause for war is national self-defense. Terrorism and the exigencies of asymmetrical warfare bring these principles into conflict insofar as the pursuit of a non-state entity like a terrorist network almost necessarily requires violating national-sovereignty and may entail a recovery of the older—and still just—notion of offensive war.

Such, however, is not the case with just war as a form of Christian discipleship. This is because the Christian community, constituted as it is by virtues such as charity and fortitude and practices like hospitality, is much more other-directed than modern nation states. Indeed, Christianity has consistently qualified the legitimacy of self-defense, authorizing armed action principally on behalf of the neighbor. Accordingly, intervention and crossing national boundaries presents no particular difficulty for Christianity, and not simply because the church is in fact already present in most lands. Rather, it is because states and statecraft are rightly affirmed only as an aid to loving our neighbors, and never as an obstacle to such love. In this way, war against a terrorist organization as a interventionist and perhaps offensive war (as understood in the older tradition, not as an excuse for preemptive or preventative war) presents no intrinsic difficulties.

The challenge to the church that would embody the just war tradition as a form of Christian discipleship in the midst of terror is otherwise and surfaces not in response to some changed context but as part of the perennial challenge to inhabit the virtues that constitute the Christian life. It is the challenge of inculcating the courage that is willing to risk our lives and the lives of our loved ones for the sake of others, even when our immediate interests are not at stake. It is the challenge of preaching and teaching not pious irrelevancies and assorted self-help nostrums but a Word of justice and love that invites us beyond ourselves. Much is made today in certain circles of churches needing to identify and satisfy the felt needs of target populations. Unfortunately, such a focus is not likely to move us out of our recliners for the sake of our neighbor. In this regard, when the lives of the saints who gave themselves for others are lifted up in our communities and when we encourage service to those in need around us (e.g., the works of mercy) we are contributing to the formation of the kind of people on whom the just war tradition as a form of discipleship depends.

After all, if we do not desire justice, if we do not care about our immediate neighbors who are unemployed, uninsured, homeless, battered, etc., it should come as no surprise when the terror suffered by Croatians, Sudanese, Haitians, or Timorese fails to move us. It should come as no surprise that we fail to respond to terror and its sources unless and until it comes crashing into our front door, as it did on September 11, 2001. The criterion of right intention has also faced tough scrutiny of late. There is widespread skepticism that simple disavowals of revenge coupled with equally simple declarations of a desire for peace adequately embody this criterion. This skepticism is heightened in the midst of a war on terror as it is revealed that some of the terrorists sought today were aided and abetted in the past and that some of the means as well as the allies in this war might themselves appropriately be characterized as terrorist. In other words, just war as statecraft has yet to articulate an account of right intent that is capable of warding off the charge of cynical mendacity or rank hypocrisy.

By way of contrast, just war as Christian discipleship associates right intent not with perfunctory declarations but with the enemy neighbor love and desire for a just peace that distinguishes the ongoing life of the Christian community. Indeed, just war is driven neither by hatred nor by a desire for the death and destruction of the enemy but by the love that desires to bestow the benefits of a just peace upon the enemy. What makes this account less susceptible to cynical manipulation is its connection to the ecclesial practice of confession. Intentionality is often a difficult matter to evaluate; for this reason it is properly associated with considerations of character and consistency of behavior. Thus, evaluating right intent in waging war includes queries such as: Is this a people who characteristically and consistently seek justice or is their appeal to justice selective? Is justice carried out to completion?

Complete justice entails looking forward—how justice will be implemented after the shooting stops—and backwards—bringing the past before the bar of justice. Here the practice of confession assumes a central place in right intent, as a just war people may be required, as a part of their pursuit of justice, to confess and amend their own failures of justice, even as they seek justice for their neighbors. So configured, right intent suffers no particular challenge from an age of terror. Whereas the injustice that mars our life tends to be minimized, denied, or ignored in the dominant approach, with the result that claims to wage a war on behalf of justice are frequently met either with deep suspicion or open derision, the recognition of complicity with injustice and terror does not short-circuit just war as Christian discipleship.

To the contrary, the confession and amendment of such injustice is an integral part of what it means to wage a just war. In this sense, a war on terror presents opportunities for self-examination and reform of life that might otherwise go unremarked and that may actually increase the likelihood that a just war against terrorists will be successful. Of course, if the changed context of terrorism presents no particular difficulties to just war as Christian discipleship, there are other challenges that attend this criterion. For example, in light of the demands of right intent, we might ask ourselves, how seriously do we take the call to love our enemies? Do we pray for our enemies or only for "our side"? Can we even name our enemies, or do we shy away from that because it is impolitic, impolite, or offends societal canons of sentimentality? Does the church model and encourage ways of dealing with enemies that neither shy away from addressing problems forthrightly nor simply cut off those with whom we disagree?

This is to say, do we model the desire for and pursuit of a just peace between enemies, or do we perpetuate a harsher politics where the winner takes all and the loser is simply silenced or encouraged to leave? Learning to name and deal with enemies on a daily basis is crucial to the formation of a people who can love their enemies in war, and who can confront injustice with a holy anger that does not become hatred, that does not rejoice in the enemy's death but truly desires that they come to their senses and be reconciled in the order of a just peace. Right intent also presents us with the challenge of confession. Many churches have lost sight of the gift of confession, either practicing it infrequently or practicing it only in the most vague and abstract manner. However, if just war is premised on the intention of justice and yet we know we are not pure in our intentions for justice, examination and confession become central to the practice of just war. Only then can we avoid the charge of hypocrisy and injustice in our pursuit of justice.

The last criterion to be considered by way of example is that of non-combatant immunity. The difficulty of respecting non-combatant immunity in the midst of terror has prompted several responses from proponents of just war as statecraft. Some recognize the difficulty of waging a war in a largely civilian context and pin their hopes on a technological fix—what we need are more precision weapons. Others acknowledge the weakening of this criterion and simply shift all responsibility for this to the enemy. Still others reinterpret the criterion such that the distinction is no longer between combatants and non-combatants but between those who are deemed a threat and those who are not. These last two moves feature particularly in arguments about the permissibility of torture.

As an ecclesial discipline, the just war tradition finds nothing new in the challenge of terror and a war on terror. Rather, the challenge remains what it has always been, neither technological nor rhetorical (as in adjusting the criterion) but a matter of character. In the face of terror and warfare in a civilian setting the challenge is the old one of forming those who would be soldiers in temperance, such that their response to threats will be appropriately discriminating, and courage, such that they will abide by their convictions in this regard, even when the pressure to ignore them will be great. These challenges, of course, extend to the whole church as well insofar as we must be willing to put the lives of our loved ones at greater risk so that enemy civilians may be at less risk

Here the other directed character of the Christian life rises again to the fore. Do we resist the appeal of a therapeutic gospel to a self-absorbed culture and instead preach and teach and model a Gospel of exorbitant self-giving for others? Does our life reflect the conviction that in such giving, though we and our loved ones may die, we will not perish? And do we let the governing authorities know that we are indeed willing to bear such costs for the sake of waging war justly?

Much ink has been spilt on the question, "Can modern war be just?" and in light of the coming out of terrorism, the question has heated up again. But, as the likes of Paul Ramsey and James Turner Johnson never tire of reminding us, there is nothing inherent in the character of modern warfare that renders it intrinsically incapable of being restrained by the just war discipline. This holds as well for a war against terrorists. War remains now, as it always has been, a human act, and as such is subject to human discipline and restraint. Just as terrorism is not an inevitable response to real or perceived grievance (most aggrieved people do not attempt to fly planes into skyscrapers), so too war that exceeds the discipline of the just war tradition is not an inevitable or necessary response to terror.

Accordingly, the crisis that appears to grip the just war tradition is due less to changed circumstances than it is to problematic ends it is asked to serve. Just war as statecraft, as a public policy checklist, is in crisis, as it has been effectively from its appearance. The challenges that terrorism present to the just war tradition are neither new nor unique. In the face of terror, the church, equipped with its discipline of just war, confronts its age-old task of nurturing the virtues that make just war possible, even in the midst of terror—virtues such as justice, temperance, courage and prudence.

These are the same virtues required to navigate peacetime faithfully as well. Whether one is a retiree or homemaker, student or teacher, accountant or mechanic, we are called to be about the business of seeking a just peace for our neighbors. Whether civilian or soldier, in wartime or peacetime, the virtues of justice, prudence, temperance and courage are central to the life of discipleship. In other words, the just war tradition is not first and foremost a public policy checklist but an embodiment of the Christian life. So, what is just war good for in a time of terror? Forming disciples.

6

Responsibilities in the Age of Terrorism

When the IAC was formed in 1983, we became concerned about the possibility of a *Clash of Civilisations,* which Samuel Huntington had written about so eloquently. We did not believe that conflict was inevitable but we did believe that positive steps should be taken to make sure there was greater understanding between different countries, regions and in particular between different faiths. Therefore we convened a meeting which was held in the Vatican in 1987. The world's major religions were represented at a high level. Our purpose was to decide whether an ethical statement could be drafted — acceptable to all religions — to all faiths.

We came away from that meeting encouraged. The core values of the world's major religions have great similarity. There is a common view about what is needed for a peaceful, cohesive and constructive society, where discrimination and prejudice can be pushed aside. As a consequence of that judgement and with the advice of ethical philosophers like Professor Hans Kung, we set about drafting a Statement of Human Responsibilities. It was our view that if major states could be persuaded to accept such a statement, that it would become a companion declaration to the Universal Declaration of Human Rights and that an acceptance of universal "responsibilities" would enhance the acceptance of human rights around the world.

Human Rights are broadly understood, and, in theory at least, accepted. On one level, "human rights" are the inalienable possession of each individual. On another level, they are the "rights" the government must accord to their citizens. The most basic of "rights" go back to Magna Carta itself, to Habeas Corpus, to the Rule of Law, to Due Process under the Law, to equal access to the Law, the right to liberty and security, to freedom of thought, conscience and religion, to freedom of opinion and expression — without distinction of any kind as to race, gender, faith, language or political belief.

Our Draft Declaration on Human Responsibilities outlaws inhumane behaviour; it makes it clear that no person, group or organisation stands above good or evil. Everyone endowed with reason and conscience, must accept responsibility. What you don't wish to be done to yourself, don't do to others. There is a responsibility to respect life; to resolve disputes between states without violence; to protect each person unconditionally; to behave with integrity, honesty and fairness and to make serious efforts to overcome poverty, ignorance and inequality. No person is exempt from general ethical standards. There is a responsibility to speak truthfully, to show respect for all other people.

If we look at the Universal Declaration of Human Rights it is clear that for a person to be able to exercise these "rights" somebody or some institution in a position of authority will need to act "responsibly".

"Rights" and "Responsibilities" are indeed complementary.

The draft Statement on Human Responsibilities was completed and published in September 1997. Many countries in the East and in the developing world liked the ideas we espoused. But in the West there was considerable difficulty. The arguments largely rested on two grounds.

Some argued that it was hard enough to get nations to accept their obligations under the Universal Declaration of Human Rights and that a further declaration would confuse the issue. Others argued that some states would use a draft Statement on Responsibilities in a repressive or even a reactionary fashion. Those who used this argument had in mind the perversion of responsibility common in Nazi Germany.

There was a third argument devised by Prime Minister Blair that the Universal Declaration of Human Rights really represented a statement about the way government should behave in protecting the rights of individuals, while the draft Statement on Responsibilities was much more a matter for individual action, and it would be quite wrong for governments to be prescriptive about what individuals should or should not do.

I believe Prime Minister Blair's argument was mistaken. The Universal Declaration of Human Rights does contain some references to "duties" and "responsibilities". It does not ignore the concept of responsibility. The Draft Declaration on Responsibilities not only refers to the responsibility of citizens, as general members of society. It refers in particular to the responsibility of people in positions of power and authority whether that power comes from wealth, from institutions, from corporations or from government.

It is clear in the Draft that those in the position of greatest influence should, in the view of the Declaration, carry greatest "responsibility". It had been our hope that the Draft Declaration would be introduced into the United Nations to be a companion piece to the Universal Declaration of Human Rights so that both "rights" and "responsibilities" would be defined.

More and more political leaders are coming to talk about the "responsibilities" of their citizens but they are doing so without context, without guidelines about what constitutes reasonable, desirable, even necessary "responsibility".

Just as there has been and continues to be a vigorous discussion about what constitutes "human rights", we need a discussion about what constitutes "human responsibility". Without such a debate, the term "responsibility" is likely to be exploited for political and repressive purposes. This is not an argument to avoid "responsibilities". It is an argument to debate, and to adopt a Declaration of Human Responsibilities.

Abuse of "responsibilities" will not be avoided by postponing debate or work on a Declaration. This may not have been clear in our discussions during the 1990's. The changes to the world since September 11, 2001 have introduced new, relevant arguments. In 1948, when the Universal Declaration of Human Rights was adopted by the United Nations it was an article of hope, a light on the hill, an aspiration to work for. It is true that many of the drafters of that Declaration were Western. The world in particular needed such a document because civilisation as we knew it had nearly been destroyed.

The Declaration of Human Rights indicated to the world that nations great and small were determined to work for a better world. The Universal Declaration of Human Rights was given substance by the 1951 Convention of the Status of Refugees, the Convention on Status of Women, Conventions on Economic, Social and Cultural Rights, and on Civil and Political Rights (1966). There are then other Conventions on the Rights of the Child (1959, 1989).

These Conventions and their later protocols have had a common purpose: to give legal force to the principles of the Universal Declaration of Human Rights. They were an exposition of what governments owed to their citizens. As a parallel, the Geneva Conventions of 1949 were negotiated protecting prisoners of war from unjust and inhumane treatment. In some places prisoners of war had been abused mercilessly.

These Conventions relate to people taken prisoner in armed conflict. It was not necessarily in armed conflict between states. This has implications for the assertions of "unlawful combatants" and of "failed states". It was clear that the world had to react forcefully to the attacks on 9/11. Whether we have reacted effectively is still an open question.

A concern, even paranoia, has developed in many places about Islamic fundamentalism and indeed, in some quarters, about Islam itself. If we want to avoid Samuel Huntington's *Clash of Civilisations*, we will work to bring reason and common sense to the debate and switch off the paranoia. I will give two examples. Since September 11, fears have been aroused not only in the United States but around the world. I had people writing to me from London saying they were greatly concerned at the idea that Saddam Hussein could drop chemical or biological weapons on the city of London within 45 minutes. No one had said Saddam Hussein could do that - but the British Government had left hanging in the air, the strong impression that he could deploy such weapons within 45 minutes.

Was it just a slip, an error not corrected, or part of a general attempt to prepare people for the most extreme actions as we combat terrorism? I know my friends in London believed that concern of theirs went a long way towards justifying war against Iraq. It is also clear that the qualifications placed by intelligence agencies on the possession of weapons of mass destruction were not really heeded by the Coalition of the Willing. Possession of such weapons was depicted as a certainty.

Whatever was said about weapons of mass destruction,

the United States knew that Saddam Hussein had no missiles that could go any way towards harming cities in Europe, much less London. That was not in doubt. It was based on complete and continual observation of all missiles that take off anywhere in the world. This demonstrates the need for wise and suitable leadership. We need governments who can speak of the reality so that there can be a considered and effective response. Leaders who frighten their people, who expand the truth, who unadvisedly support extreme action, will not be effective.

The second example is from Tony Blair talking about "The Opportunity Society" in September last year. On one page he said that terrorism "is a wholly new phenomenon" .... Whose fundamental advocates..... "preach hatred of the West and our way of life."

Blair speaks of these people, of the terrorists saying "they are not provoked by our actions; but by our existence. They are in Iraq for the very reason we should be. They have chosen this battleground because they know success for us in Iraq is not success for America, or Britain, or even Iraq itself, but for the values and way of life that democracy represents, they know that, that's why they are there."

That to me is saying they are fighting because they hate us for what we are. But then a little further on in the same speech, Prime Minister Blair says: "After November 1, I will make its (Middle East Peace Process) revival a personal priority. Two States, Israel and Palestine, living side by side in an enduring peace would do more to defeat this terrorism than bullets alone can ever do."

His first statement is saying terrorists have no cause but hatred. The second statement is saying they have a cause which is their perception of a fundamental injustice suffered by the Palestinians. Both statements cannot be true. I believe his second statement is true. There are many causes of terrorism: In the Middle East, the perception of injustice to

Palestinians; In Chechnya, the desire to break away from Russia; In Basque, there are specific objectives; For decades, Britain experienced terrorism practiced by the IRA; Those wanting separatism in the Philippines, over several decades, have another reason. While techniques and practices may be similar, the objectives of terrorists are varied.

None of this should be construed as justifying any element of terrorism or any sanctioning of violence against civilians. It is a plea for our governments to ask themselves, why do people become terrorists? Unless we understand that, our fight against terrorism will fail.

We should also advance these arguments with some semblance of humility. Nearly every religion in different stages of its history has been perverted by people whom today we'd call fundamentalists; we'd call terrorists.

The United States Defence Department conducted an investigation into Lt. General William G. "Jerry" Boykin, the Pentagon's senior military intelligence official. The Report found that he had been guilty of contravening regulations.

The New York Times in August last year, and the Washington Post at the same time both used this quotation — "He said in one speech of a Somali warlord that "I knew that my god was bigger than his. I knew that my god was a real god and his was an idol". How could such a person accurately sign off on intelligence from the Pentagon to the White House?

Fundamentalism has not only been a disease of Islam, but at different times of nearly every religion. The founder of the Liberal Party in Australia in the middle to late 40's used to emphasise the Rule of Law, Due Process under the law, Equal Access to the law. As a child I had been taught to take these things for granted. But now I know that these basic principles, on which democracy depends, cannot be taken for granted.

From the end of the Second World War to September 11, democratic powers moved — falteringly and often inadequately — to establish a world governed by law. The Conventions mentioned earlier were designed to give legal framework to the Universal Declaration of Human Rights. The International Criminal Court came into being in July 2002 — perhaps the most substantive change to international structures — since the foundation of the United Nations itself.

In these years, the ideal of a world governed by law was more than a dream. Many people, many Americans, worked for it. We believe that people who do not preserve the Rule of Law deserve condemnation. Under the Rule of Law, there can be no discrimination. The law must apply to all people of all nations without discrimination, regardless of race, colour, ethnicity, religion or gender.

In today's world we've stepped back into a darker age. It is now common to argue that because of the nature of global terrorism, we must also alter the principles by which we have lived.

There are too many examples of governments legislating discriminately. In Britain — against aliens who were thought to have some links to terrorism, but who were not charged and who were held in jail — the Law Lords found such laws unconstitutional. After a great deal of debate and argument between the Commons and the Lords, this issue has now been resolved. The solution requires the closest possible supervision both by the Courts and the Parliament. Untrammelled use of Executive Power is no longer possible.

While detention or restraint without trial is always repugnant, the conditions attached to such treatment by the latest British Legislation will go a long way to prevent abuse. To go back to history, this is not a new question. There is a passage from a cable Winston Churchill sent to

Herbert Morrison, as Home Secretary at the time Sir Oswald Moseley, leader of the Nazi Party in Britain and his wife Lady Diana Moseley, were to be released from custody.

They had been imprisoned under Section 18B of the Security Legislation. The war was going a good deal better for the Allies; the Mosleys had become ill; and the Home Secretary was preparing to release them, but with restrictions. Churchill's memorandum to Morrison asked the Home Secretary to emphasise that the release of the Mosleys was also a matter of high principle.

He suggested that the great privilege "of Habeas Corpus, and of trial by jury, which are the supreme protection invented by the English people for ordinary individuals against the State - the power of the executive to send a man into prison without formulating any charge known to the law and particularly to deny him the judgement of his peers - is, in the highest degree, odious and is the foundation of all totalitarian governments..... extraordinary powers assumed by the Executive with the consent of Parliament in emergencies should be yielded up, when and as, the emergency declines.... This is really the test of civilisation."

But today, in the name of security, the most curious and frightening provisions are justified. The United States sought to put people in Guantanamo Bay, beyond the law. The Supreme Court ruled that they had access to American Courts. That was a notable victory for the Rule of Law, which implied heavy criticism of an excess use of Executive Power. Military Tribunals were established to try people from Guantanamo Bay. Two Federal Court Judges have found that those Tribunals are unlawful. Judge Green determined that despite a terrorist emergency "that necessity cannot negate the existence of the most basic fundamental "rights" to which the people of this country have fought and died for over 100 years".

Judge Green argued that the Tribunals did not satisfy demands for fairness on two counts: They denied inmates the right to hear all the evidence against them, and they allowed the introduction of testimony obtained under torture. The highest law authority in the United Kingdom, the Attorney General Lord Goldsmith has said that the military tribunals would not provide the kind of justice that the British Government would expect for all British citizens. The Australian Government has decided to support the United States Government.

The issue will ultimately be determined by the Supreme Court. In America, to America's credit, there is debate about these issues. In my country, very little. In Australia, it may be easier to do things which are unreasonable — contrary to Magna Carta, to Habeas Corpus and to Due Process — because we do not have a Bill of Rights, unlike America, Canada, New Zealand, Britain and every European Union country. A Bill of Rights provides protection against excess and repressive use of Executive Power.

The "Australian Security Intelligence Organisation Legislation Amendment (Terrorism) of 2002" has been described as the most draconian bill any Australian Government has ever conceived. It is believed to surpass anything the former Australian Prime Minister, Sir Robert Menzies, tried to do when he sought a ban on the Communist Party as long ago as 1950.

The Legislation has been compared to Counter Terrorism Legislation in the United States, Canada and the UK and many believe it exceeds the measures adopted in any of these jurisdictions. One person summed it up in this way: "....only Australia has sought to legislate to authorise the detention in secret of non-suspects".

More specifically this legislation allows our government to detain a person whom authorities believe may help in counter-terrorism enquiries. The authorities do not have to believe the person is guilty of any offence. They only have to believe that the person may know something of relevance to anti-terrorism enquiries, even if the person does not know he or she knows it.

While in some cases provision can be made for the person to access a lawyer, there is a general provision which prevents a detained person contacting anyone at all. Section 34F stipulates: "A person who has been taken into custody, or detained, under this Division is not permitted to contact, and may be prevented from contacting, anyone at any time while in custody or detention."

If the detained person fails to provide information requested, he or she is subject to prosecution and up to 5 years jail. The legislation goes on to say that if the person does not have any information, then it is not an offence; but the person has to prove he or she has no information.

The same provision applies for the production of records. Failure to produce can put you in jail for five years; but if you don't have anything to produce, it is not an offence — so long as you can prove another negative. If the authorities happen to be wrong at the outset and the person does not know anything, and does not have anything — failing to answer or to produce proof, could result in a very heavy jail term unless they can prove a negative. How does one prove a negative? It is for good reason that under British law and under our law, the onus of proof has been on the Crown and the presumption of innocence until proven guilty is accorded to all people, but no longer under this legislation. As originally introduced, the legislation placed no restrictions on who could be detained or questioned. In other words, it applied to any child. The only restriction as to age was that a child under 10 years who was detained could not be strip searched.

Now, the legislation applies to anyone over the age of 18. For young people between 16 and 18 years, the authorities need to believe that the person may commit or has committed a terrorism offence. But it is only a question of belief. There is no suggestion the authorities have to prove it to detain somebody between the ages of 16 and 18 under these provisions. So a person can disappear for the time prescribed.

You might think we have a free press and that a disappearance will get reported and perhaps notoriety, but our Government has thought of that also. The authorities have covered normal reporting of these events. Anyone disclosing somebody's detention under a warrant, commits an offence. Under the provisions of this legislation, the penalty for such disclosure is 5 years jail.

One might think that the ban on publication would only apply for the period of the warrant allowing detention, but there is a second section that makes it an offence to disclose the fact that somebody has been detained under such a provision for two years from the end of the warrant. Again, imprisonment for 5 years. There are also provisions that apply to the person subject to detention and to that person's lawyer, if that person has been permitted access to a lawyer, making it an offence to disclose the fact of detention and questioning.

How would one describe these powers? How is it that both major parties in Australia agreed with these provisions? The legislation is contrary to the Rule of Law. It is contrary to Due Process, to Habeas Corpus, to the basic rights which we have come to understand are central to a free and open society. The provisions would well accord with old-fashioned Communist States with tyrannical dictatorships.

Such actions have been justified as necessary to fight terrorism. The Australian Government is able to pass such laws significantly because we do not have a Bill of Rights. It is also worth noting that in America, Britain, Canada and New Zealand, governments are all restrained by a Bill of

Rights; every European country is so restrained, and thus their citizens are, to a degree, protected.

Where proper Executive Power is transgressed — as has been the case in the United States — the Courts come into play. This is very much to the credit of the United States. In the 70's and 80's, Germany and Italy were under extraordinary terrorist pressure from the Red Army Faction and the Red Brigades. Both countries beat the terrorists.

Despite that experience, the United Kingdom is the only European Union country which has found it necessary to suspend some aspects of the European Union's Bill of Rights. We all need to take a long, hard look at ourselves to see what our Governments have executed in our name.

When we first saw the photographs of Abu Ghraib, many rushed to condemn torture. "This is just way out soldiers acting unlawfully". But *The Torture Papers* released by New York University's Centre on Law and Security, and published by Cambridge Press, tell a different story. The Executive wanted to know how far interrogators could go without running foul of the Geneva Conventions, or of Human Rights Legislation in America or internationally.

Part of the purpose of a lawyer is to tell a client how to do what that client wants to do. And so the torture trail began. The Executive wanted to know, "How do we justify the rigorous, intrusive questioning?" Critics from the United States have offered their own condemnation of these events. I do not need to add mine. In the New York Times, a long term National Security Advisor to the first President Bush, Donald Gregg, wrote that the memorandum "cleared the way for the horrors that had been revealed in Iraq, Afghanistan and Guantanamo that make a mockery of Administration assertions that a few misguided enlisted personnel perpetrated the vile abuse of prisoners. I can think of nothing that can more devastatingly undercut

America's standing in the world or more importantly our view of ourselves than those decisions." Israel is one Western-style democracy that has acknowledged that the mistreatment of prisoners is indeed sanctioned. I am advised that in "1987, the State Commission established secret guidelines for interrogators using what was called "moderate physical and psychological pressure". In 1999, Israel's Supreme Court ruled against those guidelines." In their view, torture was illegal under any circumstances and constitutes "a greater evil than the evil it was intended to challenge." Unfortunately, Israeli authorities have shown inadequate respect for their own Supreme Court.

In the memoranda that were published, there is a clear desire to place detainees beyond the reach of any court or law; a desire to abrogate the Geneva Conventions, and a desire to make sure that those implementing or authorising the policies will not be liable for war crimes under US or International Law. The profession of law has been shamed by many of the opinions offered. The Secretary of State Colin Powell was a lone voice arguing against such policies. He was joined as far as *The Papers* are concerned by William Howard Taft IV, the US State Department legal adviser.

One opinion said that "interrogators could go very far" and not face legal consequences. "Physical pain amounting to torture" Assistant Attorney General J.S. Bybee advised the Counsel to the President, Alberto Gonzalez "must be equivalent in intensity to the pain accompanying serious physical injury such as organ failure, impairment of bodily function or even death". He added "in the Justice Department's view, actions by interrogators may be cruel, inhuman or degrading but still not produce pain and suffering of the requisite intensity" to constitute torture.

On page 134 of *The Torture Papers*, there is a memorandum signed by President Bush saying that interrogation must be "humane". This seems incompatible with other documents. Was he the odd-man-out? Anthony Lewis wrote "they are an extraordinary paper trail to mortal and political disaster; to an episode that will soil the image of the United States in all parts of the world for years to come." I happen to agree with that view, but it is also to the credit of the United States that these issues do not remain silent; that they are debated and revealed.

In *The Torture Papers* – the Red Cross Report of February 2004 and The Taguba Report concerning the treatment of prisoners – both make it clear that the mistreatment of prisoners has been commonplace. Both reports are written in careful language, but it is plain that the violations and the mistreatment has been pervasive and substantive. Attorney General Gonzalez claimed in his Confirmation Hearings before the Senate that he was against torture but the memorandum to which his name was attached in *The Torture Papers* demonstrates that he was in favour of questioning techniques that most people would say comprises torture.

Powell and Taft come out of it with credit, but a long list come out of it with shame, which includes Assistant Attorney General Jay Bybee (now a 9th Circuit Court of Appeals Judge), then-Deputy Assistant Attorney General John Yoo, new-Attorney General Alberto Gonzalez, and Secretary of Defense Donald Rumsfeld. Even more recently, the willingness to use torture has been underlined by the United States defence of "rendition" for terrorist suspects: Capture them, then take them to a country where they can be interrogated without supervision. Thus torture is well and truly on the agenda. What purpose does "rendition" have, unless it is to enable the authorities to interrogate certain suspects with torture?

There are many experts, including from the FBI and the CIA, who claim that torture is a most inefficient way of gathering information. It is claimed that it is unreliable, often false and cannot be checked. That is a practical argument against its use. So in practical terms, it is almost certainly a highly inefficient way of gathering information. There is one more disturbing aspect of these events. The speed with which many countries, especially English speaking countries, have been prepared to put aside basic liberal democratic principles — the right of Habeas Corpus, to trial by jury, to no detention without charge and trial, to the end of Due Process — is reminiscent of tyrants.

Are we really convinced that we cannot defend our free societies by adherence to our own principles? Do we really believe that the enemy — the tyrant — has an advantage by being prepared to torture, imprison and jail without Due Process? Was this an advantage for Hitler, for Stalin for Saddam Hussein? Is it an advantage for the Stalinist dictator of Uzbekistan at the present time? Or do we believe that the strongest argument on our side is a willingness to act in accordance with principle — as the United States has done through most of its history, but not, I believe, through recent years?

If we embrace the methods and techniques of tyrants, we take a significant step to becoming too like them. This is the danger we face. This is the central dilemma our leaders have not resolved. To defend freedom and democracy, can we live by the principles of freedom and democracy or do we need to embrace the mechanisms of the tyrant and the practices of the terrorists?

Since Magna Carta, since Habeas Corpus, there has been a long march to the liberty of individual citizens. There has been a longer march to establish basic rights, the Rule of Law, throughout the wider international community. It is a disturbing phenomenon that since September 11 some people in positions of great authority have been prepared to throw those principles overboard. They have been prepared to accept that we cannot defend liberty by the principles of liberty. That our principles prevent us doing what they think must be done. It shows how fragile is our grasp of the real necessities of a democratic, liberal society.

The speed with which governments in the West have turned their backs on the Due Process and the Rule of Law, the speed with which they have embraced the methods and techniques of tyrants should greatly disturb us. These events demonstrate that a debate about "responsibilities" is an urgent necessity for all countries, but in particular for Western democracies.

The provisions that relate to the fundamental principles of humanity, to respect for life, for justice and solidarity underlining the Rule of Law, to truthfulness and tolerance, to partnership well underline and reinforce the basic concept of the Universal Declaration of Human Rights.

It is worth nothing that in our Draft Declaration of Human Responsibilities, greatest "responsibility" is placed on those in positions of power and authority. Article 13 states that such people are not "exempt from general ethical standards". We would do better in the war against terror if we could demonstrate to the world that we can fight that war, and maintain the sense of "rights" and "responsibilities".

Challenges, Responses, and Visions

It could be suggested that even though the Members of the EU still have divergent policies to fight against terrorism, the EU should be a more united power by enhancing its internal and international efforts against "new" terrorism threat after the September 11 terrorist attacks. In order to be a such power, the EU has started to institutionalise its legal and administrative capacity, developed strategic objectives in line with its liberal approach, and engaged in counterterrorism cooperations with its global partners such as the US, Mediterranean countries, and Russia, despite remaining divergences and disagreements with these Partners. Thus, by enhancing its efforts, the EU has become a more cohesive and cooperative power in order to wipe out the threat of terrorism, if it is considered that the EU had never reached consensus against terrorism before the September 11 terrorist attacks.

It is commonly accepted that no single theory of international relations provides a complete account of the international system. However, these theories enable policy makers and academicians to conceptualize and contextualize both past and contemporary events. The theories that have found greatest favours with policy makers are those which provide insights into how the international system works by proposing causal explanations, describing events and explaining trends and phenomena. In this context, since the international security environment has become more complex and interdependent after the end of Cold War, the September 11 terrorist attacks of 2001 and Madrid train station bombings of 2004 have also contributed to this complexity and forced to conceptualize the international system within theories.

Analysis of the foreign and security policies of the EU, which is the main focus of this study, and of the US, indicates that policy makers of the EU are influenced by liberalism while the US policy makers are influenced by realism when dealing with the threat of terrorism after the September 11 terrorist attacks. Thus, liberalism and realism, the two traditional explanatory theories of international relations, continue to shape the ways in which policy makers conceptualize international relations after the September 11 to confront terrorism. On the other hand, since the term terrorism is very controversial, it is worth mentioning that these theories remain insufficient to explain the concept of terrorism.

The terrorism is not a new challenge to the international community. For many years, terrorism has continued to be a significant challenge with its dangerous nature, various definitions and types. However, what is striking even today is the changing characteristics of terrorism with the help of the imperatives of globalisation. In this context, today, the new structure of terrorism, the new kind of personnel and the new attitude towards violence make the situation even more challenging. These changing characteristics of terrorism have been regarded by some authors who study terrorism as the emergence of "new" terrorism, particularly employed by terrorists motivated by religious imperatives.

In the aftermath of the September 11 terrorist attacks, the new features of terrorism came into most visible scene and "new" terrorisms' incubation period has ended. The terrorism has now become an influential actor on international politics. The devastating terrorist attacks of September 11, 2001, have also given a message to the international community indicating the need on enhanced cooperation to defeat the terrorism at the beginning of the 21st century. Thus, the analyses of the challenges of terrorism are by giving great emphasis on the changing characteristics of terrorism.

The European countries that have sheltered various terrorist organizations in their continent for many years faced with the threat of "new" terrorism and the fact of the need to enhance their cooperation among themselves. In this context, the European countries, which still have different approaches on terrorism, began to enhance their efforts to counter the threat of terrorism under the framework of the EU after the September 11 attacks. The following terrorist attacks in Madrid also confirmed these facts. In order to flourish cooperation to confront terrorism, the EU has worked to improve its legal and administrative capacity. By reflecting its liberal approaches on security matters after the end of Cold War, the EU also developed liberal strategic policies to tackle the threat of terrorism. That is why the study examines the EU's internal efforts developed as a response after the September 11 terrorist attacks.

Considering the very internationalisation of "new" terrorist threat, cooperation among governments has become significantly genuine. Thus, the EU engaged in counterterrorism cooperation's with its global partners, despite remaining divergences and disagreements. With this regard, the EU and the US have divergent policies to fight against terrorism as a result of their respective liberal and realist strategic objectives, which was the very case in the dispute for the invasion of Iraq that also divided Europeans by revealing that Europeans had problems among themselves in terms of deeming the invasion of Iraq as part of combating terrorism or not, or the invasion had become inevitable fact, how to make it. However, beyond their strategic divergences, the EU and the US have a significant convergences on counterterrorism cooperation in police, judicial, and transport and security matters.

To confront terrorism, the EU also cooperates with its Mediterranean Partners under the framework of the Euro-Mediterranean Partnership which also serves as an excellent reflection of the EU's liberal approach to fight against terrorism by struggling against terrorism from its origin. Although the Euro-Mediterranean Partnership's achievements on counterterrorism remain on the declaratory level, they should not be underestimated.

In all Euro-Mediterranean Conferences, governments proved their will to cooperate against terrorism through presidency conclusions. These conclusions should probably form later counterterrorism cooperation between Partners. In addition, even though the Chechen conflict remains as a significant problem to the relations between the EU and Russia, they engaged in police cooperation and issued significant statements which may provide a framework for practical counterterrorism cooperation in the future, as in the case of Euro-Mediterranean Summit conclusions. Therefore, this examines the EU's international efforts after September 11 terrorist attacks by also giving particular attention on European countries' different approaches to Iraq dispute.

Conclusively, it is the fact that the Members of the EU still have divergent policies for dealing with terrorism. However, the September 11 terrorist attacks and the subsequent Madrid train station bombings acted as a catalyst to the EU to intensify its internal and external efforts to fight against terrorism. The EU issued various documents and legislations to institutionalize its legal and administrative policies and developed liberal strategic dimensions to fight against terrorism. The EU also adopted various agreements and issued joint statements with its partners on counterterrorism, despite the fact that divergence and disagreements among the Partners when tackling terrorism still remain as an important problem. Thus, these efforts made the EU more cooperative and cohesive for combating terrorism after the September 11 terrorist attacks.

Since the end of the Cold War, the international environment has witnessed the emergence of complex issues and more interdependent actors. Terrorism is one of the complex issues in the new era, particularly after the September 11 terrorist attacks. The new era should be conceptualised within the two traditional theories of international relations, liberalism and realism, even though they remain insufficient to explain the concept of terrorism.

In fact, terrorism poses a great challenge to the international community for many years with the lack of uniform definition and the emerging types through different motivations. Today, it is also a growing challenge that some characteristics of terrorism has changed with the implications of globalisation process, so the terrorism has been regarded as "new" terrorism by some authors who work on terrorism. Thus, in this chapter, first of all, terrorism will be analysed within the theories of international relations so as to conceptualise the EU approach on terrorism. Then, the historical development of terrorism will be studied. In the next part, the definition of terrorism will be discussed in detail. Following that, the types of terrorism will be focused on. Finally, the characteristics of "new" terrorism will be analysed with the emphasis on the September 11 terrorist attacks.

Realism versus Liberalism

Throughout the Cold War, realist perceptions were dominant and played significant role in international relations. According to the realist point of view, states are the most important actor on international relations and their behaviour is directed by their interests which are defined in terms of power. In addition, securing the national interests through military means is the main goal of all states in anarchical environment of international relations. Taking into account this perception, power maximisation and state survival were the main rationales during the Cold War in which the nuclear balance between hegomonic powers, the US and the Soviet Union, was the main concern of international agenda. In addition, during the Cold War, main struggle between hegomomic powers was to gain military superiority in the context of nuclear power. It can be drawn that the security issues determined the international agenda during the Cold War in which the continuous struggle for power and survival was the main concern.

With the end of the Cold War tension, the international agenda has started to change. In particular, globalisation has started to affect actors, issues, and the international environment. Globalisation led to an increase in trade, greater cultural exchange, advancement in technology, spread of multiculturalism, erosion of national sovereignty and national borders, increase in the share of world economy, and increase for the role of international organizations. With the above mentioned implications of globalisation, liberal perceptions gained more importance and began to challenge the realist perceptions in the post-Cold War era.

The fundamental assumptions of liberalism are as follows. First of all, international politics involves a variety of agents, including states, organizations, groups, and even individuals; second, these agents pursue interests (both selfish and collectively) through an international agenda that includes economic, environmental, developmental, and cultural matters, in addition to security matters; third, the exercise of power involves a variety of hard power and soft power instruments; finally, laws and institutions based on principles, norms, morals, and rules, play the vital function of providing order in the international system.

The US Approach

Even though the proponents of realism interpret the theory in different ways, there are several concepts that all realists adopt. Dunne and Schmidt gathered together these shared understandings in the principles of statism, survival, and self-help. According to Dunne and Schmidt, realism posits the following ideas. First, states are the principal actors in the international system, operating in an anarchical environment; second, the lack of authoritative and global government forces states to focus on the primary national interest of survival; third, in order to ensure survival, states do not rely on international institutions but actively engage in self-help arrangements which are manifested in the development and use of force, especially offensive military force. In such a setting, non-state actors are ignored. In addition, unilateralism- "a pattern of international engagement in which one nation acts outside the framework of bilateral (between two countries) or multilateral (involving many countries) agreements and negotiation"- prevailed over multilateralism- "a structure to manage international and regional affairs that constrains unilateral behaviour through institutional mechanisms (treaties, international law, and voting process) that ensure consultation and engagement"-, because realists claim that international system is fundamentally anarchical and that multilateralism cannot eliminate the basic struggle for power among states.

Moreover, military hard power has privileged mean over civilian soft power because realism sees world politics as a state of war for power among states. Taking into account the above mentioned main assumptions of realism, it should be stressed that the US foreign and security policy operated in realist framework during the Cold War and dealt firstly with the containment of Soviet aggression. The trends of 1990s increased globalization, institutionalization, and democratization which led to President Bill Clinton to expand the priorities of the US beyond traditional Cold War concerns to include free trade agreements, peacekeeping, Third World development, and environmental protection. In brief, President Bill Clinton put new liberal paradigms for the US beyond traditional Cold War concerns such as balance of power and arms control.

However, the arrival of G.W. Bush to Whitehouse ended the liberal breeze of Clinton Administration. G. W.Bush, who came to office in 2001, was influenced by realism and dedicated himself to establish a "unipolar world". By acting unilaterally in the first months of his administration, G.W. Bush refused to approve some multilateral agreements such as "Kyoto Protocol", "Biological Weapons Convention", "Comprehensive Test Ban Treaty", and to join "International Criminal Court" regardless of the opposition of the international community. Even though the Bush Administration viewed international matters through realist perspective in its first months of arrival, it was the September 11 terrorist attacks that stimulated the realist perspective of Bush administration on international matters and, in particular, created realist foreign policy instruments to confront the threat of terrorism. In addition, it was the September 11 terrorist attacks that put the terrorism to the top priority of the US foreign policy and permeated anti-terrorism to the all facets of American diplomacy.

In June 2002, President G.W. Bush endorsed his unilateral "pre-emption" concept in his West Point, New York, speech in order to tackle the threats that the US faced, in particular, the increasing threat of terrorism by stating that "[we] cannot defend America and our allies hoping for the best...Americans to be forward-looking and resolute, to be ready for pre-emptive action when necessary to defend our liberty and our lives". President's speech at West Point Academy was the forerunner of the US National Security Strategy (NSS) which was published in September 2002. In fact, even though NSS of the US includes some tenets of liberal theory of international relations, for instance, it states that the US "will actively work to bring the hope of democratic development, free markets and free trade to every corner of the world" and it also pledges that the US will work with multilateral organizations such as UN and WTO to develop and maintain a more stable world order and to champion liberal values such as human dignity, freedom of speech, and other ethnic tolerance, other elements of the NSS show that these goals will be carried out by a decidedly realist foreign policy.

The NSS indicates that the military hard power of the US as a defining factor in international affairs and in tackling the threat of terrorism underlines the importance of the US military force by stating that "[our] forces will be strong enough to dissuade potential adversaries from pursuing a military build-up in hopes of surpassing, or equalling the power of the United States". The NSS also emphasizes its willingness to use military power without multilateral support by stating that the US "will not hesitate to act alone, if necessary, to exercise our right of self defense by acting preemptively against such terrorists". The statements of G.W. Bush at West Point and the sentences of the NSS confirm an alignment of the US foreign policy with key realist assumptions such as survival and self-help when dealing with the threat of terrorism and other threats of 21th century.

The EU Approach

Before beginning to analyse the transformation of international environment and the EU approach to fight against terrorism, it is worth mentioning that the EU had never had consensus on the evolution of term "terrorism" in terms of both definition and the ways of tackling it in its history before the September 11 terrorist attacks. However, it was the effects of September 11 terrorist attacks that encouraged the EU to reach a consensus on terrorism. Therefore, it introduced a common definition of terrorism and developed liberal strategies to fight against terrorism.

One of the explanatory concepts for analysing the transformation of international environment is the concept of "Complex Interdependence", theorized by liberal school of thought. In their book Power and Interdependence, Keohane and Nye mentioned the characteristics of complex interdependence concept in order to evaluate the developments taking place in the era of globalisation and show the rise of liberalism to this end. According to Keohane and Nye, complex interdependence has three main characteristics: multiple channels connecting societies, absence of hierarchy among issues, and minor role for military power. In this part, the characteristics of complex interdependence will be analysed in order to provide analytical tool to evaluate the transformation of international environment and the EU's foreign policy to confront the threat of terrorism in comparison with realist perceptions.

The first characteristic of complex interdependence is the multiple channels which include informal ties between governmental elites as well as foreign office arrangements and among non-governmental elites (face-to-face and through telecommunications), and transnational organisations (such as multinational cooperations). These channels should be summarized as interstate, transgovernmental, and transnational relations. In this context, apart from interstate relations that are the normal channels connecting the states according to realists, new channels have emerged and affected the relations among societies. Transgovernmental channels challenge realist perceptions, which take the states as coherent units, they started to play a very influential role in world politics.

In the light of above mentioned developments, the European Security Strategy (ESS), published by Javier Solona, the High Representative of the Common Foreign and Security Policy of the EU, on December 12, 2003, underlines the fact that new threats and new international actors are emerging other than classical wars between states. Europe "faces new threats which are more diverse, less visible and less predictable in character because different interest groups and figures have emerged inside the states including non-governmental elites, which are establishing ties with other non-governmental elites by influencing other states. More importantly, transnational channels, including multinational cooperations, challenge the realist perceptions which see the states as the only units in international relations. By the impact of these new multiple channels, new multiple actors influence the international affairs apart from states.

In the post-Cold War era, multiple actors started to more affect the international politics, in particular, by the economic, social, technological and communicative impacts of globalisation. Terrorist groups should be considered as transnational groups. In the post-Cold War era, terrorist groups strengthened their network by benefiting from the transformation of economics, communication, and weapons technology and". In order to confront these threats in the era of globalisation, particularly the threat of terrorism, which the ESS mentions it as the most important threat to the European security, the ESS indicates that "the end of Cold War has left the United States in a dominant position as a military actor. However, no single country is able to tackle today's complex problems on its own", so according to the ESS, the solution increasingly depends on an effective multilateralism by upholding and developing international law especially under the framework of the UN Charter and the UN Security Council must have the main responsibility in order to maintain peace and security.

The EU's support to multilateralism is in line with liberal school of thought, because liberals hold that it is the multilateralism that shapes the behaviour of sovereign states in ways that modify the anarchy of the international system. The second characteristic of the complex interdependence concept is the absence of hierarchy among issues. It moves away from realist perceptions' focus on military force and power politics to include political and economic dimensions of the international system. Thus, the absence of hierarchy underlines the converging importance of "high politics" and "low politics". Throughout the Cold war, the military security determined the agenda of international politics. However, as liberals indicate, in the new era, the hierarchy among issues no longer exists and various issues do not subordinate to military security anymore.

This new approach gave new dimensions to foreign security policies according to liberals who argue that states must pursue their foreign policy interests through an international agenda that includes economic, developmental, environmental, and cultural matters, in addition to military matters. That liberal perception occupied one of the primary concerns of the EU's foreign policy to tackle terrorism and other key threats such as the proliferation of weapons of mass destruction (WMD), regional conflicts, state failure, and organized crime which are interdependent among themselves according to the ESS. In this context, the ESS states that "[in] contrast to massive visible threat in the Cold War, none of the new threat is purely military; nor can any be tackled by purely military means". Therefore, in order to tackle the terrorism threat and other key threats by its root causes the ESS declares that "we need to extend the benefits of economic and political cooperation to our neighbours" to promote well-governed countries around the borders of the EU.

This will help to ensure the extension of zone of security on the European periphery. This approach of the EU is a case in the EU's engagement with Mediterranean partners, through more effective economic, security and cultural cooperation under the framework of Barcelona Process. The third characteristic of complex interdependence is the minor role of military force. In the era of globalisation, military force becomes less effective to solve problems, particularly economic and social ones. In the Cold War era, nuclear power was the primary determinant of power and used as a means of deterrence and instrument of diplomacy, so the high politics dominated the international agenda. However, in the era of globalisation, division between high politics and low politics blurred and new issues emerged. This transformation of political agenda should be used to solve problems. Therefore, the international security environment requires a combination of "hard power" and "soft power" policies.

In the light of these facts, the EU focuses on both military and civilian measures to confront terrorism and other emerging threats. Even though the EU tries to strengthen its military capabilities under the ESDP framework, it emphasizes the importance of soft power and conflict prevention concepts. These liberal concepts of soft power and conflict prevention take part in the ESS which indicates that dealing with terrorism and other key threats require a mixture of instruments. The ESS declares that "the proliferation may be contained through export controls; attacked through political, economic and other pressures while the underlying political causes are also tackled" and "dealing with terrorism requires a mixture of intelligence, police force, judicial, military and other means".

Taking into account the above mentioned perceptions of realism and liberalism theories of international relations, it should be concluded that the EU approach to confront terrorism is in line with liberalism by supporting multilateralism, pursuing its foreign policy interests through an agenda including economic, cultural, developmental, and environmental matters, in addition to military matters, and emphasizing the importance of soft power and conflict prevention concepts. On the other hand, the US approach is line with realism by underlying the importance of the military hard power of the US and pursuing a unilateral preemption concept to tackle the threat of terrorism and other threats.

7

The Concept of New Age Terrorism

One of the earliest examples of terrorist acts was perpetrated by the radical Zealots, a Jewish sect active during the Roman occupation of the first century in the Middle East. The Zealots wanted to get rid of Roman Empire's rule by a campaign involving assassinations. The intent of their actions was to give a message to broad target audience. Therefore, the Zealots chose to attack wherever there were people to see their action. As Walter Lanquer puts it "the sources telling of their activities are sparse and sometimes contradictory but it is known from Josephus that Zealots used unortodox tactics such as attacking their enemies by daylight, preferably on holidays when crowds congregated in Jarusalem". Between the years of 1090 and 1272, the Assassins, an Islamic group, used similar tactics with the Zealots in combating with Christian Crusaders.

Moreover, the Assassins used the same notion of self-sacrifice and suicidal attacks as some terrorists influenced by Islamic fundamentalism do today. They used violence as a divine act to ascend to the heaven. As written in the "Almanac of Modern Terrorism" some authors argue that the 13th century's Islamic Assassins are the forerunners of modern terrorists. Religion ensured the main justification of use of terror until the French revolution. After the King

Louis XVI's execution, the Jacobins, led by the Committee of Public Safety and Robespierre, launched terrorism process that the term "reign of terror" refers an excellent example of state terrorism in the last decade of XVIII century. In this terrorism process, about 12000 French citizens were killed because of their opposition to the revolutionary regime. Indeed, this massacre was made for political reasons to protect enlightenment ideals that changed the interest from religion to nationalism and democracy.

Nationalism, anarchism, Marxism, and other secular political movements changed the situation during 1800s. These trends challenged the divine rule of monarchs. However, religious motivations were not totally lack. The most of the people in European countries rebelled against church domination of political life to construct secular societies. Indeed, the terrorism of 1800s was antimonarchical and gained its concrete meaning by "Narodnoya Volya" of Russia.

As Walter Lanquer argues "of all these movements Narodnoya Volya was the most important by far, even though its operations lasted only from January 1878 to March 1881". Even though Narodnoya Volya assassinated many government officials and Tsarist, the political police of Russia, of the highest rank, its most successful action was the assassination of Tsar Alexander II of Russia on March 1,1881, paradoxically after most of the group members had already been arrested by police. Four months after the assassination of Alexander II, a group of political radicals convened "anarchist conference" in London to discuss how to achieve revolutionary change.

The idea of the conferences was to establish "Anarchist International", it is also called as "Black International" after they adopted black flag, to support and coordinate terrorism for defeating monarchies and elected governments throughout the world. Bruce Hoffman claims that even though "this idea, like most of their ambitious plans, came to naught, the publicity generated by even a putative "Anarchist International" was sufficient to create myth of global revolutionary pretensions and thereby stimulate fears and suspicions disproportionate to its actual impact or political achievements". The individual actions or operations carried out by small cells of like-minded radicals of anarchists made detection and prevention by the police particularly difficult, thus further heightened the public fears. For instance, following the assassination of William Mckinley on September 14, 1901, by Leon Czolgocz, a Hungarian refugee, who was not the member of any anarchist organization, but only inspired by the philosophy, paved the way for enaction of legislation by the US Congress not to give permission to anarchists or anyone who influenced by this philosophy to enter in the United States. In general, the years between 1880 and 1920 were the period of "anarchist wave" of terrorism.

Meanwhile, a Bosnian Serb assassinated Austrian archduke Fracis Ferdinant on June 28, 1914, who was on official trip in Sarajevo, Bosnia, to free its country from Austrian domination. This assassination triggered the World War I. As in the case of today's state sponsors of terrorism do, it is claimed that Serbia provided some assets for this assassination.

The dictatorial regimes of Germany, Italy, and the Soviet Union terrorised their citizens by intimidation, torture, unlawful detentions, beatings, and assassinations by unknown hands during 1920s and 1930s. On the other hand, in 1930s and 1940s, systematic terrorism aroused in the Middle East by terrorist organizations influenced by Islamic fundamentalism to gain independence of their countries from colonialist states. In this context, Muslim Brotherhood in Egypt and Irgun, a Jewish terrorist organization, fought against Britons in Palestine and Front Liberation Army, Front de Libération Nationale (FLN), battled with French in Algeria.

After the end of World War II, terrorism regained its previous connotations. During 1940s and 1950s, nationalist/ anti-colonialist organizations aroused in the Middle East, Asia, and Africa in order to gain independence from European domination. Israel, Algeria, and Kenya gained their independence at least in part to their nationalist movements that used terrorism against continued rule of colonial powers.

As Bruce Hoffman indicates, it was also during this period that the politically correct appellation of "freedom fighters" came into fashion because of the international community's support and sympathy to struggles for national liberation and self-determination. In particular, many newly independent Third World states and communist block states argued that anyone or any movement which fought against colonial and/ or Western domination cannot be described as "terrorists", but they were deemed to be "freedom fighters". Indeed, this perspective was most famously explained by Yassir Arafat, chairman of the Palestsine Liberation Organization (PLO), when he addressed the UN General Assembly in November 1974:

"The difference between the revolutionary and terrorist lies in the reason for which each fights. For whoever stands by just a cause and fights for freedom and liberation of his land from the invaders, the settlers and colonialists, cannot possibly be called terrorist..."

Terrorism continued to be viewed in revolutionary context during the late 1960s and 1970s. However, this explanation expanded its meaning by including nationalist and ethnic separatist groups outside a colonial or neo-colonial framework as well as radical, entirely ideologically motivated groups. The Paletsine Liberation Organization, Québec Liberation Front, Front Libération du Québec (FLQ), Freedom for the Basque Homeland, Euskadi ta

Askatasuna (ETA), employed terrorism to drew international community's attention to their causes. On July 22, 1968, the three armed terrorists of Popular Front for the Liberation of Palestine (PFLP), one of the six groups later constituted Palestine Liberation Organization, which fought to regain Palestine territories occupied by Israel since the Six-Day War of 1967, hijacked an Israeli El Al commercial jet en route from Rome to Tel Aviv.

This incident drew enermous attention from international community to the plight of Palestinians. Bruce Hoffman argues that even though there had been several commercial aircraft hijackings before, this incident was the first political hijacking that started the internationalisation of terrorism. In addition, the hijacking of this airplane was the first example with its international character seems similar with the September 11 terrorist attacks.

In 1972, the Black September Organization (BSO), a Palestinian Paramilitary Unit, founded in 1970, attacked on Israeli athletes at the 1972 Munich Olympic Games, that resulted the death of 11 Israeli athletes, ended the indifference of Western World toward terrorism. Despite international community's condemnation of Munich massacre, it generated spectacular publicity that the PLO exploited.

Indeed, two years after Munich events, Yassir Arafat, the leader of the PLO, was invited to UN to address General Assembly and the PLO subsequently gained the observer status in the main international body. Moreover, the PLO, as a non-state actor, had more diplomatic relations with countries than Israel, an established nation-state, had by the end of 1970s.

In this time of increasing ethnic and nationalist movements throughout the World, other nationalist groups such as Quebec Liberation Front, Front de Libération du Québec (FLQ), French-Canadian separatists effective at

Quebec region of Canada, and Irish Republican Army (IRA), effective in United Kingdom, started to emulate the Palestinian example to get international publicity.

The internationalisation process of terrorism in the late 1960s and 1970s was not only the product of Palestinian success but also the activities of other movements. During these years political extremists started to oppose American occupation of Vietnam and economic and social inequities of modern capitalist liberal-democratic state. The Red Army Faction (RAF) in Germany, known also as Baader-Meinhof Gang, and Red Brigades (RB), Brigate Rosso, in Italy, its famous act was the murder of former Italian Prime Minister Aldo Moro in 1978, were the most active radical paramilitary leftist movements in this period, which tried to establish socialist regimes by destroying their capitalist governments.

In the beginning of the 1980s, the right-wing terrorism, or neo-fascist terrorism, perpetrated in response to left-wing movements that arose in some parts of the European countries and the United States. However, the right-wing groups could not get the support like left-wing groups enjoyed, so the violence perpetrated by the right-wing groups remained mostly short-lived and periodic. The most famous actions of these groups were the bombing of Munich October fest Celebration, in 1980, perished 14 and injured 215 people; Bologna rail station bombing, in 1980, killing 84 and injured 180; track bombing of Alfred Paul Murrah building at Oklahoma City by Timothy McVeigh, a Gulf veteran, in 1995, killing 168 and injured over 800 people which was the most lethal terrorist attack in the US borders before the September 11 terrorist attacks.

The most important development in international terrorism was the resurgence of religious terrorism that was reinforced, in whole or in part, by state-sponsors in 1980s. David Rapoport argues that the Iranian Revolution and

Muslim resistance in Afghanistan against the Soviets provided necessary conditions for religious terrorism in terms of supporting and accommodating the religious terror groups. However, the 1990s were the golden age of religious terrorism. During the 1990s, the number of religious terrorist organizations increased appreciably. In addition, the characteristics of terrorism changed in these years. In this context, some foremost academicians and authors who study terrorism argue that terrorism has become a "New" Terrorism by its new network structure, increase willingness to cause mass casualty, and mostly religious imperatives. The "new" terrorism led to more casualties than the violence perpetrated by secular terrorists. The most notorious acts of new terrorism should be exampled as follows:

- The series of 13 simultaneous car and truck bombings in Bombay, in February 1993, by radical Islamists, killed 400 people and injured more than 1000.
- On September 11, 2001, unprecendent terrorist attacks on World Trade Center, New York, and Pentagon, Washington D.C., by Al Qaeda, killed nearly 3000 and injured more.
- On November 19, 2003, track bombing attacks on British Consulate and the HSBC Bank in Istanbul by Islamic extremists, killed 27 people and injured more than 400.
- On March 11, 2004, Al Qaeda's terrorist attacks to three different train stations in Madrid, killed up to 200 and injured more than 1250 people.
- On September 1, 2004, Chechen militants' horrific school siege in Beslan, North Osetia, killed at least 335 and injured over 700, mostly children.

Even though terrorism exists in history for many years, there is no single definition of terrorism. The definitional weakness helps terrorists to find weak points in administration and politics of states so that they commit their crimes. In this context, it is also common to ask what issues in the definition of terrorism remains unresolved. According to Alex P. Schmidt and Albert I. Jongman, some of the answers of this question are as follows:

- The boundary between terrorism and other forms of political violence.
- Whether government terrorism and resistance are part of the same phenomenon.
- Separating terrorism from simple criminal acts, from open war between contesting groups, and from acts that clearly arise out of mental illness.
- Is terrorism a sub-category of coercion? Violence? Power? Influence?
- Can terrorism be legitimate? What gains justify its use?
- The relationship between guerrilla warfare and terrorism.
- The relationship between crime and terrorism.

Indeed, among these unresolved issues for the definition of terrorism, the relationship between guerrilla warfare and terrorism is the most striking one and therefore merits further attention. The relationship between guerrilla warfare and terrorism is the most important reason for why the international community cannot find single definition for terrorism. This problem mainly stems from the fact that, on the one hand, many Third World states call the groups, who involve guerrilla warfare to gain independence or to oppose Western oppression, as freedom fighters not terrorists, on the other hand, most of the Western states, especially former colonial ones, call these groups as terrorists not freedom fighters. Even these states have different perspectives on the issue depending on their changing national interests and point of views. Therefore, as Boaz Ganor argues, the definitions of terrorism remain state-centric and the statement of "one man's terrorist is another man's freedom fighter" becomes cliche and most important difficulty to define and confront terrorism. Academics, international organizations, journalists, individual states, and politicians use a variety of definitions of terrorism. These definitions mainly focus on terrorist organizations' motivations, mode of operation, and characteristics. However, it is common to define the term by its motivations, especially as political violence. For instance, according to Brian Jenkins:

"Terrorism is the use or threatened use of force designed to bring about political change". Like Brian Jenkins, Walter Lanquer defines the term as political violence:

"Terrorism is the premeditated, deliberate, systematic murder, mayhem, and threatening of the innocent to create fear and intimidation in order to gain a political ot tactical advantage, usually to influence an audiance".

The lack of universally accepted definition of terrorism hinders to coordinate international cooperation on fight against terrorism. In order to solve this problem, United Nations (UN), as the main international body, adopted its definition as below:

"any act intended to cause death or serious bodily injury to a civilian, or to any person not taking any active part in the hostilities in a situation of armed conflict, when the purpose of such act, by its nature or context, is to intimidate a population, or to compel a government or an international organization to do or to abstain from doing any act".

However, the UN definition cannot bear the complexity of the problem. According to Martha K. Jordan, the first reason to this complexity is sovereignty. States reserve their rights to define bounds of activities and policies in their own borders, so each state reserves the right to determine, politically and legally, what terrorism is. No country wants to be limited by a definition that will constrain its own foreign and domestic policy. Secondly, some members of the UN use terrorism for their purposes. Therefore, the UN will not be suitable forum to develop definition or policy for terrorism, if not the UN members agree to stop sponsoring, harbouring, and training the terrorists.

Even though Europe faces terrorism on the continent for many years, there was no consensus among European countries on the definition of the term. However, the September 11 terrorist attacks increased the fears among European countries and the European Council provided a common definition of terrorism for the EU Member States by adopting "Council Framework Decision of 13 June 2002 on Combating Terrorism", In the Framework Decision, terrorist offences are defined, before the lists of punishable terrorist offences in the same article, as offences must be committed with the aim of:

"- seriously intimidating a population, or

- Unduly compelling a government or international organization to perform or abstain from performing any act, or

- seriously destabilizing or destroying the fundamental political, constitutional, economic or social structures of a country or an international organization".

It is clear that the adoption of the framework Decision is a significant step for European cooperation on fight against terrorism. However, taking into account the fact that the EU's Framework decisions only put the standards that Member States are expected to follow, the success of this framework decision would depend on the insertion of the Framework Decision's provisions into Member States' legislations. In the case of individual state level, every state defines the term in accordance to their national interests and point of views. Thus, the definition of terrorism differs from one state to another. A uniform definition does not exist even in the agencies of countries. For instance, there is still no common definition between various agencies of the US.

Different Types of Terrorism

Before beginning to explain different types of terrorism, it is necessary to point out that it is impossible to distinguish some types from each other because some of them are interdependent. In addition, terrorism is typed differently by academicians and authors. As Murat Karagöz argues, like the challenge in defining terrorism, typing the terrorism with one single classification is impossible. However, it is common to type terrorism as state-sponsored, anarchist, nationalist, ideological, and religious.

In the case of state-sponsored terrorism, radical states practice terrorism as a foreign policy tool- as Bruce Hoffman puts it, as "a cost-effective way of waging war covertly, through the use of surrogate warriors or guns for hire". The Iranian Islamic revolution had a very impact on the emergence of state-sponsored terrorism.

Paul Wilkinson argues that after the end of Cold War, state-sponsored terrorism has dramatically reduced, especially employed by the former Soviet Union and its Warsaw Pact communist regimes. However, in 2002, only five states, which employ state-sponsored terrorism, remained and all of them are in the Middle East: Iran, Iraq, Syria, Sudan and Libya. But in fact, it is clear that countries listed as state-sponsors of terrorism differ from one country to another in the world.

Anarchist terrorists employ terrorism to overthrow established governments. These groups, variously defined, want to replace capitalism by dictatorship of proletariat as inspired by Marxism. From 1870 to 1920 anarchist terrorism practiced its golden age. Indeed, in that period anarchist terrorists involved in very successful actions by directing their plans to the heads of some states, including the assassination of Tsar Alexander II of Russia in 1881, King Umberto I of Italy in 1900, and US President William McKinley in 1901.

The aim of the nationalist terrorism is to form a separate state for their own group, often by drawing attention to a fight for "national liberation" that they think the world has ignored. The characterization of nationalist terrorism is very contentious because, most importantly, many groups claim that they are not terrorists but "freedom fighters" engaged in "assymetric warfare". The most important nationalist terrorist organizations include Basque Fatherland and Liberty (ETA), terrorized Spain to get independence for Basque region, Irish Republican Army (IRA), employed many terrorist attacks on British society in the aim of getting independence for Northern Ireland, Palestine Liberation Organization (PLO), wants to stop Israel invasion in occupied territories of Palestine in order to establish independent Palestinian state.

Ideological terrorists want to change the existing political, social, and economic system. The most devastating actions of ideological terrorism are practiced by left-wing terrorists. The left-wing terrorists seek to establish communist or socialist regimes by destroying capitalism. The Red Brigates (RB), in Italy, Japanese Red Army (JRA), in Japan, and Red Army Faction, in Germany, were the important practioners of left-wing terrorism. On the other hand, the right-wing terrorists want to destroy liberal democratic governments to create fascist states, or to protect the existing system or to help the system return to an earlier status from which it has. Cindy C. Combs indicates that right-wing terrorism, unlike that of the left, has been stronger in the US than in Europe throughout the history and, in addition, terrorist organizations like Aryan Nations (AN) and Christian Identity Movement (CIM), both active in the US, began to gain strength due to the diminish of left-wing movements in the 1980s.

Religious terrorist groups use terrorism to overthrow the dominant religious order that they claim evil and corrupted. Today, religious terrorists, as Magnus Ranstorp argues, are also motivated by political considerations within their context. Therefore, distinguishing the religious and political sphere of these terrorist groups is very difficult. For instance, political origins of some groups in Israel/ Palestine, Chechenya, and post- Saddam Iraq, which see themselves freedom fighters rather than terrorists, demand statehood and self-determination.

On the other hand, the differences between religious and secular terrorists, as Bruce Hoffman argues, lies in their "radically different value systems, mechanisms of legitimization and justification, concepts of morality, and Manichean world view that holy terrorists embrace.

For religious terrorists, violence first and foremost is a sacramental act or divine duty executed in direct response to some theological demand or imperative". Throughout the history, religious terrorism is employed by many major faiths and small cults.

What is striking today is the recent upsurge of terrorists influenced by Islamic fundamentalism. Al-Qaeda, Hamas, Hizballah, and Palestinian Islamic Jihad are the examples of contemporary terrorist organizations influenced by the Islamic fundamentalism that apply very violent and devastating actions such as the September 11 terrorist attacks in 2001, Istanbul bombings in 2003, and Madrid train station bombings in 2004.

The "New" Terrorism and the September 11 Attacks

The bombing of World Trade Center in 1993, the bombing of Oklahoma city federal state building and Tokyo Sarin gas attacks in 1995, American embassy bombings in 1998, bombing of US destroyer in Yemen in 2000, the September 11 terrorist attacks, Istanbul bombings in 2003, Madrid train station bombings, and Beslan School siege in 2004 were the indication of a new and more threatening terrorism influenced, in part or in whole, by a religious motivations, one that aims to produce casualties on a massive scale.

Terrorist threats exist throughout the history but, as Kostas Infantis argues, it had never been considered so seriously as an actor or even a polar in the world arena since after the end of Cold War. The "new" terrorism can be accepted as an actor in world politics because "new" terrorists' operational area is the world not a limited region of one part of the world. Even the aim of these "new" terrorists is to change the whole world system, not to change political system of one country. They are trying to influence the world politics. The consequences of the actions of "new" terrorists have influenced not only the country that the terrorist action occured but also the whole world politics. For instance, the September 11 terrorist attacks changed all the international politics. On the other hand, the "new" terrorism has pursued their above mentioned aim of demolishing the world order through its own special characteristics.

Indeed, it was these characteristics that made the actions of "new" terrorists more dangerous and also more difficult to avoid. In that context, this section will try to analyse the characteristics of "new" terrorism in order to identify the threat correctly.

Firstly, according to David Tucker, network structure is a good place to begin analysing the characteristics of "new" terrorism. The "new" terrorists are now capable of developing network forms of organization for the same reason that business are. The information revolution by lowering the cost of communication, allows terrorist organizations to operate outside a controlling hierarchical structure. Therefore, terror organizations can flatten out their pyramids of authority and approach a network form like dispersed entities, linked by advanced communications and common purpose.

The structural transformation of terrorist organizations from hierarchy to network is the advantage that an organization acquires, because it becomes more flexible, adaptive, and resilient by its loose coordination with others, so if its one or several constituent entities are destroyed, the others carry on. In sum, the network structure of the new terrorists cannot be decapitated like former terrorists' hierarchical structure. Secondly, as Michael Whine argues, the recent innovations and inventions assisted to network form of "new" terrorists. Because of the communication revolution, the "new" terrorists are able to find more political and individual support and provide knowledge, resources, and money. Even they could search the internet to get information on how to build nuclear bomb.

Thirdly, the "new" terrorists are mainly amateurs. They become together in *ad hoc* groups and then disband, so it is difficult to follow and counteract them. In addition, less of these "new" terrorists are getting training from state-sponsors but rely on networks of supporters, they get what they need from World Wide Web or publications. Fourthly, the "new" terrorists do not limit themselves on the casualty of their attacks. The "new" terrorists want to cause terrifying lethality on their victims. Bruce Hoffman indicates that even though the total volume of terrorist incidents worldwide declined in the 1990s, the percentage of terrorist incidents with fatalities increased. Bruce Hoffman also adds that there are some reasons to explain terrorism's increased lethality. First, terrorists want to get more attention than their early colleagues.

Second, they are getting profit from past experiences, so they become experts on killing. Third, the amateur terrorists participating in terrorist acts increased. Fourthly, the combination of new tactics, motivations, and adversaries cause mass casualty. Fifthly, the "new" terrorists are mostly religious motivated. In the 1990s, religious motivated terrorist groups dramatically increased. The very majority of terrorists motivated by religious imperatives are Islamic fundamentalists. They believe they are carrying out the mandate of God to kill unbelievers in order to dominate Islam in the world. On the other hand, as Steven Simon argues, even though recent years witnessed the proliferation of terrorists influenced by Islamic fundamentalism, the threat of violence by other religious terrorists has also increased including Japan's Aum Shrinkyo, American Christian Patriot Movement, and Isreal's Jewish messianic militants. Moreover, as most importantly for humanity, the increase in religious motivation correlates with an increase in lethality.

Finally, the "new" terrorists frequently do not claim responsibility after their actions. They do not need to claim responsibility because they believe that they are only responsible to God and God sees their action. No one else matters. Jonathan Stevenson argues that what derives "new" terrorists to kill is particularly hatred unlike the classical terrorists that present their demands clearly and generally by taking responsibility for their actions in order to threaten their advarsaries that the bloodshed would not stop if their demands are not met.

In September 11, 2001, four terrorist groups hijacked four airplanes, two of them Boston's Logan Airport and other two from Dulles Airport of Washington. Two airplanes crashed to World Trade Center that is located in the hearth of Manhattan, New York City, and one dove into Pentagon at Washington. The other plane was destroyed by the US Air Forces on Pennsylvania. The attacks left nearly 3000 death and more injured people. The September 11 terrorist attacks in which the airplanes were used as weapons of mass destruction were the "bloodiest day on American soil since the civil war". Osama Bin Laden's Al-Qaeda was declared as responsible. However, most importantly, the US President G.W. Bush declared war on terrorism. The threat of "new" terrorism was on the highest points of international politics then. Indeed, the "new" terrorism, which emerged after the end of the Cold War, gained its meaning with the events of September 11. The "New" terrorism's many characteristics can be seen in September 11 terrorist attacks.

Firstly, the "new" terrorism's network structure could be seen in the September 11 terrorist attacks. According to Cindy C. Combs, it is clear that these 19 terrorists were part of a much larger network and that years of planning had been a part of September 11. In addition, the terrorist cells, that operates autonomously, did not aware the identity of each other. Moreover, their leader cannot be captured and some supporters of these actions, logistically and financially, were arrested in different parts of the world such as Germany and Philippines. Secondly, they probably used internet to reach each other and learnt flight plans of airlines companies. As Murat Karagöz argues, "the September 11 attacks were accomplished by using open information". The center of the "new" terrorism is information technology's blessings. As Andrew Cotey indicates, by using information technology, they even hit the Pentagon.

Thirdly, the perpetrators of September 11 were amateur and they gathered in *ad hoc* organization. They gathered just for the September 11 attacks as four separate groups. They were the "sleeper agents" waiting for order in some places to make their action. Even they took amateur flight lessons in some parts of the US to successfully fulfill their action. Fourthly, the September 11 terrorist attacks caused horrific, unprecedented lethality in which nearly 3000 people were perished and more wounded. More horrifically, about 1100 of 3000 death bodies were not identified. It is clear that the terrorists wanted to kill as many people as they could successes so that they proffered to hijack transnational flights with full of oil and dove into the middle of the World Trade Center that is located in the downtown of Manhattan, New York City. Indeed, limitless casualty is the most dangerous characteristic of the "new" terrorism.

Fifthly, it is very clear that the perpetrators of September 11 were religiously motivated. They saw themselves as the sword of Islam, even though Muslim religion prohibits killing someone. After September 11, some of the terrorists' video cassette was captured in which they declared they were ready to die for God and they would punish the big evil, the United States. On the other hand, it was also unhumanistic that there had been a demonstration on the streets of some capital cities of Middle East countries, such as Baghdad and Tahran, to celebrate the attacks. They believed that God took their revenge.

Finally, none of the terrorist organizations took the responsibility of the September 11 attacks in the beginning. Even though in a few minutes later attacks Japanese Red Army took the responsibility, they did not insist on. It does not matter for "new" terrorists to take the responsibility because they only believed that they fulfilled their sacramental duty and, most importantly, God saw their action. However, even though Osama Bin Laden, the leader of Al-Qaeda, in his September 16, 2001 speech, stressed he did not carry out these attacks, he took the responsibility after 48 days from September 11, on October 29, 2004. He stated in video speech that was sent to Al-Jazeera Television:

"I say to you, Allah knows that it had never occurred to us to strike the towers. But after it became unbearable and we witnessed oppression and tyranny of the American/ Israeli coalition against our people in Palestine and Lebanon, it came to my mind...And as I looked at the demolished towers in Lebanon, it entered my mind that we should punish the oppressor in kind and that we should destroy towers in America in order that they taste some of what we tasted and so that they be deterred from killing our women and children".

Every terror attack wants to give a message. Beyond

the message of September 11 attacks to the US government, attacks revealed for international community that the "new" terrorism is the most challenging threat to the international security at the beginning of the twenty-first century. On the other hand, the message for the EU was clear: requirement of enhanced security efforts both internally and externally. To this end, the EU that fought against terrorism by realist perspective at the Member State level for many years, tried to institutionalize its legal and administrative capacity and developed liberal strategic objectives at the EU level, and enhanced its international efforts in line with its liberal approach to fight against this "new" terrorism after the September 11 terrorist attacks.

Internal Efforts Against Terrorism

As a response after the September 11 terrorist attacks, the EU has intensified its internal efforts for fighting against terrorism. Thus, in this chapter, following an analysis of the EU's internal efforts after September 11 as an overview, the EU's internal efforts to institutionalise its legal administrative capacity by adopting European Arrest Warrant and Framework Decision on Combating terrorism, enhancing the role of Europol, and creating Eurojust and Joint Investigation teams would be examined. After that, as part of its internal efforts, the EU's introduction of European security strategy, appointment of Counterterrorism Coordinator, adoption of Solidarity Clause and Conceptual Framework for the ESDP dimension of terrorism in order to develop liberal strategies to tackle the threat of terrorism will be analysed.

As Nora Bensahel argues, the unexpected result of the September 11 terrorist attacks was that it furthered integration within the EU Member States, particularly in improving the legal and administrative capacity to combat the "new" terrorism threat. The EU had been developing some measures particularly since 1999 Tempere Summit, but disagreements among the EU Member States on Justice and home affairs matters such as extradition procedures and immigration, and security and defence matters such as the role of the ESDP in fight against terrorism had hindered it. However, after the September 11 terrorist attacks, the EU realised that cooperation is vital to prevent terrorist attacks from occuring.

The EU reacted swiftly to the attacks and tabled concerete measures. The main lines of the EU's normative reaction were set out in the "Plan of Action", road map, by the Extraordinary European Council of September 21, 2001, and in the conclusions of the Justice and Home Affairs Council the day before. With the adoption of Plan of Action, 68 measures were listed in a road map as blue print, which was to be updated regularly, and "the Council has decided that the fight against terrorism will, more than ever, be a priority objective of the EU".

The larger part of the road map measures were dedicated for the cooperation in criminal matters within the scope of Justice and Home Affairs, most importantly, including the adoption of European arrest warrant and a common definition of terrorism, in line with 1999 Tempere Summit conclusions; creation of joint police investigation teams across the EU, enhancing the Europol; and the establishment of Eurojust.

In addition, the European Council adopted the European Security Strategy in December 2003 in order to determine the key threats that the EU faces, strategic objectives that the EU carries out, and consider policy implications of creating a security strategy. After Madrid train station bombings on March 11, 2004, the European Council, in its March 25, 2004, session, adopted "Declaration on Combating Terrorism" to get new protection measures against terrorism. These measures include, most importantly, the appointment of Counterterrorism Coordinator Mr. Gijs de Vries, declaration on solidarity against terrorism as laid down in Article 43 of the draft Treaty establishing a Constitition for Europe, developing the contribution of the ESDP for fight against terrorism, and agreement on the EU plan of action to be revised. In the light of these facts, it should be concluded that the EU enhanced to institutionalise its legal and administrative capacity and developed liberal strategies to fight against terrorism after the September 11 terrorist attacks as a response.

European Arrest Warrant

Even though the EU had been discussing adoption of a common arrest warrant long before the September 11, the idea had been stagnated in the face of opposition from several member states such as Italy, the UK, and Greece. However, as Susie Alegre indicates, the September 11 terrorist attacks spurred the adoption of common arrest warrant allowing for political agreement on the highly controversial area of the EU law, European criminal law. On September 19, 2001, the European Commission once again submitted a proposal for the "Framework Decision on European Arrest Warrant". On September 21, 2001, the Extraordinary European Council directed the JHA Council to flesh out an agreement on this framework decision. The JHA Council adopted the framework decision on June 13, 2002, and agreed that it would come into force no later than January 2004.

The essence of the decision is stated in Article (1):

- The European arrest warrant is *judicial decision* issued by a Member state with a view to the arrest and surrender by another Member State of a requested person, for the purposes of conducting a criminal prosecution or executing a custodial sentence or detention order.
- Member States shall execute any European arrest warrant on the basis of the *principle of mutual*

recognition in accordance with the provisions of this framework decision".

Therefore, the aim of European arrest warrant is to provide that trails of suspected criminals, including terrorists, are not held by messy extradition procedures.

The scope of application of the Arrest Warrant is set out in Article 2, which states in Article 2 (1):

"A European arrest warrant may be issued for acts punishable by the law of the issuing Member State by a custodial sentence or a detention order for a maximum period of at least 12 months or, where a sentence has been passed or a detention order has been made for sentences of at least four months".

The most important difference among other European Conventions on Extradition and European Arrest Warrant lies in the fact that in European Arrest Warrant, "double criminality" is not required. This means that it is not necessary that the offence concerned is also punishable under the law of executing Member State. However, for offences not listed in Article 2 (2) the executing state may require that the acts for which the European arrest warrant has been issued constitute an offence under the law of executing member state. Article 2 (2) listed that in 32 offences double criminality may not be required, if these offences are punishable in the issuing Member State by a custodial sentence or detention order for a maximum period of at least three years.

These crimes include *inter alia* terrorism, a number of offences related to terrorist activities, such as illegal restraint and hostage taking, illicit trafficking in nuclear and radio active materials, kidnapping, illicit trafficking in weapons, munitions and explosives, unlawful seizure of aircraft/ships and sabotage, laundering of the proceeds of the crime, and a number of other offences, e.g. fraud, murder, racism, corruption, illicit trafficking in narcotic drugs.

One of the biggest problems to modernize and modify the extradition system is the question of ground for refusal, for the surrender of the requested person. The European Commission and the Council solved this problem in the way very much along the traditional lines of the extradition legislation by inserting *compulsory* and *optional* grounds for non-execution into the European Arrest Warrant.

Framework Decision on European Arrest Warrant lists three grounds for *compulsory* non-execution:

(1) The offence is covered by amnesty in the executing State and that State had jurisdiction over the offence; (2) the requested person has been finally judged in respect of the conduct concerned in a Member State and, if he/she has been sentenced, the sentence has been served, is being served or may no longer be executed according to the law of the sentencing State; (3) the requested person can, by reason of his/her age, not be held criminally responsible for the offence under the law of the executing State.

There are also a number of grounds for *optional* non-execution:

Firstly, as mentioned above, in some cases double criminality may still be required- for acts which fall outside the list of 32 types of specific offences.

Secondly, there are a number of grounds for refusal which broadly can be regarded as applications of the double jeopardy prohibition *(ne bis in idem)*.

Thirdly, the executing State may refuse execution if the offence is concerned is statute-barred according to its own law and it had itself jurisdiction over this offence.

Fourthly, the executing state may refuse execution if it undertakes to execute itself the sentence or detention to which the requested person has been condemned if that person is a national or resident of the executing State or is staying in that State.

Finally, a refusal to execute is also permitted for offences committed in whole or in part in the territory of the issuing Member State which are not punishable extraterritorially according to the law of the executing Member State.

Indeed, one of the greatest achievements of the European Arrest Warrant is the abolishment of nationality-based exception, even though it is not listed. This means that requested person's nationality of the executing Member State is not a ground for rejecting execution.

The Terrorism Framework Decision

On September 19, 2001, the European Commission submitted a proposal for a framework decision on combating terrorism. The Extraordinary European Council, on September 21, 2001, agreed that the EU had to adopt a common definition of terrorism. On October 19, 2001, the Ghent European Council called that this definition to be reached by December 6-7, 2001. JHA Council reached a provisional political agreement on the framework decision in its December 6-7, 2001 meeting. After the consultation of European Parliament and parliamentary scrutiny in Sweden, Denmark, and Ireland, the Council adopted the decision on June 13, 2002.

The framework decision on combating terrorism provided the common definition of terrorism, terrorist groups, and sets uniform minimum and maximum penalties across the EU. Before the adoption of framework decision, only 6 of the 15 EU Member States had legislation that criminalised terrorism. This was the case in France, Germany, Italy, Portugal, Spain, and the UK.

The Article 1 of the decision ensures the definition of terrorism offences that says, each EU Member State according to its national law shall ensure that the following offences which are committed to:

- Seriously intimidate a population,

- Compel a government or an international organization to perform or abstain from performing any act,
- Seriously destabilize or destroy the fundamental political, constitutional, economic or social structures of a country or an international organization will be punishable as terrorist offences:
    - Attacks against the life of a person, which may cause death;
    - Attacks against the physical integrity of a person;
    - Hostage taking or kidnapping;
    - Causing extensive damage to a Government or public facility;
    - Seizure of aircraft, ships or other means of public or goods transport;
    - Manufacture, possession, acquisition, supply, transport or use of weapons, explosives or of chemical, biological or nuclear weapons, as well as research into, and development of, biological and chemical weapons;
    - Release of dangerous substances, or causing fires, floods or explosions;
    - Interfering with or disrupting the supply of water, power or any other fundamental natural resource;
    - Threatening to commit any of the acts listed above.

According to Elisabeth Symeonidaou-Kastanidou, the definition of Framework Decision is the most comprehensive one and it helps better to understand terrorism's socio-political nature, if it is compared with previous attempts to define terrorism either in the context of international treaties or domestic legislation. For instance, the European Convention on the Suppression of the Terrorism, signed on January 27, 1977, classifies terrorist acts as, among other crimes, all serious offences involving an attack against the life, physical integrity or liberty of internationally protected persons, as well as offences involving kidnapping or taking hostages.

Therefore, it defines terrorist acts with regaid to the identity of the victim or type of the offence, while the motive of the perpetrator or the damage possibly produced by his conduct at the expense of a State or an international organization are not taken into account. In the same vein, the UN Convention For the Suppression of the Terrorist Bombings, signed on December 15, 1997, states that any person commits a (terrorist) offence, if that person unlawfully and intentionally delivers, places, discharges or detonates an explosive or other lethal device in (*inter alia)* a place of public use, with the intent to cause death or seriously bodily injuries. Thus, the treaty only refers to specific crimes, which can most definitely cause an entire population to be seriously intimidated, but it does not take into account the political objectives which make terrorist crime distinguishable from other types of criminal conduct.

Apart from terrorist offences, the Article 3 of the Framework Decision makes reference to certain actions of lesser gravity, such as aggravated theft or extortion that are the crimes linked to terrorist activities on the condition that they are perpetrated with a view to committing a terrorist offence.

The Framework Decision also defines the terrorist group and determines offences relating to terrorist group. In that context, terrorist group is defined as "a structured group of more than two persons, established over a period of time and acting in concert to commit offences". Directing and participating are deemed as offences relating to terrorist group. Even though these terms are not fully described in the text, "directing" a terrorist group is the act of guiding this group to the choice of the offences which are to be committed. On the other hand, "participation" covers any act of cooperation or contribution to the offences planned by the organization including supplying information or material resources, funding the illicit activities. Inciting, aiding or abetting these acts is also regarded as punishable behaviour.

A common maximum penalty of deprivation of liberty is only provided for offences relating to terrorist groups. To this end, maximum penalties are determined as no less than fifteen years for directing terrorist groups and no less than eight years for participating terrorist groups. Terrorist offences, on the other hand, should be punishable with "custodial sentences heavier than those imposable under national law for such offences in the absence of the special intent required".

Indeed, the common definition of terrorism is a great achievement for coordinating and cooperating counterterrorism efforts among the EU Member States. However, it is worth mentioning that the Framework Decision on Combating Terrorism does not give the EU any new supranational powers. Instead, the Framework Decision improves efforts to deal with terrorism by putting standards that the EU members are expected to follow. For instance, the role of the EU in defining and criminalising terrorism is similar to its role in customs policy: the EU determines common policies but leaves the enforcement of this policy to national judges and police authorities. Thus the successful implementation of the Framework Decision depends on the insertion of the provisions into national legislations by the EU Member States.

The Europol

The establishment of Europol was agreed with K.1 (9) of the Maastricht Treaty, on February 7, 1992, to fight with the problem of European trans-national crime. TREVI Ministerial Meeting in Copenhagen on June 2, 1993 created Europol Drugs Unit (EDU) that started working in January 1994. In 1995, the Europol Convention was concluded and the mandate of Eurpol extended, which defines the objective of Europol as:

"Improving...the effectiveness and cooperation of the competent authorities in the Member States in preventing and combating terrorism, unlawful drug trafficking and other serious forms of international crime where there are factual indications that an organized criminal structure is involved and two or more Member States are affected by the forms of crime in question in such a ways as to require a common approach by the Member States owing to the scale, significance and consequences of the offences concerned".

The Europol Convention came into force on October 1, 1998, and Europol has started its activities on July 1, 1999. Even though terrorism is not a new competence for Europol, its role in fight against terrorism was strengthened after the September 11 terrorist attacks. In this context, a special anti-terrorism unit has been set up within the Europol with the task to collect and analyse data concerning current threats and provide operational and strategic analysis and Europol is financed by supplementary budget for 2002 of more than three million Euros. In addition, on April 24-25, 2002, the JHA Council agreed to amend the Europol Convention to allow it participating in "Joint Investigation Teams".

This allows Europol to ask members to initiate investigations into specific cases but without giving Europol independent coercive powers. Therefore, the EU Member States can decide not to accept the request of Europol because of their security interests or such a request would jeopardize the success of investigations or the safety of the individuals. As a response to Madrid train station bombings, on March 11, 2004, the Council decided to reactivate the closed "Counter-terrorist Task Force" within Europol. The aim of Counter-terrorist Task Force is to facilitate the direct exchange of information between national representatives to get a more complete picture of the criminal activities of terrorists. In fact, it should be questioned that whether these measures, taken after September 11, significantly increase the authority of Europol on the EU Member States. Europol should now ask the member states to launch investigations, but it cannot order them to do so. Europol personnel cannot detain or arrest any suspects but can join in investigations of crimes only within their specified mandate.

The Eurojust

Judicial cooperation in criminal matters was first included as an EU objective in the Maastricht Treaty. The European Council of Tempere, on 15-16 October 1999, in point 46 of its conclusions, made a decision to establish permanent judicial cooperation unit called Eurojust, to enhance fight against serious crime. On December 14, 2000, provisional judicial cooperation unit, with the name of Pro-Eurojust, Eurojust's forerunner, was established by the decision of Council of the European Union, which started work on March 1, 2001. The September 11 terrorist attacks stimulated the creation of Eurojust and Eurojust was finally established by a Council Decision on 28 February 2002.

Eurojust, a "unit" with legal personality, composed of one prosecutor, judge or police officer seconded from every member state with equivalent competence. The objective of Eurojust is mainly to stimulate and improve the coordination between the competent authorities of Member States, of investigations and prosecutions in the Member States, taking into account any request emanating from competent authority of a Member State and any information provided by any body competent by virtue of provisions adopted within the framework of the treaties concerning two or more Member States, or in certain conditions a Member State and non Member State, in relation to serious crime, in particular by facilitating the execution of mutual legal assistance and the implementation of extradition requests.

Eurojust does not have authority to launch or execute investigations, but instead relies on a system of lateral links among its members. Like Europol, whole is greater than the sum of its parts principle is also valid for Eurojust and that cross-border issues such as terrorism and organized crime require increased cooperation among judicial authorities. Eurojust seeks to improve cooperation between the different legal systems of the EU Member States rather than harmonize them. After Madrid train station bombings, the European Council adopted Declaration on Combating Terrorism on March 25, 2004, in which the "European Council calls on Member States to ensure that the optimum and most effective use is made of existing EU bodies, in particular Europol and Eurojust, to promote cooperation in fight against terrorism".

The European Council also called the EU Member States to designate Eurojust national correspondents for terrorist matters and use Eurojust to the maximum extent to cooperate in cross-border terrorism cases. Furthermore, the Council called Eurojust representatives to associate with the work of Joint Investigation Teams as far as possible.

Joint Investigation Teams

The Tempere European Council on October 15-16, 1999, called for joint investigation teams to be set up to combat trafficking in drugs and human beings, as well as terrorism. Following the September 11 terrorist attacks, the Council Framework Decision of June 13, 2002, provided the establishment of joint investigation teams. The competent authorities of two or more Member States can now set up a joint investigation team for a specific period and a limited period in order to carry out criminal investigations in one or more of the Member States setting up the team. A joint investigation team should, in particular, be set up where a Member State's investigation requires difficult and demanding investigations having links with other member states, and "a number of Member States are conducting investigations into criminal offences in which the circumstances of the case necessitate coordinated, concerted action in the Member States involved".

European Security Strategy

In order to determine a common security strategy in the face of the threats that the Europe challenges, High Representative Javier Solona presented as a draft the European Security Strategy (ESS), also intitled as "A Secure Europe in a Better World", at the Thessaloniki European Council meeting on June 19, 2002, which was subsequently adopted by the Brussels European Council on December 12, 2003. The ESS is divided into three parts:

The first part of the ESS deals with "key threats" facing the Europe after the end of Cold war. In that context, the ESS puts terrorism on the front of the threats by indicating that today's terrorist movements are well-resourced, connected by electronic networks, and incline to unlimited violence to cause mass causality to destroy democratic structure of the EU Member States. Proliferation of weapons of mass destruction is set out below terrorism as a second key threat in the ESS by pointing out the race in the WMD and serious possibility of using them in any terrorist attacks. The ESS handles regional conflicts as the third key threat to European security. In this respect, it is stressed that the regional conflicts, neighbouring to Europe or above all in the Middle East, can cause extremism, terrorism, state failure, and provides opportunities for organized crime. State failure is the fourth key threat. The ESS indicates that the bad governance- corruption, weak institutions, and civil conflicts are the reasons of state failure and lead to obvious threats, such as organized crime and terrorism and adds to regional instability. Lastly, the ESS point out that Europe is a prime target for organized crime. According to the ESS cross-border trafficking in drugs, women, illegal migrants and weapons are the internal threats to European security which have significant external dimension and linked to terrorism.

The second part of the ESS is dedicated to "strategic objectives". Three liberal strategic objectives are determined for the EU. The first objective is to extend the "zone of security" around Europe to the East, to the South and beyond by extending the benefits of economic and political cooperation to troubled countries, because in the age of globalization key threats stem from distant threats and they are as important as threats created at home. The second objective is to strengthen the international order by developing and supporting an "effective multilateralism" with well functioning international institutions. In this context, the ESS stresses the importance of upholding and developing international law and points out the UN Charter as the fundamental framework of international relations.

In addition, the UN Security Council has been taken as the primary responsible body to maintain peace and security in the world. The important role of other key institutions of international order such as WTO, NATO, OSCE, Council of Europe, ASEAN, MERCOSUR, and the African Union are also handled in the ESS for more multilateral international order. The third objective for the EU is to be prepared against new dynamic threats before a crisis occurs. It is indicated that conflict prevention and threat prevention cannot be started too early. In this respect, "preventive engagement" is at the heart of the EU approach against key threats in order to avoid them by acting at the first signs of trouble.

The final part of the ESS considers the policy implications for the EU of establishing a security strategy.

While the ESS stresses that the EU has been made good progress in the development of coherent foreign policy and effective crisis management capability, it is also emphasized that the EU must be "more active, more coherent, and more capable" in these areas. Developing a "strategic culture that fosters early, rapid and when necessary, robust intervention" are specified to make the EU more active in order to counter the new dynamic threats. For more coherent EU, the ESS underlines the importance of the CFSP and the ESDP, and puts that the challenge is now to bring together the different instruments and capabilities that the EU created over recent years.

This should be done by bringing together the European assistance programmes, European Development Fund, military and civilian capabilities from Member States, and other instruments. On the other hand, according to the ESS, transforming the EU military forces into more flexible and mobile structure, and enabling them to deal with new threats should provide more capability to the EU. Moreover, the ESS specifies the need to engage in co-operations with international partners to make a contribution to the EU's foreign and security policy and crisis management. In this respect, the ESS indicates the necessity of developing the relations with the US, Russia, and countries of the Middle East, Africa, Latin America and Asia.

Strategic Achievements of Declaration on Combating Terrorism

Following the Madrid train station bombings, on March 11, 2004, Brussels European Council meeting of March 24-25, 2004, resulted with the release of the Declaration on Combating Terrorism in order to provide more effective counter-terrorism measures. The impressing achievements of Declaration on Combating Terrorism for the EU's strategic objectives to fight against terrorism are the creation of counterterrorism coordinator and early activation of solidarity clause that is laid down in the draft Treaty establishing a Constitution for Europe. In fact, the EU Member States by creating the position of counterterrorism coordinator and adopting solidarity clause proved an important degree of political will on establishing a liberal multilateral cooperation on fight against terrorism at the EU level in terms of counterterrorism coordination and mutual assisstance.

The Counterterrorism Coordinator

Following the proposal by Javier Solona, Secretary-General of the Council of EU and High Representative of the CFSP, Mr.Gijs de Vries, a former Dutch deputy interior minister, was appointed as counterterrorism coordinator through the release of Declaration on Combating Terrorism on March 25, 2004. The function of the coordinator, who works within the Council Secretariat, is to "coordinate the work of the Council in combating terrorism and, with regard to the responsibilities of the Commission, maintain an overview of the all the instruments at the Union's disposal with a view to regular reporting to the Council and effective follow-up of Council decisions".

The Solidarity Clause

EU Member States were not eager to debate the involvement of the EU military force in fighting against terrorism, however, the September 11 terrorist attacks led to such a debate at the beginning of the 2002. After the US's Afghanistan operation, the Spanish government insisted on the fight against terrorism could be put in the Treaty on European Union, Maastricht Treaty, along with other Petersburg Tasks. However, other EU Members were suspicious on the inclusion of that new mission, because of practical reasons, the EU force was not yet prepared to contribute usefully to the fight against terrorism, and legal reasons, no treaty reform was envisaged at that time. After discussions among the EU Members, particularly, on that reasons, European Council's Seville meeting in June 2002 adopted a Solemn Declaration that examined the terrorism and the ESDP issue indicating that the CFSP and the ESDP can be used in fight against terrorism.

Even the time of disagreements among Europeans on Iraq crisis, there was a growing convergence of new thinking on how to confront terrorism in the security and defence field. For instance, the UK and France agreed on need of solidarity against possible terrorist attack at Le Touquet Summit on January 4, 2003, by declaring that they committed themselves from now on to mobilise all their available assets in order to provide help and assistance to the other country against terrorist acts. The France and the UK also invited other EU Member States to join this committment and to support the proposal to include in the draft Treaty establishing a Constitution for Europe a solidarity clause against terrorism.

In the name of same solidarity, after Madrid terrorist attacks on March 11, 2004, agreement was reached at March 24-25, 2004, Brussels European Council Summit, in which the Declaration on Combating Terrorism released, to early activate the solidarity clause, that is laid down in the draft Treaty establishing a Constitution for Europe. The European Constitution was signed on October 29, 2004. In the European Constitution, solidarity clause is laid down in Article 1/43 which states that if one of the EU Member States becomes the object of a terrorist attack, the EU shall mobilise all the instruments at its disposal, including the military resources made available by the Member States in order to

- Protect democratic institutions and the civilian population from any terrorist attack;
- Assist a Member State in its territory, at the request of its political authorities, in the event of a terrorist attack.

In addition, arrangements for implementing the solidarity clause, Article 1/43, are set out in Article III-329 of the Constitution for Europe in which it is stated that the nature of the assistance is not automatic, but depends on a request for assistance from the victim member state.

The Conceptual Framework of the ESDP

The European Security Strategy (ESS), Declaration on Combating Terrorism, and the adoption of solidarity clause by the EU Constitution laid the foundations of the "Conceptual Framework on the European Security and Defence Policy Dimension of Fight Against Terrorism" endorsed by European Council on November 22, 2004.

As a response to crisis, the EU can mobilise civilian, military means and instruments which encompass crisis management and conflict prevention capacities in support of the CFSP objectives. This facilitates "a comprehensive approach to prevent the occurance of failed states, to restore order and civil government, to deal with humanitarian crisis and prevent regional conflicts".

Thus, the main objective of the ESDP tasks target failed states that pose security threat indirectly from the periphery of the EU. However, the Madrid train station bombings brought the danger into the heart of Europe then the ESDP missions were reevaluated in order to address the terrorism issue. In this context, four main areas of action were determined in line with the EU's liberal approach of ensuring the combination of hard power and soft power instruments to tackle the terrorism by the endorsement of Conceptual Framework on the ESDP dimension of the fight against terrorism. These are:

Prevention: Under the framework of an EU-led crisis management operation, prevention of an assymetric threat is to ensure that the Member States of EU would support an operation by providing necessary level of effective intelligence and information gathering.

Protection: Protection is a fundamental aspect of any EU-led crisis management operation. In the case of a terrorist threat, the aim of protection is to minimise the vulnerabilities of EU personel, material, assets and civilian targets in the operation area.

Response/ Consequence Management: In the context of a crisis management operation, it is mentioned that EU-led ground forces would be available to cooperate with local authorities. *Third Countries:* A wider spectrum of the ESDP missions can be evaluated to incorporate supporting the third countries in the fight against terrorism. In addressing the fight against terrorism, the wider issue of the protection of the EU citizens in third countries, especially in the case of hostage taking, would also be considered.

One of the basic principles of the ESDP dimension of the fight against terrorism is its voluntary nature. The voluntary nature of EU Member States' contributions is one of the basic principles of the EU capability development process. It depends on each Member State to choose the most appropriate means to fulfill their solidarity commitment such as in ways that pooling, sharing and coordinating often scarce resources in this field.

8

The Future of World Society

First of all most writers tend to equate globalisation with the expansion of markets, the expansion of free trade if you like across the world which for me however is only one narrow aspect of what's happening in the world, that one wants to subsume under the ideas of globalisation and the global age. Globalisation is about more far than that and second, most writers today do something which they shouldn't do I think, that is they treat globalisation as something out there for the industrial countries.

Globalisation is like either a synonym for what's happening in the international arena or it's a kind of synonym even for the developing world but I've tried to argue through these lectures that globalisation fundamentally influences and changes the nature of the industrial countries too, our societies in which we live and one of the prime reasons for that is that the driving force of globalisation or the global age, in my view anyway, is not markets, it's the impact of communications and media which means we seem to have a different texture of experience from previous generations where the kind of immediacy of communication that we have now, which is only really constructed over the past 30 or so years, this is something really new in people's experience and it's a new feature in the structuring of our societies too and as I will be arguing in this lecture it is very intimately related to the rise of the new terrorism and the impact of terrorism in our lives today.

Think back to the American election. Just before the American election Osama Bin Laden produced a video which played some part, we don't know what, in the electoral process. I don't think you'll find any previous selection with an analogue to this where many quite serious commentators in the newspapers were asking who did Osama want to win in the American election. Did he want Bush to win or did he want to Kerry to win and there are commentators who took both sides of that argument. Not only that, I don't know how many people here have either seen the Bin Laden video or read the text of it but that's also extremely interesting because the text of the video seems to imply that Osama probably saw Fahrenheit 9/11 because there's one telling phrase in it. How many people here have seen Fahrenheit 9/11? Well, that's a lot.

You remember what to me was one of the most transfixing parts of the film was when George Bush himself was transfixed in the school classroom when he was listening to the story about a goat and he stayed, for what was it, about 4½ minutes in a classroom when the twin towers were attacked and Bin Laden in his video says what kind of leader is this when his country is under intensive attack, sits in a classroom being preoccupied with a story of a goat. There is something about the immediacy of this relationship which I've argued, it's not just a political thing, it's a kind of everyday thing for us and I called that in the first lecture, everyday culture shock.

Everyday culture shock is not always shock but its an everyday contact between the different cultures of the world which are no longer out there for us, they're here and they're present and they're everywhere and their manifestations are everywhere. Think of the horrific murder of the journalist that just happened in the Netherlands, a journalist who spoke out very forcefully against what he saw as the intolerance of Islam and was murdered in a brutal way, in a way which has a clear analogue to the kidnapping and murders that have happened in the context of the Iraq war, it might have happened before who knows, but there seems to be a tele-visual link in these occurrences.

Everyday culture shock is something that we have to live with but something which sort of very much influences, our decisions, our lives and even the political process in western societies today. What you can say here that we no longer have to go out and get to the world. You can't insulate the problems of the world from our societies. Those problems will come to you. If you don't deal with those problems those problems will now come to you and you should remember 9/11 is perhaps the most, still the most dramatic expression of that because it was the first major successful attack on the American mainland since the British raised the capital Washington some 200 years previously. America seemed to be territorially secure, way different from the big conflicts of the world which to some extent it had sponsored and certainly had been involved in during the cold war period. Those things never came to America. Of course the threat of nuclear annihilation was always there, those missiles could come to America but this was a kind of coming to America which really shattered people's sense of security and geographical integrity.

One of the things Europeans on hold still find it difficult to grasp is what dramatic impact September 11 had on the American psyche and it's no doubt that impact was a continuing feature really of the results which are for better or for worse, propelled Mr Bush back to power. So part of my theme in this lecture is the intrinsic connection between communications and violence just as a whole theme of all the lectures really is significance of communications and transformations in our lives. Now when you look at the origin of the term terrorism, ask yourself can the term terrorism have a reasonably objective social scientific meaning, very important issue I think, the term terrorism seems to have its origins in the French Revolution, in the revolutionary terror perpetrated during that process.

The term terror wasn't invented by the revolutionaries themselves, the term terror was invented by the counter-revolutionaries, the people who despise the French Revolution and what it stood for and believe the blood letting which went on was a form of as they said terrorising the population so the term terror seems to have been invented at that period but of course you could say the phenomenon of terrorising people through violence is as old as history because if you look back into the history of ancient civilisations, everybody here will know I think that when one army invaded a city held by the enemy they would sometimes raise the entire city to the ground and kill all the men, women and children in the city. This was not at all uncommon in traditional civilisations and the point of it was terror.

The point of it was not just to dispose as it were physically the enemy within the city, the point was to create terror in those living in other cities and show the power which that terror represented and of course terror was used in the practise of putting severed heads on pikes outside city limits in Britain until surprisingly late time in European history, these sorts of things were a fairly common phenomenon. So the phenomenon of using violence with the idea of terrifying populations, especially civilian populations is obviously old but the term is new and I'll be arguing that essentially the phenomenon is new and especially what we now call terrorism is much newer phenomenon than even the French Revolution. Terrorism as a term doesn't date for the time which terror was first coined.

Terrorism only became widely used in the early years of the 20th century and when you have a fairly recent term which becomes fairly widely used, it normally reflects changes in the phenomenon and I'll be describing a bit later why I think the notion of terrorism and the fact of terrorism in a certain modern sense is relatively recent and a particular form of terrorism which I'll call new style terrorism or the new terrorism is actually very recent and linked to the phenomenon of the global age which I was discussing a bit earlier. Now there are two questions which arise when you consider the problem, can terrorism be a useful concept for the social scientist. That is can you use it in a reasonably objective way.

First of all there is the question of moral valuation. It's famous that one person's a terrorist, another person's a freedom fighter and another person's freedom fighter is a third person's terrorist so you can use these terms in shifting ways. It is also very well known that people who were terrorists at one point themselves can later come to condemn terror just as violently as they practised it and you could say, some reservations in the early history of Israel for example, was punctuated by terrorist activity but today of course the Israeli leadership is part and parcel of self declaredly of the war on terror and regards terror and terrorists as its primary enemy. You also have moral shifts because its not that long ago that Nelson Mandela was widely regarded as a terrorist and wildly reviled actually as a terrorist leader, potential terrorist leader within the ANC, but of course Nelson Mandela has now become one of the most revered figures, if not the most revered figure of the late 20th century so there is that kind of issue.

Can you free the term terrorism from a certain level of moral valuation where that moral valuation shifts across time or shifts according to the perspective of the observer. The second issue I think is that the role of the state, can states be said to practice terrorism because whatever people now say about the big corporations or whatever, states have been responsible for far more deaths in human history than any other type of organisation. States have brutally murdered populations and this includes civilian populations. I mean states have certainly, in modern times, carried out the kind of analogue that the raising of cities that happened in traditional civilisations. You only have to think of the Queen's visit to Germany a couple of weeks ago where the issue of Dresden was raised.

Dresden was fire bombed, many thousands of people died. The city was at that point was largely raised to the ground and it had no strategic advantage many historians think at that time of the War so it could be described as an act of wanton terror, certainly by the critics of the allies action it has been described in that way in which many people died and which the purpose was to produce terror within the wider society of Germany.

So, the question of whether you can have an objective definition therefore is a difficult one and it raises lots more issues than I can really discuss here so I am going to offer what is a fairly dogmatic conceptualisation of terrorism because I think having thought about the issue quite a bit that you can have a reasonably objective definition of terrorism and terrorism defined as I'll try to do in a minute is a major force affecting our lives today and it is different from other kinds of violence which are practised in other contexts. So let me just say what my definition is, you've got these various elements.

First of all I think terrorism should be separated from the activities of the state. Maybe there are contexts in which one can use the term state terrorism but I'll separate that from the activities of the state and I'll define terrorism as the following. Terrorism, first, involves acts of violence, physical violence, second, used by non state actors whatever these be, whether they be quasi-combat units or what, normally targeted at civilian or non-combatant targets. Normally targeted at civilians or those who are not themselves fighters and crucially where the violence involved is more symbolic than strategic.

Where the violence involved is more symbolic than strategic because the point of terrorism is to terrorise the point, is to instill fear and anxiety in a principally a civilian population so the main characteristics will be violence used by non state actors directed mainly at civilian or non-combatant populations where the violence involved is more strategic than symbolic but like any concept that terrorism is fuzzy round the edges and there will always be definitional problems around what terrorism actually is. I want to argue that terrorism in this sense as I mentioned a bit earlier a specifically modern phenomenon. I would therefore would want to separate it from acts of violence designed to terrorise that happened in previous periods of history. The reason why I think terrorism in the sense in which I'm using it as a relatively recent phenomenon is again its connection with communications.

If you are going to terrorise populations on a fairly wide spectrum you need to bring the information about the violence quickly to those populations affected. So terrorism to me is largely contingent on the rise of modern communications which makes it possible to do this. The rise of modern communications as I mentioned is essentially a sort of late 19th century process with the invention of the electronic telegraph which made possible transcendence of time and space. Once this happens then you tend to get the rise of symbolic acts of terrorist violence which can be projected at distance. You don't have to be local in order to know about them. It's very important, I don't know how far people are familiar with the sort of history of communications and geography but before the invention of the electronic telegraph it took a long, long while for news or information to percolate around.

You couldn't have an immediate influence on a situation process or acts of violence in an immediate sense before something like the middle of the 19th century. Even in the early part of the 19th century, late 18th century, battles were fought in wars where peace had actually been concluded but it took so long for the news to get back that the battles were fought without people realising that the wars had ended. One of the main battles in the American Civil War for example fought our in the South, actually happened something like 2 months after the War had formally ended and this was the nature of communication in those times. So I think terror is a phenomenon that tries to influence civilian populations at distance, is a creation of modern mass communications, especially electronic communication and of course it links in with these fantastic transformations in recent times which I've mentioned in previous lectures and which I'll come back to a bit earlier. The bulk of what I want to say in this lecture is that we have to make a distinction between what I call old style and new style terrorism.

Old style terrorism is the kind of terrorism which has been dominant for something like 60, 70, 80 years in the early part of the 20th century, still exists today but has distinctive characteristics. Old style terrorism is largely associated with the rise of nationalism and with the somewhat artificial process of the establishing of nations. There are many views about nationalism and its origins but my view anyway for what its worth is a kind of Ernest Gellner type view that nationalism is a creation of modernity. It's a phenomenon of something like the late 18th century onwards although you find residues early on. Anthony Smith argues this very strongly in the LSE, he says it goes back earlier but I think it's more of a modern phenomenon. The rise of the idea of the myth of the nation, integrity of sovereignty, the idea of bounded territories associated with national identity. Now in all nations the boundaries of nations were fixed somewhat arbitrarily. They were fixed either as lines on a map as happened in Africa or Asia, essentially by western colonisers or they were fixed through conquest battle struggle.

Think of this country for example, the United Kingdom. The United Kingdom is a nation with territorial integrity but of course it involved history of warfare. Scotland was brought in after several wars and the Act of Union, the Welsh were never completely integrated into wider British society and felt themselves to be to some extent subjugated people and Ireland was the crucial arena for the British in terms of its desire to have a separate national identity. I'm going back to at least the mid 19th century. Now when you have patchwork nations, all nations to some extent are founded on force and a kind of patchwork, then you have many examples of what you can call and students in the field call nations without states.

Nations without states are nations with a claim to having a common cultural identity, a claim to the sort of myth of the nation but without the territorial and state apparatus which normally belongs to a nation and most forms of old style terrorism are linked to nations without states and the point of old style terrorism is to establish states in areas where nations do not have control of the territory state apparatus. This is true of Northern Ireland for example or one side of the combatants in Northern Ireland, the Basque country in Europe for example and various forms of violence associated with national identity. There are issues like Kashmir and many other situations like that where the main issue is territorial integrity and identity in the formation of a state. What terrorists want to do is to have integral state in normally a sovereignty of an existing state where the existing state lays claim to overall territorial sovereignty and where terrorists are prepared to use violence to achieve their ends.

Old style terrorism is fundamentally local therefore because its ambitions are local. It wants to establish a state in a specific national area and once that ambition has been realised of course that's the situation under which terrorists can then become heroes or those who once were reviled as terrorists can become national leaders of the state which emerges and can then become as it were perfectly responsible politicians leading the new nation. Now old style terrorism especially in recent years has had a kind of international component to it because countries like Libya or Syria and some of the East European countries for example and groups in the United States have supported the IRA in Northern Ireland and Basque terrorism to some extent has become international so you couldn't say old style terrorism is wholly local but it is mainly local, it's ambitions are local although it might involve a wider global network of supporters. It might involve the filtering of arms and drugs from different parts of the world to fund armaments and so forth.

Old style terrorism is fundamentally limited in its ambitions and normally in old style terrorism the violence involved is relatively limited. Many people have lost their lives as the result of the conflict in Northern Ireland but the proportion of people killed in Northern Ireland including British soldiers is actually less than those who die in road accidents each year so although quite significant numbers of course of people who have been maimed and injured and killed, there's never been a massive extension of that level of violence and this is characteristic normally of old style terrorism because it has relatively limited aims, the violence itself tends to be relatively limited, fearsome and horrific though it may be because it is often aimed at completely innocent populations.

Old style terrorism is difficult to combat as the British have found for such a long time in Northern Ireland. For various reasons its difficult to combat because of the strong moral compulsion of the myth of national identity. It has a very energizing component to it, national identity, which can continue to fuel devotees of a movement which seeks to establish a state where there is a nation without a state and its also especially difficult to come to terms with when there are contested claims on the same set of land and the same territory. This is true in Northern Ireland, difficult to produce a settlement or a settlement hopefully seems to be emerging because what the parties want is completely different. One group wants to be part of the United Kingdom, the other one wants to be part of Ireland.

The same is true in Israel where you could say, many neutral observers anyway say that both sides have legitimacy in their claim to large chunks of the land which they occupy or of course this is very heavily contested from those on both sides of the argument, extremely hard to resolve because they are fighting over large parts of the same land not just trying to get a state where one didn't exist when there aren't subsidiary claims as there are in the Basque country for example, it's much more like a movement which seeks to go a bit further beyond the autonomy which the Basques already have. However difficult it might be to eradicate old style violence however, myself I think it's really important to draw to a fundamental distinction between old style terrorism which if you like is 20th century terrorism and new style terrorism which is essentially the terrorism of the global age because it deploys the very techniques of communication and global spread which have constructed this new global period for us and Al Qaeda, but not only Al Qaeda, are examples of new style terrorism.

Let me list the main characteristics as I would see them of what new style terrorism is. First, new style terrorism is different from old style terrorism in respect of the scope of its claims. One of the distinguishing features of Al Qaeda's view of the world for example is that it has geo-political aims, it seeks to restructure world society. As you'll know what the proponents of certain chunks of Al Qaeda leadership want to do is to reconstruct an Islamic society, a caliphate going all the way from Pakistan into Europe, to effect regime change in the Middle East. One of the origins of Al Qaeda is to change the regime in Saudi Arabia but also to re-establish strongly Islamic governments throughout the Middle East. It's also to recapture Northern Africa and if you look at the various Al Qaeda websites, it's also partly to re-conquer Europe. Al Qaeda takes a long view of history and says that over a period of a thousand years the West has expelled Islamic groups from those areas which it has legitimate claim to. It includes for example the Balkans or they include about half of Spain because half of Spain was ruled by the Moors for a long period.

Quite large chunks of what we now regard as Europe were previously Islamic, were ruled either by the Ottoman Empire or were ruled from Northern Africa and the point is to re-establish the global role of Islam in these regions and areas. So where as old style nationalism is local and linked to particular states, normally quite small states, new style terrorism is global or is geo-political in its ambitions. It wants to reverse the tide of world power. An interesting thing about Al Qaeda and similar organisations is that it is a kind of modernist anti-modernism because the new terrorist organisations make great use of modern communications. They make use of the whole palpably actually of modern communications but to criticise modernity but to reverse the tide of modernity, reverse what is seen as a corrupt style of society emanating from the West has lost the moral compass which a true society have.

Second, if the first feature is geo-political scope in terms of aims and ambitions, the second is organisation. Mary Kaldor, who is one of the heads of the Centre for Global Governance in the LSE, the very organisation to which I am also now attached, has quite interestingly pointed to the similarities between new terrorist groups and NGOs. New terrorist groups she says and I think this is quite right, Al Qaeda is like a kind of malign NGO because it deploys the same global forms of organisation as NGOs do. It's driven by a sense of mission and commitment, just like say, I don't want to say, you shouldn't draw this parallel too closely, it's an organisational parallel. If you take an organisation like Friends of the Earth, it's a very powerful global organisation because it's driven by a sense of mission and commitment and that sense of mission and commitment allows for a fairly loose global organisation to flourish.

It's a network type organisation just like Al Qaeda is driven by a sense of mission and you know Al Qaeda has been very substantially weakened by the American attacks in Afghanistan but its also strong still because the moral conviction further which drives the sense of mission can keep cells functioning even when some aspects of the overall organisation have been weakened or broken and that's we're seeing in many parts of the world today. So there is a lot of autonomy in local cells and these can sort of breed without really necessarily being in any strong sense directed from the centre. Another characteristic is that these cells exist in many countries or these groups exist in many countries just like NGOs have global spread so does Al Qaeda. It's very contested what Al Qaeda is now especially after Afghanistan but many students of Al Qaeda, a specialist book called Inside Al Qaeda, which is one of the best ones I read, claims that there are still cells in something like 60 different countries with something like 20,000 people to die violently for the cause.

Not all of them suicide bombers but a certain proportion certainly prepared to sacrifice their lives for the cause and existing semi-autonomously from as it were the centre. The final characteristic just like NGOs is that the new terrorist organisations intercept with states. No NGO could flourish completely as a non state organisation. They all have some contacts and support from states and this is true, Kaldor says of new style terrorist organisations to and so it is so support from states say like Libya or certainly

Iraq for some kinds of organisations and so forth has been quite important to the survival.

Thirdly, the third difference between old style and new style terrorism is means. Old style terrorism as I mentioned because it had relatively limited objectives, the violence involved was normally fairly limited and continues to be, normally fairly limited. Chechyna is an example where it is becoming radicalised and the two are overlapping for some substantive attempt degree. The new terrorism seemed to be much more ruthless in the means it is prepared to use and again if anyone is concerned or interested in this, which I hope in some sense everybody will be, if you check some of the Al Qaeda websites they talk in extremely destructive language of the enemy.

The enemy being principally the United States but for some extent the West as a whole and they do explicitly say we should whatever means we can, we will kill as many people as we can. It's very, very different from the style of violence characteristic of old style terrorism. Now in my view, it's these two second characteristics, organisation and ruthlessness which links new style terrorism to mass destruction, the possibility of mass destruction. It's not as such weapons of mass destruction, about which I want to, well, I want to speak a bit, already the time seems to be sort of running out slightly. You have to regard the connection between mass destruction and weapons of mass destruction as a problematic one. Let me tell you why.

If you look at the example of 9/11, what happened in 9/11? Well about 3000 people were killed in the Twin Towers but if the planes as they were designed to do, had hit at a slightly different angle and the Towers had collapsed immediately, 50,000 would have lost their lives in the Twin Towers. I remember what Al Qaeda was doing was striking at the centres of American economic power, military power and political power.

The second plane hit the Pentagon but it didn't hit the part of the Pentagon where much more destruction could have happened if the plane had hit the right part. Where the networking capabilities of the Pentagon are, they could more or less have paralysed America military capability at least for a while because it's very dependent on networks communication.

The third plane was only stopped from hitting the White House, you remember, by the bravery of some of the passengers on it, who brought it down before it could actually hit that target but if it had hit the White House and destroyed the White House, it would have been, at the outer edge of the possibility of 9/11, is a possibility of massive destruction with something like 60,000 people losing their lives and a kind of strike at the main nerve cells of American political, economic and military power. You see you don't need weapons of mass destruction to kill a lot of people if you're ruthless enough and you're well organised enough because only planes were used in that attack.

So the connection between weapons of mass destruction and modern mass terrorism is more problematic I think than many people assume. But what about the issue of the weapons of mass destruction? What kinds of weaponry are there around and what likelihood is there that new style terrorists could use them. Well, I was going to say more about this than I actually have time to. You have to treat not just the connection between weapons of mass destruction and modern mass terrorism, problematic, but also the concept of weapons of mass destruction. The concept of weapons of mass destruction is actually not a useful one I think when you look at the literature on weaponry can be employed. One of the things that is stunning when you to start to look at the literature is however, if you combine organisation, ruthlessness and modern weaponry there could be truly horrendous events which could be threatened by the rise of new style terrorism.

Summarising very briefly because I did want to say a lot more about this, summarising briefly, you have to distinguish among the various categories of what are ordinarily regarded as weapons of mass destruction. Chemical weapons are dangerous, yes. They could hundreds of people, who knows, thousands of people if deployed in certain ways but they don't have ultimate destructive power. The destructive power of chemical weapons, when you are talking like civilian populations rather than on a battlefield is relatively limited. Much the same is true of biological weapons. Biological weapons, for example, ricin, are pretty fearsome and could certainly have destructed potential. They could cause panic as to some extent even the original letters, you know involving Anthrax did in the United States three or four years ago, about 5 people died then.

You could certainly kill hundreds of people by chemical or biological weapons but their lethal potential does not extend beyond that therefore I sympathise very much with people who say you must draw attention between biological and chemical weapons on the one hand, dangerous though they are and nuclear weapons on the other and the most significant problem facing the world and the most horrific conjunction between new style terrorism and modern weaponry is in the field of nuclear weapons and nuclear proliferation and it's nuclear proliferation which should primarily worry us because nuclear weapons give terrorists the chance to destroy a whole city. Nuclear weapons, certain kinds of nuclear weapons, if they get in the hands of the wrong groups, could kill millions of people, not just a few hundreds of people and so much of the effort which is being directed on the so called war on terror should instead be directed not just to contain proliferation but actually produce de-proliferation in the world because the proliferation of nuclear weaponry is really dangerous and it comes not from rogue states primarily.

It comes from two sources, the ex Soviet Union and to some extent Pakistan when Pakistani scientists were involved in passing nuclear secrets to some extent to different countries. In the Soviet Union it has been calculated that it has something like 50,000 nuclear weapons and something like possibly a quarter of these are unaccounted for. We know many of them have been stolen, some of them have been recovered, we don't know who stole them. General Abed who is a famous general come politician in Russia, after the collapse of the Soviet Union gave evidence before an international committee in which he said over half of the so called suitcase bombs that existed in the Soviet Union, which were 1 kiloton bombs, have gone missing. You can take those bombs in a suitcase literally and leave them in a middle of a city.

Incidentally, you have to separate these from dirty bombs. Dirty bombs are simply conventional explosives packed inside radioactive materials. Dirty bombs are relatively easy to make and its almost certain that a dirty bomb will be exploded somewhere at some point but dirty bombs do not kill large numbers of civilian population. Other nuclear weapons can do.

Al Qaeda was trying to acquire nuclear weapons way back in the early 1990's and we have evidence that they made connections with a range of countries in order to seek to do so. If Al Qaeda, and there is not only Al Qaeda, there are several other such groups out there in the global internet network, if they brought a van into Times Square with a 10 kiloton bomb in it and exploded it, they could kill something like half a million people in the centre of New York City and they could devastate also wider areas around. So, it's this outer edge which is the most fearsome possible connection and therefore we need a much more rigorous regime of nuclear non-proliferation and de-proliferation than we have so far. Since I have to accelerate, let me just conclude by a number of brief observations that summarise at least my position on this. First, as I said, the notion of weapons of mass destruction has itself to be deconstructed is not really useful notion. It least has to be deployed with some care partly because you can produce great destruction anyway without using such weapons but partly because of the differentiation between them. Second, I don't believe in the war on terror. I don't believe in the war on terror because the whole point of new style terrorism, asymmetric violence is that it is different from conventional war. It is not a war in the conventional sense. You do have to fight it and in some parts through the use of violence. I think it was necessary for the Americans to destroy the Al Qaeda networks in Afghanistan because they were planning nuclear attacks on Western countries but it's not a war in the conventional sense and the most problematic thing, within it, it's not just a war on terror, it's the problematic edge especially of containing the possibility of nuclear violence and nuclear proliferation.

Thirdly, we all have to be alert to what I call the phenomenology of risk and violence in the kind of world I'm describing, a mediatised world where you have mass terror which is deployed through modern techniques of videos, television and so forth. The phenomenology of terror and threat is a difficult one to manage. The phenomenology of threat and terror is that often you have to announce a threat in order to get people to change their behaviour or to take action against it. However if you announce a threat and nothing happens or if you announce a threat and through announcing that threat you neutralise it, then people will accuse you of scaremongering and this is exactly what a series of Channel 4 programmes recently made about global terror did I think.

Part of the reason of why the impact of global terror is less than it was is because the organisation of Al Qaeda, in it's original sense, has been in some part crippled but of course as soon as your successful, people will say why are you scaring us in the first place but if you don't give information then they will say cover up. They will say you weren't providing enough information in the public domain and all governments have to struggle with this difficult relationship between cover ups and scaremongering which is very difficult for us a civilian population to deal with.

Next, we do have to have pre-emptive doctrines but these pre-emptive doctrines should be in no way confined to terrorism. It's absurd I think the position of the Bush administration, pre-emptive doctrines against terrorism, no preemptive against global warming, you need a whole variety of pre-emptive doctrines if you are going to face up to the risks and threats that we have in the world.

Finally, there is the problematic issue of civil liberties. What happens to our civil liberties in the age of the war on terror? Well, I think what is happening is wrong because first of all Guantanamo Bay is surely just a scandal, it's a kind of off shoring, an equivalent of industrial banking off shoring really and to avoid the kinds of democratic rights that surely the whole point of fighting terrorism is to sustain those rights. That's surely a scandalous thing but also I think you get an attack on civil liberties if you bracket all weapons of mass destruction as the same and you bracket all terrorism as the same.

We should be concentrating far more as I've said several times upon nuclear options and upon nuclear proliferation. We should not be just producing a blunt defamation of civil liberties in order to do that because it has to be in some part geo-politically organised, not just a matter of vetting people when they come into a particular country so I think the struggle against terrorism does not necessarily mean a complete denial of human liberties and we should stand up for the things which our society asserts as against new style terrorism, human rights, democracy, political participation, equality and therefore we must resist some of the entrenched reductions or reverses of human rights that have been carried out in the name of terrorism.

Visions from the EU Perspective

International security environment has been transformed by emerging complex issues and more interdependent actors since the end of the Cold War. Terrorism takes place as one of the most complex and serious threats to the international security in this new security environment. The EU, as an interdependent actor, was affected by this complex security threat and designed liberal strategic policies in response to the September 11 terrorist attacks of 2001 such as supporting effective multilateral international order, adopting foreign policy agenda comprising developmental, economic, cultural, environmental matters, in addition to security matters, in order to pursue its interests, providing the combination of "hard" power and "soft" power instruments for its preventive engagement strategy. In fact, the history of terrorism dates back to the early centuries. However, although the threat of terrorism has existed for many years, there is no single definition of it.

Academicians, policy makers, international organizations and individual states have defined the term in various ways. This complexity stems from the fact of the term terrorism's political connotation. To this end, there are lots of issues remained unresolved to ensure a uniform definition of terrorism for the international community. However, among these unresolved issues, the most important one is the relationship between guerrilla warfare and terrorism in which the Third World states describe guerrilla warriors as freedom fighters and Western countries call them as terrorists. Thus, the definitional weakness poses significant challenge to the international cooperation against terrorism. As in the case of the challenge in defining terrorism, it is impossible to type terrorism in one single categorisation because terrorism exists in various motivations throughout the history.

Therefore, many types of terrorism have emerged such as state-sponsored terrorism, anarchist terrorism, nationalist terrorism, ideological terrorism (left-wing and right- wing), and religious terrorism. It is also a challenge to distinguish these types from each other, because some of them are interdependent. Beyond above mentioned challenges, what is disturbing today is terrorism's emergence as an international actor affecting world politics after the September 11 terrorist attacks. By the help of globalization, the characteristics of terrorism have changed to a great extent and terrorism has become "new" terrorism according to some foremost authors who study terrorism.

The characteristics of the "new" terrorism are quite different from the old one. The terrorism's new structure is a network, facilitated by information technology, new personnel are amateurs, who often come together in *ad-hoc* or transitory groups, and new attitude is an increased willingness to cause mass casualties, perhaps by using chemical, biological, nuclear or radiological weapons (CNRB). In addition, the employers of the "new" terrorism are mostly terrorists motivated by religious imperatives, especially terrorists influenced by Islamic fundamentalism who frequently do not claim responsibility because of their belief that God sees their action.

The characteristics of the "new" terrorism should evidently be seen in the unprecedented September 11 terrorist attacks in which the "new" terrorism's incubation period has ended. In fact, the September 11 attacks revealed the necessity of international cooperation to confront terrorism. In this context, the EU Member States, which still differ on the ways to combat terrorism, have come together under the EU in order to intensify their efforts for fighting against terrorism, both internally and internationally. Therefore, it is worth mentioning that

September 11 attacks acted as a catalyst for the EU efforts to tackle terrorism and the following Madrid train station bombings also contributed to this fact. In the light of these facts, as a response to September 11, the EU adopted concrete measures to institutionalise its legal and administrative capacity to cope effectively with terrorism. In this context, the EU adopted the European Arrest Warrant to reduce the prospect of terrorists evading justice by exploiting differences in national legal systems.

By the adoption of Framework Decision on Combating Terrorism, the EU ensured a common definition of terrorism, which is the most comprehensive terrorism definition when compared to the other definitions of domestic state legislations or international treaties, set out minimum penalties for terrorist offences, and criminalised the direction of, support for and incitement to terrorist activity. To enhance the role of Europol for fighting against terrorism, a special anti-terrorism unit has been set up under Europol framework to collect and analyse operational information. In addition, Counter-terrorist Task Force has been reactivated under Europol to provide direct exchange of information between the EU Member States. Moreover, Europol's participation in Joint Investigation Teams has been provided without giving Europol an authority to launch an investigation by its own.

In order to improve coordination between magistrates and prosecutors, the EU established Eurojust and its association with Joint Investigation Teams have also been accepted. By furthering its efforts, the EU ensured the creation of Joint Investigation Teams, in which the Europol and Eurojust have been allowed to link as mentioned above, by the involvement of one or more EU Member States with the aim of implementing criminal investigations. On the other hand, it is worth mentioning that the EU's framework decisions set the standards for the EU Member States are expected to follow. Thus, taking into account the fact that

European Arrest Warrant, a common definition of terrorism, and Joint Investigation Teams have been introduced through framework decisions, the implementation of these achievement would depend on how much the EU Member States would be successful to insert them into their own legislations. In addition, because of its intergovernmental and voluntary structure, Europol challenged the dilemma of sharing multinational information on the issue of security for fighting against terrorism. Moreover, Eurojust's mandate is limited to provide cooperation rather than harmonization.

As part of its internal efforts, the EU developed liberal strategies to fight against terrorism. To this end, the EU published European Security Strategy document in accordance with its liberal approach, in which the EU underlined the importance of effective multilateral cooperation under the framework of the UN, extending the zone of security by extending the benefits of economic and political cooperation to its neighbours, and preventive engagement strategy incorporating various soft security instruments. In addition, through the release of Declaration on Combating Terrorism, the appointment of Counterterrorism Coordinator Mr. Gijs de Vries and the early activation of solidarity clause that is laid down in the draft Treaty establishing a Constitution for Europe have been introduced, in which the EU Member States gained their cooperation a liberal multilateral dimension as a result of their political will.

Moreover, the EU reevaluated the missions of the ESDP to address the fight against terrorism by combining hard power and soft power instruments in line with its liberal approach. In this context, four main areas are determined for the development of the ESDP's civilian and military crisis management capabilities related to terrorism. These are prevention, protection, response management, and support to third countries in fighting against terrorism. To fully confront the threat of terrorism cannot be achieved only by enhancing internal efforts. Thus, the EU also enhanced its international efforts with its global partners. To this end, the EU engaged in cooperation with the US. However, there are some divergences between Partners that stem from each side's different strategies related to the EU's liberal approach and the US's realist approach to tackle terrorism.

While the EU, in line with its liberal approach, supports effective multilateral system under the UN framework, pursues multidimensional foreign policy agenda including economic, developmental, cultural matters, in addition to security matters, and develops a conflict prevention concept by combining hard power and soft power instruments, the US, on the other hand, in line with its realist approach, makes its military hard power a prominent factor and pursues its foreign policy unilaterally by also emphasizing the role of preemptive strike that was the case in Iraq war which also proved the divisions among Europeans. Indeed, the international Iraq dispute showed how the Europeans could not reconcile their differences. Throughout the Iraq dispute, the Europeans divided among themselves on whether to give the US a support for the invasion of Iraq or not.

On the one hand, the countries like France, Germany, Belgium, Luxembourg, and Greece, and the most majority of the European public, by supporting multilateral consensus, insisted that the invasion of Iraq would be unlawful if it is not explicitly authorised by the UN and the invasion could damage the international efforts to wipe out terrorism. On the other hand, the publishers of the "Letter of Eight" and the "Vilnius Ten Text", notably the UK, Spain, Italy, Poland, Denmark, Estonia, Latvia, Lithuania, and Slovakia, supported unilateral US military operation by indicating that the Iraq regime had breached the resolutions of UNSC for 11 years, which forced Iraq to disarm.

That is why these perspectives of Europeans on the Iraq dispute were a distinct slap at the very notion of the CFSP that the EU was meant to be developing and which even the proponents of military operation against Iraq claimed to support. Beyond the divergences between the EU and the US, convergences should be seen in their counterterrorism cooperation. Indeed, the counterterrorism cooperation between the EU and the US is in significant degree. The EU and the US signed two information sharing agreements including the sharing of intelligence and personal data for police cooperation. In addition, the EU and the US concluded Extradition and Mutual Legal Assistance agreements for their judicial cooperation. As a result, requests for extradition are handled much faster, the EU and the US agencies are in direct contact, extradition is possible for many offences and authorities can access to bank accounts on the other side of the Atlantic, the joint EU-US investigative teams can be set up, and usage of modern communication techniques for assistance are provided.

Moreover, in order to improve transport and border security, the EU and the US concluded customs cooperation agreement which extend customs cooperation to cover container security, and agreement on the transfer of PNR (Passenger Name Record) data for transatlantic flights. Southern Mediterranean is one of the most important regions of the world with its terrorist breeding. The EU believes that the breeding of terrorists in the region stems from the fact of region's economic, political, and cultural instability. Thus, the EU gives great importance to providing stability in region to eradicate the root causes of terrorism. In this context, the long-standing Barcelona Process and its reinvigoration with Valencia Action Plan in 2002 reflects the EU's liberal approach to tackle terrorism by pursuing multidimensional foreign policy including developmental, cultural, economic matters, in addition to military matters.

On the other hand, the EU and its Mediterranean Partners also involved in counterterrorism cooperation under the framework of Barcelona Process after the September 11 attacks. However, the Euro-Mediterranean Partnership on counterterrorism could only be seen at the declaratory level. In fact, the reason for this insufficiency mainly stems from different definitions of terrorism used by the Partners. After September 11, the EU and the Mediterranean Partners called the requirement of counterterrorism cooperation in all Euro-Mediterranean Summit conclusions. In these conclusions, both sides accepted to bring justice the perpetrators, planners and sponsors of terror actions, pledged that differences regarding terrorism definition could not prevent to identify cooperation areas, committed to fight against terrorism in all its forms and manifestations regardless of who perpetrated, underlined the importance to adopt all terrorism related the UN Conventions and to accomplish the largest possible consensus on the draft of the UN Comprehensive Convention Against Terrorism which also tries to ensure universally accepted definition of terrorism.

In fact, these statements can be regarded as important steps in terms of showing both sides' willingness to beat some problems, especially the problem of defining the term terrorism, and to improve counterterrorism cooperation. Thus, the conclusions of summits should not be underestimated; they should pave the way to create future concrete counterterrorism cooperation. The EU-Russian relations have proved to be an important step since the end of the Cold War. Even they signed Partnership and Cooperation Agreement which form the basis of EU-Russian strategic partnership. As a response after September 11 terrorist attacks, the EU and Russia also involved in counterterrorism cooperation. In this context, Partners issued two joint statements on terrorism in which the both sides agreed to exchange information on terrorism matters and determined areas of cooperation that should found the framework for counterterrorism cooperation between the EU and Russia in the future, as in the case of Euro-Mediterranean Partnership conclusions.

In addition, the EU and Russia signed an agreement on the exchange of technical and strategic information to enhance police and judicial cooperation, which does not include exchange of personal data. On the other hand, the Chechen conflict still remains as a significant problem between Partners. The reason of the disagreements on Chechen conflict stems from the fact that from the beginning of the conflict, the EU, in line with its liberal approach, wants a solution of the problem through political settlement, while Russia uses its military hard power as a defining factor for the solution of the conflict. Thus, the EU's internal and international efforts against terrorism after the September 11 attacks made it more cohesive and cooperative organisation in order to collaboratively come up with solutions to deal with terrorism, if it is taken into account that the EU had significant disagreements to reach consensus to fight against terrorism before the September 11 terrorist attacks.

Bibliography

Adams, James. *The Financing of Terror*, New York: Simon & Schuster, 1986.

Alexander, Yonah and Richard Latter, eds. *Terrorism and the Media: Dilemmas for Government, Journalists & the Public*, Washington, DC: Brassey's, 1990.

Andersan, Sean and Stephen Solan. *Historical Dictionary of Terrorism*, 2nd ed. Lanham, MD: Scarecrow, 2002.

Atkins, Stephen E. *Terrorism: A Reference Handbook*, Santa Barbara, CA: 1992.

Bell, J. Bower. *Transnational Terror, Washington*, DC: American Enterprise Institute, 1975.

Burton, Anthony. *Urban Terrorism: Theory, Practice, Response*, London: Cooper, 1975.

Chaliand, Gerald. *Terrorism: From Popular Struggle to Media Spectacle*, Atlantic Highlands, NJ: Saqi, 1987.

Comb, Cindy C. *Terrorism in Twenty-First Century*, 2nd ed. Upper Saddle River, NJ: Prentice Hall, 2002.

Crelinsten, Ronald D. and Denis Szabo. *Hostage- Taking*, Lexington, MA: Lexington Book, 1979.

Crenshaw, Martha. *Terrorism, Legitimacy, and Power*, Middletown, CT: Wesleyan University Press, 1983.

Gay, Kathleen. *Encyclopedia of Political Anarchy*, Santa Barbara, CA: ABC-CLIO, 1999.

George, Alexander, ed. *Western State Terrorism*, New York: Routledge, 1991.

Gurr, Ted Robert. *Handbook of Political Conflict: Theory and Research,* New York: Free Press, 1980.

Harmon, Christopher C. *Terrorism Today,* London: Frank Cass, 2002.

Hoffman, Bruce. *Inside Terrorism,* New York: Columbia University Press, 1998.

Jenkins, Brian. *International Terrorism: The Other World War,* Santa Monica, CA: RAND, 1985.

Kushner, Harvey W. ed. *The Future of Terrorism: Violence in the New Millennium,* Thousand Oaks, CA: Sage, 1998.

Laqueur, Walter. *History of Terrorism,* New York: Transaction Publishers, 2001.

Lesser, Ian O. et al. *Countering the New Terrorism,* Santa Monica, CA: RAND, 1999.

Lewis Bernand. *The Political Language of Islam,* Chicago: University of Chicago Press, 1988.

Miller, Abraham H. *Terrorism and Hostage Negotiations,* Boulder, CO: Westview, 1980.

Moss, Robert. *Urban Guerrilla Warfare,* London: International Institute for Strategic Studies, 1971.

Netanyahu, Benzamin. *The Terrorism Reader,* New York: Meridian, 1986.

O'Neill, Bard E. *Insurgency and Terrorism: Inside Modern Revolutionary Warfare,* Washington, DC: Brassey's, 1990.

Peters, Rudolph. *Jihad in Classical and Modern Islam,* Princeton, NJ: Markus Wiener, 1996.

Picard, Robert G. *Media Portrayals of Terrorism: Functions and Meaning of News Coverage,* Ames: Iowa State University Press, 1993.

Pillar, Paul R. and Michael H. Armacost. *Terrorism and U.S. Foreign Policy, Washington,* DC: Brookings Institution, 2001.

Rashid, Ahmed. Jihad: *The Rise of Militant Islam I Central Asia,* New Haven, CT: Yale University Press, 2002.

Rosie, George. *The Dictionary of International Terrorism*, New York: Paragon House, 1987.

Schamis, Geraldo Jorge. *War and Terrorism in International Affairs*, New Brunswick, NJ: Transaction Publishers, 1980.

Segaller, Stephen. *Invisible Armies: Terrorism in the 1990s*, San Diego, CA: Harcourt Brace Jovanovich, 1987.

Sofaer, Abraham D. and Seymour E. Goodman. *The Transnational Dimension of Cyber Crime and Terrorism*, Stanford, CA: Hoover Institution, 2001.

Sonn, Richard D. *Anarchism*, New York: Twayne, 1992.

Stern, Jessia. *The Ultimate Terrorists*, Cambridge, MA: Harvard University Press, 1999.

Tanter, Raymond. *Rogue Regimes: Terrorism and Proliferation*, New York: St. Maytin's, 1998.

Tucker, Jonathan B. *Toxic Terror: Assessing Terrorist Use of Chemical and Biological Weapons*, Cambridge, MA: MIT Press, 2000.

U.S. Department of State, *Patterns of Global Terrorism*, Washington, DC [Annual].

Venzke, Ben N. *First Responder Chem- Bio Handbook*, Alexandria, VA: Tempest, 1998.

Wardlaw, Grant. *Political Terrorism: Theory, Tactics, and Counter-Measures*, New York: Cambridge University Press, 1989.

White, Jonathan R. *Terrorism: An Introduction*, 3rd ed. Belmont, CA: Wadsworth, 2001.

Whittaker, David J. *The Terrorism Reader*, London and New York: Routledge, 2001.

Zinn, Howard. *Terrorism and War*, New York: Seven Stories, 2002.

Index

W